Sex & the Zodiac

Helen Terrell

CRCS PUBLICATIONS
Post Office Box 1460
Sebastopol, California 95472

Library of Congress Cataloging-in-Publication Data

Terrell, Helen.
    Sex and the zodiac.

    Originally published: Roslyn Heights, N.Y. : Libra
Publishers, c1976.
    1. Astrology and sex. 2. Zodiac--Miscellanea.
I. Title.
BF1729.S4T47 1988   133.5'83067   87-34854
ISBN 0-916360-41-5 (pbk.)

INTERNATIONAL STANDARD BOOK NUMBER: 0-916360-41-5

First Paperback Edition
    Published by CRCS Publications
            Distributed in the United States and internationally by
                    CRCS Publications
            (Write for current list of worldwide distributors.)
Cover Design: Image and lettering by Rebecca Wilson.

Dedicated to the Unseen Trio—ever watchful, ever protective!

And with deep appreciation to:

Jack D. Sheley (my brother) whose knowledgeable advice on
the rhetorical aspects of the book was invaluable;

Linda Waldrop, an excellent typist, remarkable in her ability
to decipher marginal scribblings—and a loyal friend as well;

The many, many persons who opened their minds and hearts to
me in their search for a solution to their problems;

And my husband to whom I am especially grateful because of
his unquestioning faith. (Asked if he believed in Astrology
or Women's Lib, he replied, "I don't know but I believe in
Helen");

And my son for his perceptive interest and our frequent discussions which helped to keep my viewpoint flexible. Without their encouragement, my Taurus persistence, constantly
hampered by Gemini restlessness, might never have overcome the difficulties in completing this work.

CONTENTS

Foreword

Almost everyone who reads the following pages will have had some previous knowledge of the precepts of astrology. He is aware that it existed thousands of years ago in many countries of the world and that today its principles are utilized as an instrument toward better understanding of oneself and others.

If there are those who would refute these theories, it is only because of the human propensity to reject the new rather than change preconceived ideas.

Although some of our finest astrologers are men, and well-known physicians, researchers, mathematicians and astronomers have attested to the truths therein, the average man is sometimes slower than a woman to accept such tenets, refusing to concede that any element outside himself could play a part in his accomplishments. With the same reasoning, he can deny his ancestral heritage, not bothering to look for the source of his drives and ambitions.

It is amusing to hear him vehemently disclaim the possession of traits which imply certain Zodiacal affiliations since in his very indignation he often betrays not only those in question but others which are even more indicative of his planetary genesis.

One thing that misleads one of logical mind is the reading of "General Horoscopes" which predict a trip, the meeting of a new "love object" or other happenings on a particular date. Obviously, not all residents of a given sign will have such experiences at that time. It is merely that the location of the planets makes favorable the possibility of such events.

When one takes his first breath, he is like a blank page of a book, on which he must describe himself. It is the ability to do this creditably, with pride and not too much inner conflict which makes of him a happy person. In his early years he usually learns to adapt himself to the world about him in one of three ways: by being placating or seeking to please; by aggressively dominating people or situations in which he senses opposition; or by withdrawing emotionally in an attempt to avoid disturbing confrontations. The better adjusted he becomes, the greater his capacity to use the three methods interchangeably as the need arises.

However, it has been found that in the course of maturing, reactions to the same sort of conditions do differ according to the varying Zodiacal signs—the signs of the parents also being pertinent.

Astrology teaches that although one has a certain potential, he is responsible for the use he makes of it.

While psychologists impute a man's characteristics to his geneology and early environment (and in any dependable Birth Chart one must take into account the circumstances of the subject's family, race, group or religion), there is conclusive evidence that hand in hand with these factors, there is the one created by the position of the Sun, Moon and planets when he is born.

The stars alone may not completely determine his leanings, but they do initiate certain tendencies while modifying or strengthening others and channeling them into specific directions. He begins his life with a nature peculiarly his own and within a special framework of latent inclinations which includes those of sex and power drives, these in turn affecting not only himself but all those with whom he is closely associated. Since the sexual phase of his life is secondary only to the will to survive, it behooves each of us to know what to expect from a loved one—his dreams, his fantasies and his relation to reality because only then can there be a sharing which is mutually rewarding.

Does astrology explain the sex games men play? Indeed it does (as well as those by women, whose motives, however, are usually unlike those of men).

A man could ask himself:

Why is he charmed by almost any girl on some days, having an immediate quickening of the senses at any close proximity, when as a rule in these casual contacts, he avoids such reaction. Why does unfaithfulness to a loved one distress him more in one instance than in another? Why does betrayal seem normal to many men but not to all? Why is one man good "husband material" while others remain married bachelors? Does a man not wonder why his sexual temptations are of unequal intensity? Why, at one period of his life, although basically interested only in heterosexual relationships, can he be led into a homosexual incident but never have any wish to repeat it—or, if he does, why is the impulse only intermittent? How can he condone one "deviation" but feel guilty thereafter at thoughts of this nature? (If he actually tends to "love" men rather than women, or even to be bi-sexual, it might be revealing to investigate the reasons in the realm of astrology.)

In areas not pertaining to sex, there are questions to be asked also:

Why does a world famous ball player go for weeks without being able to "get a hit" but suddenly gets one whenever he goes to bat? Why do those who follow the races have no explanation for having days when they (rightly) "feel" which horses will win? What of the player who knows nothing of roulette but suddenly sees himself winning at almost every turn of the wheel and the salesman who sells nearly every "contact" on one day but finds most prospects "out" or indifferent to him or his product on another? (In the latter case, one can say that the answer lies within the man himself and may be due to his manner at that time, but what prompts the manner?) Is there a more appropriate explanation of these few illustrations (of which there are hundreds more) than ascribing it to the influence from the heavens?

At Duke University, through studies of parapsychology, there has come a conviction of a force at work outside our general knowledge or voluntary efforts. We accept with ease the fact that all other life is affected by the Sun and the

Moon, so why should we question the impression they probably make on us? There is much that we do not know about this science of the Ancients, but the same is true of many secrets of the universe.

Long discarded beliefs regarding medical and psychiatric suppositions are again being examined. There is every indication of machinations beyond our ken. Why should the principles of astrology be rejected just because we do not know why they are operative?

Astrologers speak of the "Rulers" of various signs, although there are some who now set up horoscopes without giving tribute to the planets, simply pointing out that there is a "synchronism" between their vibrations and the activities upon the Earth.

However, having long used astrology for a greater comprehension of human nature and having accumulated hundreds of "case histories" to verify the facts, this writer subscribes to the idea that the powers to which people respond in unique patterns are planetary (whether designed thus or incidental) and that each individual's reaction to them is of utmost importance.

Only by knowing *why* a person reacts as he does, can one understand him. To resolve the problems which plague the families of today, all available assistance is needed. The information herein is based not only on historical research, but on facts gleaned from the confidences of thousands of subjects, both men and women. In the beginning of the conference some were completely disillusioned, openly recriminative and vindictive; others were disarmingly cheerful but implacably hostile beneath the mask of their pretenses. Some, more mature and honest in their desire for adjustments, struggling valiantly toward an amicable union, did find better methods of compromise and communication when armed with the tools for assessing others *as they are*.

Many books have been written on the premises of astrology, including the variances of individuals according to their Zodiacal signs. Yet, added to these are the great attitudinal differences between men and women. The resulting injustices are numerous, among them women's outside working conditions as well as those of their private lives. The following chapters deal with such matters, but since so many difficulties initially arise because of disparate outlooks on sex and love, emphasis is placed upon this aspect and more data given which (hopefully) will lessen the dissatisfactions.

Before going into an analyzation of astrological elements which directly affect all situations, it seems imperative to focus attention on sexual attitudes in general. Only after much deliberation and "soul searching" has this been done.

It is not intended as a diatribe against men, who are certainly not the beasts that some of the more radical feminists have proclaimed. They are, though, frequently inconsiderate or unbelievably ignorant about that most intimate of relationships. (Considering their constant preoccupation with sex, one can find very little to excuse such lack of perception.) The sexual adventuring indiscriminately enjoyed by many men is untenable to women and this they most protest. With considerable justice, they also decry men's bedroom manners, in which the aesthetic concept is so often lost.

Undoubtedly, there are many kind, thoughtful, trustworthy, lovable men (albeit there may be but few to whom all of these adjectives could honestly be applied), and ruefully, it must be mentioned that being thus sensitive, gullible and unsuspecting, they may be led into regrettable indiscretions by women of as little moral fiber as the unethical self-oriented man.

The wife of a man without a sexual conscience sails a marital ship without a rudder. Hers is a lonely vigil in the dark hours of night—a perilous journey upon unchartered seas where love, her only beacon, may not be enough to assure her safety. She is forever denied the emotional security which feeds the ego and nourishes the spirit.

Her unmarried counterpart may not assume all the burdens of the woman with a family, but she faces the same fears and desolation if her lover is not constant.

Despite the disadvantages women have suffered in all areas, their resentments continue to run deepest where they have had to contend with sexual callousness, insensitivity, or faithlessness. If solutions to these problems could be found, their other myriad complaints would seem less serious. Granted that there may be many happy marriages (though one questions the validity of any poll on the subject since for reasons of expediency, many pretend to a contentment which they do not feel), but there are many women of all ages, backgrounds, and life styles who are unhappy. They are embittered and frustrated, yet caught hopelessly, inextricably, in the web of their own love or loyalty. It is because of them and from their viewpoint that most of this book was written.

Chapter 1

The Chemistry of Sex

Little Jack Horner, the eternal egotist, so aptly typifying youth with its natural exuberant presumption, abetted by his innate masculine conceit and arrogance, appropriated with gleeful audacity, that which he desired, bolstering his self-esteem with such obvious pride that he not only excused his conduct but actually glorified the deed!

Thus it is that many a man deludes himself and seeks to delude women, glamorizing his forays into areas of promiscuous sexual indulgence and experimentation. (The little boy's mama may have thought him very cute then but later on his wife or sweetheart would not have found that boyish charm sufficient compensation for his peccadillos if the plums he coveted were other women!) This is the man, however, the adorable, sweet-talking, Peter-Panish Lothario, often safely married to a mother surrogate, who usually manages to have his (pie) and eat it too.

He is unconcerned about any woman's angers or complexities (if she is not readily amenable there is always another one just around the corner) nor does it disturb him that he is instinctually polygamous, since he gives it little thought. Probably he would be amusedly disbelieving if told that a specific planet lends impetus to his maneuvering and plays a dominant part in his motivational impulses concerning sex.

We all know what sex is! It is that intangible mystery that used to lurk secretively in the dark, sometimes causing coy giggles or ecstatic moanings in the night but which parents so reluctantly discussed with their children that an aura of sinfulness and shame seemed always to surround it.

Now, however, in our changing world the word is on the lips of everyone. Newspapers, magazines, books, television and the films all portray its many facets in uninhibited and lengthy detail.

Yes, we all know what sex is and if there is anything about it which requires explanation, Dr. David Reuben can be relied upon to supply that, unless, of course, one is interested in discovering how a certain person is apt to react to sexual stimuli and whether or not he is addicted to philandering behavior or to involvement in illicit or serious affairs. For these answers, one must be very well acquainted with the individual or informed through astrological data of his propensities.

Hearing of the art theaters, the pornographic books, the pseudo massage parlors and their bold advertising claims, the licensed prostitution in some well-known resorts and the pressure to have it in other places—even listening to the various opinions expounded on the "talk shows" of television, one is apt to conclude that sex is a purely physical "fun thing," although few women of the past ever accepted this evaluation without some qualifying reservations. Currently many are beginning to wonder if the "game is worth the candle."

True, the instance of orgasm might be termed "fun" by many persons, both men and women; admittedly, the definition is especially fitting for the antics of those men whose ideas of "love making" still take the form of hasty, limited or ritualistic procedures which were all they knew in adolescence, all they have taken the trouble to learn since and which, incredibly, they often still employ, never even being remotely aware of that mystical rapport which can (and sometimes does) attend such unions!

The pathetic performances of these self-satisfied, unenlightened men reminds one of an amateur blithely playing a musical scale on a Stradivarius when the audience is expecting a symphonic composition. Under these conditions, it is doubtful whether the nebulous word "fun" would apply to the woman's interpretation.

Yet, women do not disparage sexual pleasure. Indeed, they now have a greater conception of its importance than their mothers or grandmothers dared to acknowledge. They do, though, question men's attitudes concerning it. Just as those older women were chagrined at the unflattering, impersonal elements of these contacts, so too do the women of today take umbrage at this indignity which tends to emphasize their sense of injustice in many other areas.

Although there is a general rebellion among them which has culminated in Liberation groups and Women's Rights Organizations designed to lessen their burdens and give them the remuneration and opportunities which should have been theirs long ago, it is not to be denied that discontent with the more intimate aspects of their private associations lies at the heart of much of their resentment. Certainly this is the prime cause of many divorces, although previously women remained silent or gave other explanations for their difficulties.

Still, although in this age of frankness there is far more complaining and airing of disagreements between couples than there was in the past, women themselves may seem to ignore the absence of chivalry and that gentle, frothy sentiment called romance that once inspired them in song, film and story. They may appear to do so but their concept of love and sex has always differed from men's and that has not greatly changed.

Here, they have two serious grievances against men: their infidelities and the fact that they are impercipient lovers, but their criticism is often focused upon the smugness that accompanies these faults. Even when needing a more discerning approach to intimacies than most men are wont to give, they have been able to adjust to the prevailing insensitivity except when a prurient attraction to other women became too obvious—an inclination which a man rarely disdains or makes an effort to control.

Unfaithfulness, women have always lamented and have never learned to overlook; they are apt to depend upon loyalty, despite all evidences to the contrary and even though it is well known that the male nature keeps him forever looking at women with appraising eyes. However, as Dr. Reuben has said, "A woman is the most sexual being on earth" (a statement that must have surprised most men who heard it), and furthermore, her need of love is so great that if her husband bestowed upon her the courtesies which he saves for extramarital affairs, she might then even condone his perfidy or at least refuse to admit to herself the truth of his imperfection.

(He may be as complacent toward a sweetheart with whom he has an amour as he is with his wife, it seldom occurring to him that his usual "home-style love-making" is wanting in any respect.)

She who is lucky enough to have a husband or lover she can trust, has a scintillant manner that is unmistakable and which only a sense of security can induce!

When irate women call men "animals," this description could sound bitterly overdrawn but there actually are those so totally unversed in the sexual amenities that their actions do greatly resemble males of less intellect.

There are some who grant to "pick-ups" and to their wives alike the same quickly depleted attention that a boasting rooster confers upon one of his harem and are just as ignorant of the ridiculousness of their insolent preening as is the prideful fowl! This is an intolerable affront which is nothing short of rape, though in truth they may not realize it. If not in actual physical discomfort, the outrage in a woman at that moment is so great that no matter what her feelings had been just previously, unless she herself is especially callous, she cannot be expected to enjoy her partner's ludicrous assault.

Those who evoke such anger are no wiser than the sea otter, who, though well intentioned, in the excitement of the nuptial moment, often clutches his mate's face so desperately that he bloodies her nose! However, the male otter has been programmed for procreation only, while his human counterpart has been given other options and with them a reasoning ability which should lead to some finesse in intimate matters.

He would do well to look to the domesticated cat for advice! This is a species of animal that could teach him patience! This roving Casanova with his own reputation for promiscuity still knows the rules of the game. He understands the rituals of courtship and will gladly forego food and sleep as he waits, poised in tense watchfulness, anxious for the object of his wooing to give him the signal that the flirting period is over and that his tentative but formerly aborted overtures are at last welcome. However, too many men had their only lessons in sex from another little boy behind the bathroom door and have continued to think about it in the same way most of their lives.

Whence comes men's conceit? Can it really be that their appendages for procreation have convinced them of their superiority over women whose paraphernalia for this purpose is hidden within themselves? (This is quite possible since Freud and other psychiatrists later on accused women of envying men for their anatomical structure—a male assumption as laughable as it is unbelievable. No woman other than a lesbian would want the bother of such a member!)

Unquestionably, everyone enters life wanting admiration or at least respect from others, but the two sexes have not had identical avenues through which to achieve either. Aside from the injustices in social and public life to which women must submit, they have been denied the amorous victories of men who have solved their ego needs through sexual dominance, made easier by an innate mystical, charismatic portrait of themselves as superior human beings.

To be fair, the need for this masculine assessment is not as irrational as it may seem. In the past, for a man to be effective, vigorous and successful in meeting the challenges of the world it may have seemed a necessary precept. Also, this need might derive from the knowledge that women are said by scientists to be physically stronger in their ability to adapt themselves to their environment, to resist disease, stress and death. Perhaps, then, men have been provided with more active egos to balance this inequity.

Whatever the source, the myth persists, at least in the minds of many men, that as Gods of the earth they surpass women in almost every way and therefore, are far more privileged, particularly in the realm of sex.

For years, sex was considered to be the exclusive "property" of the male. "Nice women" were not supposed to think about it; they were suspect if they indicated any pleasure even when obliging their husbands. A dutiful permissiveness was the custom and so prescribed in whispered instructions to the new brides by those already indoctrinated.

It was an era when many men patronized the prostitutes, found conspirators among the more indiscreet, discontented married women, or sought out the girls "beyond the tracks" where fewer opportunities for marriage supported a more lenient moral code. Men's earthy approach often startled and dismayed the fair damsels whom they had married for their sweet innocence. (Yet, even the gently reared, along with those of lesser social advantage, were taught that they must cater to their husbands' desires.)

Contrary to the thinking of today, the first "sexual revolution" in America came about at the time of World War I. Word had trickled back from "Gay Paree" that the husbands and sweethearts were having quite a ball with the French girls; hence the "Red Hot Mama" was born in this country. She planned to be ready and waiting when "Johnny Came Marching Home." (The truth is that she was only too glad to shed her cloak of naivete! Women have never been so stupid as men liked to think.)

With the rolled-down hose, the feather-edged hair, the dangling earrings and the fancy cigareete holder, she was a sight to behold!

The "it" and "Umph" Queens of the Screen were never more popular than was the girl who readily joined in the continuous round of dances and bath-tub gin parties. Her playmates might be the returning "Dough boys," the racoon-coated, flask-carrying college students, or the married business men of her vicinity. It was fun time for them all, and in the rumble seats of the new cars many a baby was conceived!

Yet, the "Flapper" of the twenties, as she was often called, was a strange unpredictable phenomenon. While flaunting her cigarette smoking and drinking of bad "hooch" as if they were badges of great accomplishment, seeming to say that she was "thoroughly emancipated," sometimes the reticent, virgin-like feeling that lay beneath that gay demeanor was in conflict with the image, and she was quite capable of walking home from a displeasing situation.

This was puzzling and annoying to males. They did not understand a "date" who could say "no" when her mood prompted, since with the crumbling moral structure of the times there were many who did "give their all" without reservation.

It had not taken any girl long to discover that those who sought her company offered little romance with their pseudo "love making," and that to them she was only a moment's diversion, the realization of which was as mortifying then as it is today. She had found that the male's only interest in "pitching woo" (as they so cutely called it), was to quickly obtain satisfaction for themselves. Certainly it had little to do with "wooing" and no personal significance whatever! Most astonishing was the assumption that if there had not been mutual orgasmic pleasure the fault could have been only hers. If the jaunty blades of the twenties had not been so appallingly obtuse, they would have known how little erotic excitement they caused! They even might have been somewhat chastened, though their natural self-assurance makes this seem unlikely.

Some girls, wanting gaiety and fearing ridicule if they would not go along with the prevalent ideas, learned to pretend a passion that rarely surfaced with such inadequate partners, yet there were those whose physical needs were deeply aroused and completely unassuaged.

By then women had begun to wonder at the absence of the chills and thrills mentioned in novels. (They had more tingles as they watched screen lovers tenderly embracing than they had in the arms of those fellows so bravely defying their marriage vows or when submitting to the clumsy acrobatics of the self-styled lovers of the younger set.)

It is possible that at this time the average woman was not

sufficiently knowledgeable to recognize the extent of a man's awkwardness in sexual matters. She knew only that his apparent confidence accompanied by such lack of discernment left her baffled, usually unsatisfied, and very angry.

It was not for a lack of expertise that she mourned, but for the lost visions of romance she had harbored through her adolescent years.

As the big depression became reality, women's viewpoints wavered and fluctuated and life often seemed dull and drab in comparison with their expectations. Though they might love their husbands, something indefinable was missing.

These mothers of a newer generation, apprehensive of the many dangers and "heartaches" awaiting their daughters, knowing full well that the price of popularity far outweighed the advantages, began seriously to question a woman's place in the scheme of things, to ponder the unfairness between the sexes. They may have said little, but indignation had become a smoldering, threatening secret within them.

When the next wars came along, many of all ages worked in the factories, which revived self motivation but produced the usual disappointment in associations with men, many of whom though of a later era were as determined in their attempts at conquest and just as immature in sexual behavior as their fathers had been!

Girls in secretarial pools or other places of employment where there was little privacy had only to evade unwanted invitations. But those in small businesses or other places with dark corners, basements, seldom-used "show rooms" or other hideaways were often besieged with importunate urgings for "quickie" assignations.

It is true that some were as avid as the men and had as few qualms in the sharing of disloyalties, though nearly always they were disappointed by the impersonal nature of the intimacies. Many, though, were affronted by even a suggestion that they could be taken so easily. These varying attitudes are almost the same today as they were then. Adding to women's discomfort, when they are not so quickly aroused as are males by casual contact, they are accused of being either "cold" or teasingly coy. A man, hoping to charm a girl into an amorous affair or ensnare her for a purposeful moment (ten or fifteen maybe?) may mistake her hesitancy, not realizing that women are more discriminately selective than men (including those who can ultimately be persuaded), and do not give themselves as readily to sex alone. They look instead for associations based upon mutual liking, and the development of something more serious, feeling that the gift of sex is too intimate, too complex, to be given or accepted otherwise.

If men fail to understand this, it is because they are almost completely motivated by sexual instincts. Being unaware that those who play at love are often the poorest lovers, they wrongly think of themselves as eminently fitted for such roles and blindly rush into precipitous action which does not inspire the expected results. (Unfortunately, even in this enlightened age, they may know as little at 40, 50 or 60 as they did at 15.) Being quite certain as to the infallibility of their procedures, they seem never to learn that a woman wants to be wooed, not only at the first seduction but in all the phases and instances that pass for "love making" throughout her lifetime. The whispered "nothings," the tender caresses, the early moments of sweet togetherness—it is these that are the open sesame to warm response.

Yet the lure of brief stolen moments is strong and men's predisposition to look for diverting sexual meetings seems to be as compelling as is their need for other conquests. (Our nomadic ancestors, who pillaged the villages of those of more agrarian pursuits, did so as much for the novelty and variety of captured females as for plunder.)

Although many a man's search for flirtatious episodes resulting in erotic fulfillment often depends upon the station he holds in his own household or the strength of the bond shared with his sweetheart or mistress, his Zodiacal sign does push him in certain directions, and even when deeply woman conscious, he is not necessarily promiscuous. His astrological heritage could be such that his sexual leanings are nullified or guided into a one woman channel. Also, there are often restricting agents in his genes.

To be sure, sometimes he remains in love with his wife even though the newness, the glamour, and the sense of wonder have long since faded in the repetitious and benumbing rituals of every-day living. Remaining mentally loyal, he may establish erotic contacts which have no lasting meaning; or out of fear of destroying his image as a family man and responsible citizen, may sublimate such urges through work, recreational pursuits, civic affairs or sports.

For some it is just too much trouble to make the arrangements for a "love nest;" their energies may be so depleted from other activities that there is little left over for dalliance (though rarely is a man so exhausted that a fluttered eyelash by a mini-skirted charmer, or a come-hither glance from even a less appealing but sympathetic co-worker, could not quickly revive his libido.)

In the early days their games usually were played with unmarried girls but later, women of both categories joined them in their "fun"—although the majority of wives did so either in retaliation for their husbands' infidelities or to find that elusive ingredient which seemed to be missing in their "love making" once the marriage vows were said. Most preferred affairs of serious nature or still endeavored to maintain a marital status not fraught with too much anxiety.

Many women had lost their outside jobs when the men returned from Service but by then they were taking courses which led them to seek vocations hitherto not available to them. As they thought more and more about the "brainwashing" that for so long had kept them from these desirable positions, making it seem that they were unqualified, their hostilities were not mitigated by the continuing sexual injustices.

They lamented the many illegitimate children, the irremediably bungled abortions and often doubted that the company of men was recompense for all the trouble to which it led. Unsettling thoughts as to their husbands' or lovers' inconstantcies haunted each waking hour. Alas, passing years have brought little surcease in this respect.

Every woman knows that the man she calls her own is never that. He is a separate entity, almost entirely self-oriented, and a law unto himself. (It is this trait of separateness and complete concentration upon his work or the business at hand which makes possible his unique success in many fields.) His perspectives, preferences, ideals and ethics are very unlike hers. Given the proper set of circumstances, he will likely yield to his natural instincts for clandestine foolery; there is always someone waiting to fulfill his purpose; although she may be impelled by reasons other than his.

New situations develop from day to day, and a woman wonders how to cope with them. It seems that the sexual complexities of life are increasing and outweigh all else in the resulting frustration which many experience. Suppose her husband suggests that they engage in a group sex experiment or even attend a mate-swapping gathering? Should she comply? (It is said that women are slower to like such practices, but that some eventually come to enjoy them more. Is this because of disappointment in their husbands' "love making," a search for something more romantic than marriage, or does she only pretend, through motives that few men would understand?)

What should her reaction be when the husband, after a few drinks at a party, invariably begins "smooching" with another guest or following her around in a state of schoolboyish enthrallment? Certain that every man present thinks her a fool and that every woman pities her (even those who may be flattered by his alcoholic attentions) she cannot hide her embarrassment. Often a warm, loving human being, perhaps having much more to offer than the others for whom he is momentarily drooling, she understands that when in search of ego refueling, he naturally turns to those who do not know his faults so well. Is he really worth the humiliation which she knows will always be hers?

Then there is the husband who goes out after dinner, ostensibly to buy a pack of cigarettes, but goes instead to a street where he can make a quick homosexual contact. (It is one thing to accept the idea of homosexual alliances and to see the justice in a protective law for "consenting adults" but quite another to condone one's own husband's participation in incidents of a surreptitious, shoddy nature.)

While some men are not too strongly libidinous, others are so preoccupied and obsessed with sensuous titillation that they neglect their talents and all other aspects of life, apparently following what they find to be the most stimulating, hedonistic pattern.

The exploitation and enticements of sex are everywhere, but not only in the topless restaurants, the "skin" shows, the houses of prostitution and the bars with their suggestive nude dancers is there an overabundance of temptation to males. The fierce, ever-growing competition of "the other woman" is also a menacing challenge!

Some husbands, more and more regularly, call to say that they are working late, or neglect to phone at all and later have no reassuring explanation for the delay.

Lying awake and watching the clock at night, each woman asks herself the same depressing questions: "Has he stopped loving me?" "Is he sitting in a bar with some seductive stranger?" "Is he parked in a remote spot with a new secretary?" "Could he be in a motel with one of my best friends?" Or—"Is he out on the town with the boys?" (The question she is most reluctant to phrase stems from her fear of his involvement in a *real* love affair.)

These are the disquieting questions of lonely women during their nocturnal waiting. Though aware that the answers may very well be in the affirmative, they constantly strive to deceive themselves. After a time they become so weary, they feel that knowing the truth, however damaging, would be better than uncertainty. But husbands, artful in maneuvering, frequently reason that "what they don't know can't hurt them" and have no intention of breaking up their homes. Moreover, having a wife in the background provides the protection many a man wants as he goes about his self-indulgent adventures which are as instinctive and natural as a firefly's on a summer night.

It is not the wives alone who are filled with misgivings. Sweethearts, lovers, paramours, mistresses—all have the same problems. Rivalry is so overwhelming that no knowledgeable female is absolutely secure in any man-woman relationship. After all, what has she to offer that someone else might not offer with more tantalizing guile?

The young unmarried girl can be greatly perplexed. As the

mores and customs change, this allows her less leeway in making her own choices according to her preference or conscience. Though reluctant, greater pressure is brought to bear upon her to enter questionable unions.

She hears sex discussed unceasingly, yet dislikes believing that this is all that intrigues her favorite man. Certainly its expression is earthy, satisfying for the moment and biologically necessary in most normal lives, but when she hears a demure woman celebrity on television prattling about the beauty of sex, she must be somewhat astonished at the over-simplification, feeling that it is only as beautiful as the spirit in which it is enacted.

She may feel harassed when confronted with the necessity of making decisions. Notwithstanding today's greater freedom in many areas, the sexes still retain extremely different ideas about this freedom as well as the delights of its privileges. Recently, in a questionnaire presented to university students, the gap of understanding between the sexes was clearly exemplified. Whereas the women unfailingly spoke of love in connection with sexual communication, the men's replies suggested a much more "relaxed" viewpoint. While the students expressed the conviction that every individual has a right to his own code, when asked their opinion about the custom of some married couples who take separate vacations and have consorts—perhaps actual affairs—almost as many men disapproved as did the women. (One must not forget that it pertained to both wives and husbands. While many men would applaud the husband's vacation fun, many of them would not excuse similar conduct by the wife!)

Actually, the most note-worthy information to be drawn from the questionnaire is that *a larger percentage of women rejected the idea of extra-marital exploits than had done so in a similar query almost thirty years ago!*

Radical changes must be made and are indeed preferable to the hypocrisy of previous generations, but while some women can willingly accede to men's wishes for "temporary commitments," there are those who are hesitant, knowing that the double standard still persists in the minds of many men. Often, confused by these dissident views, a woman can hardly know what is best for her.

Hopeful of marriage, she may agree to a prior sexual relationship, and discover later that the man actually wants a wife with stricter views. Still, had she refused him, he might have deduced that she was not compatible with him physically. She can never tell just what his thoughts on the subject are, for in any case, he will not refrain from using any persuasive measures to obtain his objective.

It has always been easy for the man to make his own rules, and although some women will do so now, can anyone be sure at this particular period whether or not they will have profited from their decisions, or how many will be irreversibly scarred? It is one thing for a really mature person to chart her own course and abide by the consequences, and quite another for someone younger to be coerced or ridiculed into accepting ways which are against her natural instincts.

Women have been pretending to concur with men's views since the beginning of time. No matter their age or the circumstances of their lives, they seem destined to be plagued by doubts. For instance, there were great differences in the thinking of women themselves after the advent of the "pill" and other contraceptives, yet they were faced with new and startling problems. Pandora's Box had inadvertently been opened!

Now that they were less worried about unwanted pregnancies and so had more liking for sexual activity, they were surprised at the reactions of their partners. Having believed that they would be pleased and grateful, they found instead that as their interests quickened, men's often declined.

Hundreds of books on such matters had flooded the markets, but these women whose longings had been disregarded before, still did not find the response in men that they had anticipated.

Expecting greater skill, or at least a more perceptual approach, they foolishly looked for subtlety but were thwarted here as before. (This was more attention than the average man was accustomed to giving! Without warning, he had suddenly found himself in an alien position and on the defensive, the responsibility for his partner's pleasure, as well as his own, being unaccountably his. Most husbands thought that it all seemed somewhat silly, although some, having read the books on anatomy and erotic techniques at their wives' requests, now recoiled from the memory of their meager uninspired gestures at trysts with younger acquaintances who could only have been amused at their unworldliness.)

As the young people began to unashamedly admit the truth regarding their own behavior, and women to require more effective performances from their spouses, there were men—especially those who were somewhat older in years and marriage, who were astounded and even secretly dismayed at what they thought of as "a woman's lack of modesty."

It was all very well for a man at a convention to cavort with a "call girl," an office acquaintance whom he had surreptitiously taken with him, or a bar "pick up"—to even indulge in orgies of various kinds (he could not be blamed when he was drinking, could he?). But when his wife, whom he thought he knew so well, seemed to be emulating such girls not only in her capacity for enjoyment but in a knowledge new to him, and even was asking him to reciprocate, it was just too much!

Vance Packard in his book about the corporation man in "The Pyramid Climbers" quotes Lester Dearborn, Director of the Counseling Service of Boston, and former President of the American Association of Marriage Counselors, as saying that "an executive can take off his dignity with his clothes (at a convention) and be just a devilish playboy." He continues along these lines saying that such men "may be at the top of the ladder vocationally, but they are at the foot when it comes to making love."

In this connection, he speaks also of the fact that the executive, once he is successful, seeks to maintain his dignity even with his wife. (This attitude is still not uncommon even though some authorities stress the fact that an older man has more time to devote to his family, which should make for greater harmony.)

Although once he may have been eager to cooperate in his "love making," as time passes, although his wife may be her

most enchanting self, such a man will not allow her to
penetrate the insularity with which he houses that decorum
and pride of vocational accomplishment. He often seems
somewhat chagrined if reminded of his former enthusiasms
and spends less and less time and effort in the gentler
nuances that lead to more intimate communication. Some
change could undoubtedly be attributed to a lessened sexual
drive due to the aging process, but this does not explain the
diffident, restrained manner that many men adopt. Nor does
it answer the question of younger women whose husbands,
ardent and affectionate before marriage, almost immediately
afterward find that the petting which should precede coitus
is too boring or time consuming.

Can it be that many men are having difficulty living up to
their vaunted image as lovers? Or is it that with the passage
of time, sex with the same person loses its fascination?

In former days, when a man went to a brothel, it was assumed that his wife was not cooperative or that she was incapable of complying with his wishes. Sometimes this was so,
but usually their dilemma was a result of his own untoward
procedures rather than due to aberrant malfunctioning on
her part.

Possibly he preferred to think as some do now that there
are two kinds of women—those one marries and those with
whom one "parties." Often men marry fine, gentle women
with whom they cannot fully relax because they are reminded of their mothers. In some instances, however, women's recent more aggressive actions may be inhibiting. It
could be that deep within many men, there is still that need
to conquer and because this is so much a part of their impetus to sexual accomplishment, the female's eagerness
dampens their desires and motivations. They may require
resistance so that they can subdue or override their partner's
defenses as a stimulus to their ardor.

Undeniably, persons differ in their sexual drives and
moods because of their zodiacal affiliation and the tendencies
thus activated. Everyone, particularly women, should know
more about this in order to understand those they love, since
in spite of recent innovations or perhaps because of them,

there is even more dissension than before.

For one thing, books on the subject changed few men. One serious, widely-read writer, Desmond Morris, the zoologist, in his book "The Naked Ape, which has to do with the origins and development of our species, has included in a chapter on our sexual habits (based upon a number of studies carried out in North America) an extraordinary pattern of erotic performance describing the average (?) couple "making love." Therein he lists three phases of sexual behavior: "pair formation" (or courting), "pre-copulatory" and "copulatory", which surely must have amused or amazed the many wives whose husbands had never heard of the second, or if they ever had, thought it almost entirely superfluous soon after marriage, often reverting to the ways of our monkey and ape "cousins" in which this preactivity is so brief that it provides no sexual stimuli for the female and allows her no possibility of climax. (A woman under the same conditions could be charged with being frigid, while strangely enough if she were even shown the "indulgencies" of the courtship period—the kissing and holding of hands, the soft playful nuzzlings, she might respond with such ardor and appreciation that she would astonish her partner and even find complete fulfillment herself!)

Any woman who reads Mr. Morris' narrative would realize the futility of discussing it with her husband, however, and as for her lover, if he were not already employing at least part of the tactics mentioned, he would be perturbed at the suggested criticism of himself if asked to read the provocative passages.

In truth, the elaborate rites as well as similar ones mentioned by other authors, could but seem unrealistic (however captivating and entertaining) to many couples under the conditions of normal family life.

What manner of man or maid could settle down to such involved sessions, with young children running in and out of the bedroom every few minutes begging for "one more dink?" Or older ones peering through the keyhole? (Voyeurism may have begun in the home.)

As for the suggestions on the same subject in "The Sensuous Woman," one might assume that "J", the author, was writing with tongue in cheek (no pun intended), and the onanistic practices she advanced for increasing a woman's sensuality surely could not have been designed to make her more alluring to either her husband or a lover, since most men would be repelled—indeed, forever "turned off" if they knew of her self-induced pleasures. (Having spent hours by herself in orgiastic experiences, would she not be so completely satiated as to lose all interest for a time in any form of erotic communication?)

Women do want sexual expression, yes, but are we not missing the point here? It is not that women need to be more sensuous to appeal to men, but rather that men should know more about the women with whom they have such unions— not only their potentials but their individual, specific requirements.

If a woman must go to such lengths as "J" advises, she might well dispense with her lover altogether. Her testing indubitably would have resulted only in a greater discontent with his feeble efforts. (It has already been determined by experts that in terms of pure "lustful" enjoyment, an individual may pleasure himself much more than he is pleasured by another) But this is not the objective of the average woman, few of whom would ever find onanism the complete answer to their personal needs. (Kinsey indicated this and anyone who knows women well would reach the same conclusion.) It should be reiterated again and again that most women require much more than the physical aspects of sex to alleviate their hungers. This is what men must learn.

Single women of affluence may have gigolos or even marry younger men, but often they wrongly credit their partners with emotions comparable to their own. (This does not apply to those rare, sincerely loving couples of disparate ages among whom is the woman who has the means to support the husband or lover while he perfects a talent or pursues further education. However, such a man must be of a special nature not to feel his pride of superiority usurped.)

If women followed men's lead in finding excuses for sexual assignations outside the home, Bordellos for them would be flourishing everywhere. Men's lack of concern or desire to please, their infidelities, their eventual impotence (usually long before their mates' passions have subsided—though all men hate to concede this and do not discuss it in conversations with each other)—surely these are reasons enough, yet this alternative is one that men would never countenance nor the women themselves condone. Since it is this very concentration upon the physical side of sex that they have criticized in men, it is hardly likely that great numbers of them would patronize such "houses" (although in all honesty they might be shown more astute consideration than has been granted them elsewhere.)

No, a woman is looking for something more than lustful gratification. She is often worried because her husband's attempts in her behalf seem halfhearted and begrudging, serving to separate them even further spiritually.

Sexual freedom is many faceted. Could it be that the emphasis on sex has tended to crowd out other important phases of family life; that a change of bedroom manners is not enough to reconcile their multiplying differences? Besides, if it has become necessary for couples to look for new special enticements in order to continue to enjoy their initial intimate moments together, is not something missing that once was unifying or at least promising?

Those persons most deeply in love have rarely sought advice from textbooks. In their absorption with each other they have found their own raptures with an ingenuity and spontaneity far removed from mere techniques. What a woman wants in the marital bed is a blending, a fusion of mutual desire, long moments of fond *love* play and meaningful caresses—not learned practices or lascivious orgies.

She may feel strangely alienated today, aware that in seeking greater thrills, she may have defeated her real purpose since the closeness she once shared with her husband now seems somewhat lessened, and that intangible emotional bond—the delicate thread of loving communion has become frayed, and almost severed.

There was a time when she deplored men's negligent "blindness," yet did she not most bemoan his impersonal attitude? And is it not just as pronounced now as it was earlier? Are the days gone forever, she sometimes wonders, when a knowing conspiratorial glance across the room could give them the heady "lift" of several cocktails? When just holding hands while watching television or sitting together in a darkened theater could cause a thunderous pounding of the heart?

While some wives have acquired more modernized ideas of marital bliss, how many husbands have made any attempts toward improvement of their intimate relationships? Instead, are not more of them looking for other companions with whom they hope to find greater rapport?

Although the number of divorces is increasing, only about thirty percent of these are by young people. (The exception is the tripled divorce rate in the last ten years for young executives earning over $25,000.) As women have fewer children and preferably only at an early age, marriage to a new spouse will be more feasible and more easily effected.

Margaret Mead on a television "talk show" intimated that in the near future many men will be seeking younger wives (when the children have finished school), but it appears that this is already happening since statistics show that among marriages that have lasted twenty to twenty-four years the divorce rate is up twenty-eight percent, and thirty-five percent for couples married twenty-five to twenty-nine years.

Is divorce then the panacea for marital unhappiness? As one thinks of these older men, one wonders just how long younger wives will tolerate their ways. How soon will the men tire of catering to them or even trying to satisfy their demanding passions? Among older women, many are dismayed at the thought of divorce; they have invested years in their marriages, and to form new alliances would be almost impossible.

To them it seems that too much is happening too fast, and none of it in their favor—that the world is moving on and leaving them behind. Albeit this is not true for those women who themselves seek new lives—another chance to find what they want through marriage to other men, or in careers if they were free to pursue them, but to the older women it spells tragedy. Added then to their list of anxieties is the present dread of ultimate finality. They suspect secret plans for imminent departures.

Once it was their supposed frigidity that was criticized, then their awakened, "undignified" interest in sex, and now their husbands for whom familiarity has brought restlessness and boredom, want their freedom so that their waning sexual appetites may be revived by younger women.

One cannot help smiling when reading of "authorities" recommending "a sexual life" for those well into their eighties—as though this might be a recommendation for the marriage tradition. These male octogenarians are the ones who knew so little about incitements in their heyday. Can they be expected to have learned much through the years, with the diminishing of their desires? Along with the "wildness" attributed to the past era there was much false modesty, especially between marriage partners. There were taboos and "hangups" and men in general did not display what they thought of as their baser natures to their wives or even to the "playgirls." (Prostitutes were then the solution.)

The present generation, perhaps even the previous one, may look forward to continued sexual activity as they approach the centenary mark, but those of the Prohibition Era? Oh no! it is difficult to believe that human nature can change to that extent.

Younger wives with their liberated views may change the picture for some, but one thing is sure, the average man of years will not risk humiliating himself in clandestine affairs, however many he may have had in the past. Too, the young "sex expert" may be surprised when at the age of eighty-plus he finds himself much more devoted to keeping his heart beating or his hypertension within reasonable bounds than he is in the attainment of orgasm.

A man with the Sword of Damocles hanging over his head can relinquish erotic pleasures without too much regret, and if he is at all intelligent, he will have developed mental and spiritual resources to more than offset the loss. (As for that aging wife, she has probably found ways of adjustment and sublimation long before she reached those later years.)

With all her problems, if a woman knew what to expect as to the dissimilarity in men's passions or their various methods of contending with them, if she were cognizant of the vast differences in individuals and the reasons for the differences, if she could see her own partner's urges and actions in proper perspective, she could better avoid the disappointments that are so often hers. (A man himself is often unable to understand his puzzling moods.) She suffers agonizing uncertainties when she could have been spared much of her sorrow or regret had she possessed a workable knowledge of his leanings before becoming entangled.

A few earlier astrological facts could have provided her with important measures of compromise if she felt irresistibly and unalterably bound to him, or she could have avoided her pain by marrying someone more suitable to her own nature. Even now such information would be helpful, perhaps offering the key to a richer life for both.

The unmarried girl has little excuse for not looking ahead and planning wisely. Such knowledge might not prepare her for every problem with a certain individual, but it can give her pertinent facts regarding herself and him which can strengthen the promise of their creating and maintaining a more compatible relationship.

That any man's predilection for amorous experiments is written in the stars cannot be contested when one has the proof at hand. Too little has been written along this line. Other than mentioning Scorpio's sensuousness and Libra's thirst for pleasure and variety, many astrologers seem to have thought little about it.

Should one then conclude that natives of the other ten signs are passionless? Or that all those of a given sign are equal in their responses to erotic stimuli? Certainly not! Nor must it be intimated that all men are equally faithless, though much depends upon the amount of inducement and the individual's current mood. Sometimes it is the man one would least suspect of infidelity who inexplicably becomes ensnared in circumstances to which even he himself is intrinsically opposed, or feeling that marriage has lost its glamour, allows himself to "fall in love" with someone new.

A man normally in command of his own maneuvering and often preferring the chase to the prize and always fixing the terms as to the extent of involvement according to his personal convenience, might still be an unsuspecting "victim" of a sparkling, eager Libra girl, looking for diversion. A warm, vibrant Scorpio woman with her incomparable charm could capture his wayward senses and his heart. The naivete of a tender Geminian or the romanticism of an Aquarian in their perpetual search for storybook endings, could arouse his amused curiosity.

While any man might capitulate to such pressure, his birth bequeathment may have counterbalancing influences to help him overcome temptation. He may be firmly resistant, for as the Sun and Moon affect the tides, so too do the Sun, the Moon and the planets determine the ebb and flow both of sexual desire and the need for adventure and excitement. They may prompt a man's participation in bacchanalian delights or suggest a cautious, more serious approach to love and sex.

This applies to a woman as well as to a man, but her motivations are more complex and her reactions as an adult are almost entirely dependent upon the various men she has known. No wonder she is more and more concerned in learning the astrological reasons for all behavior!

In the next chapters there are brief profiles of men under each of the twelve Zodiacal signs (followed by *very important decanative divisions of each—the triplicities and cusps*) with suggestions as to their respective attitudes toward women. Further on there is a more detailed discussion of the effects of these attitudes upon the women of each sign.

Yet whatever one's proclivities, each of us has within himself the essentials for controlling his own destiny. One should never feel resigned to any condition not favorable to his well-being.

Although we have been programmed through our instincts to "be fruitful and prolific," because of over-population, pollution and ecology breakdown, we must find new ways in order to survive.

At the moment, there still remains vast sexual and

psychological differences between the sexes, and difficulties these give rise to must be resolved so that there can be vital communication between them.

When men stop thinking of women either as mother substitutes or as objects for lustful enjoyment, and accept them as equals, worthy of respect, with ambition, ability, dignity and pride as natural as their own, women's antagonisms will be quelled for want of fuel. Surely it will at last be recognized that their fulfillment must include that spiritual and emotional harmony, without which the sexual bread is dry.

They are weary of tolerating in so many men of otherwise fine qualities, the smugness of "Little Jack Horners" and are in search of that generosity which indicates real maturity. They hope for the day when there can be more meetings of unselfish, affectionate regard—a genuine mutual solicitude for the happiness and welfare of one another. Belief in such love as this is the woof of most women's girlhood dreams and is not easily destroyed even though it may never be shared or ever fully comprehended by most of the men they encounter. (Zodiacal residence of the men themselves can be of utmost important.)

Chapter 2

Men's Varying Inclinations Based Upon the Zodiacal Signs

ARIES

Rejection is a brackish taste
Upon my trembling lips
Our yesterdays are lost in now's dismay
Your wintry glance doth scourge as cruelly as
A thousand whips
The passion which was yours is gone today.

E'en birds have stilled their lovely songs
And sit in silent grief
And flowers have bowed their heads in deep concern
They share with me my incredulity—
The disbelief
That fires so bright, so quickly cease to burn.

THE ARIES MAN
March 21 through April 20 = Chief Ruler—Mars
Decanative Co-Rulers = The Sun and Jupiter

Mars bequeaths to this man a goodly share of the attributes which make for worldly success and personal satisfaction, yet simultaneously chastens him in the fiery furnace of his own emotions.

It gives him the intellectual capacity to plan and develop a wide variety of business activities and lends him the enterprise, ambition, energy and determination to bring them to fruition, thereby achieving his own goals and aiding those with whom he is associated. He functions best in directing others, leaving to them the mechanics and details of a project.

Complementing his ambitious qualities are those of optimism, humor and generosity. To him life is a constant challenge—a concept which proves equally helpful in business affairs and in those of the heart. The Arien tends to look ahead from early manhood, knowing just what he wants in life if not yet sure just how he will attain it. Few young people apply themselves so early and so diligently or with such indefatigable zeal. His seriousness is evident even in his choice of feminine companions.

Whereas most young men initially are attracted only by exciting, alluring figures, Aries, though of strong libidinous feeling and usually choosing a girl of substantial sex appeal, is moved also by her shy glances of approval. She must admire him and believe implicitly in his worth and his ambitions.

Unless she understands his vulnerability and his unceasing need to see that adoration in her eyes, she cannot hope to long retain his interest. Since he is variable in his affectionate moods, exacting, possessive and jealous, much more flexibility is required of her than the average young woman has yet attained. This usually means that he has a number of romances and casual contacts before becoming overly serious about any one girl.

Actually, his changeability stems from his own Mars moods, and when the rhythm of his emotions is at a depressingly low ebb he may misinterpret some unwitting word or action of another as a threat to his pride, and being deeply hurt, will affect a coldness of manner which is not always understood.

This explains, perhaps, the fact that the Arien often marries at a later age than his peers, and although he may be compulsively flirtatious and indulge in many previous light affairs, in marriage his standards of conduct are usually more strict and he will not condone promiscuity in himself or tolerate it in his companion.

Even from the beginning, his avocation is of prime importance, his amours occupying only a small part of his waking hours. Any serious alliance must be carefully considered since, as he plans his career, so too does he envision the home life he desires.

When he has oriented himself in a field which promises continual progressive achievement, his erotic dreams become more purposeful and he seeks a mate who will "complete the picture" of the life pattern he foresees in correlation with his own self image. Although he may be tempted to turn aside for a woman of flamboyant nature because he is attracted by this type, usually he chooses one who is conservative in manner, appearance and outlook.

Obviously she must be above reproach where other men are concerned. His pride demands this, and though earlier he may have enjoyed the challenge of wooing a popular, sexy woman away from another suitor, he cannot now endure the indignity of such pursuit, feeling that his own proven worthiness should obviate such procedures. Also, the idea of frivolity in a wife does not appeal to him. His need to be the aggressor is ever present and one who pursues him can only expect disappointment or at best, a brief response.

While the Arien may notice every curvacious feature of other women, when he is wife-hunting, the effect is only a momentary pang of nostalgia. He seeks a woman of his own meticulous tastes and interests, one who is quietly congenial, hopefully, physically desirable and whose personal accomplishments and varied abilities will make him proud. She may even surpass him in some field of endeavor and his generous reaction will be one of real pleasure since seeing her as a projection of himself, her success is also his.

Though he expects her to play a subordinate role as to his business and finances, he will be delighted at any talents she may display as long as they do not intrude upon their relationship. She must be wise in her knowledge of him so that she will rightly interpret his moods. (Mars elevates his spirits to great heights at times and as quickly reverses them.) This gives him the appearance of being emotionally fickle, spontaneously warm at one moment and chillingly indifferent at another, a tendency of which he himself is often unaware. Therefore, one who loves him must withhold judgment in order to retain her own equilibrium.

If he strays into philandering ways it will be only because of deep disappointment. If his mate fails to live up to his expectations, he may look for another; if insurmountable obstacles have kept him from fulfilling his ambitions, he may allow temptation to overcome his scruples and be led into trivial, meaningless affairs. (Even these would disturb his peace of mind and deep sense of loyalty.) Rarely will he commit himself to a *serious* extra-marital affair. The restless, adventurous spirit that served him well in those years when the chase was as important as the conquest, becomes buried under many layers of serious habit.

If in his troubled dreams a beautiful "golden girl" offers warm, silken lips and even more tantalizing inducements, a deep sigh might betoken a passing regret for his cautious ways, but when he has awakened to full awareness, the dream content will have been suppressed.

The lucky Aries man is one who finds the dreamed of Love Goddess hidden within the woman who is his "wife image." Being keenly perceptive, he often does.

TAURUS

So busy he, the prescience which he feels
Is fraught
With quickened interest as he turns the wheels
Of action which he sense will bring gold
But naught
Of this keen insight was he ever told
Or taught

So busy he, he does sometimes forget
To say
The words so deeply etched within, and yet
The ladies seek him out and neither are
They fey
In offering their love; whate'er their star
They stay

THE TAURUS MAN

April 21 through May 21 = Chief Ruler—Venus
Decanative Co-Rulers = Mercury and Saturn

Venus awakens in this man a love of natural beauty and harmonious sounds, a quality of delicate balance puzzling to one who remembers that he is the Head Sign of the Earth Triplicity with finance significantly pronounced and solid fundamentals figuring in all of his well considered judgments.

It is true that of first importance on his adult agendum is the attainment of sufficient funds and income for complete independence. No man has greater determination regarding this accomplishment and no man succeeds better.

His wants or needs are not necessarily beyond reason nor his accumulations always spectacular, although his money-making abilities are often phenomenal; his motivation, however, derives from an emphatic wish to remain free by having no obligations.

Indominitable of purpose, reliable, conscientious and industrious, he is able to recognize the possibilities of a business proposition where others would fail to perceive them, but prudently delves more deeply into issues and circumstances than is common to some, arriving at definite decisions more slowly. Only after a thorough investigation will he lend his support to an enterprise.

This very patience which makes for success in practical affairs also leads him into such diversified fields as acting or musical entertainment. Preoccupied with the sober face of life, with its problems and demands, and having a steady concern to fulfill his personal commitments (yet urged by Venus almost contradictorily toward the creation of beauty through musical or artistic channels), automatically he turns often toward such expressions in ways which he knows to be of real commercial value.

The Taurian can be charming when circumstances warrant the effort but he can be extremely obstinate if one attempts to override his opinions or thwart his plans. He remains oblivious to any advice or ideas counter to his own.

Deeply resenting and fearing criticism, he sees suggestions from others as a frightening attempt at manipulation—an "impudence" he cannot abide. It is because of this trait that he can be hurt through his own infidelities.

If he suspects that his female companion is trying to "manage" him, he may deliberately seek solace with other women, though his primary motive will be to obtain sympathy or support for his belief of unjust treatment.

Yet, prizing loyalty and being much more romantic than would be indicated by his calm, well studied approach to affairs of the heart, when he has allowed himself the indulgence of such pleasures (mostly to assuage dissatisfaction with his marriage partner or regular consort), he still finds no surcease to his unhappiness. Added to the emotional chaos which he formerly endured is now a nagging discomfort and continuous need to rationalize his course of action. Although he feels guilty in the role of the transgressor, understanding his unfairness in expecting allegiance and constancy under these circumstances, he would be stunned at any hint of deception or insincerity on the part of his companion and find it difficult to forgive or forget unfaithfulness.

Still, while adament in his various decisions and almost fanatic in his desire to pursue his own choice of action, the Taurus native is nonetheless kindly, pleasant and even pliable in his personal relationships as long as this freedom is not jeopardized.

It is plain that any woman in love with this Venus-ruled man needs to be uncritically discerning in order to fortify his self-assurance, the lack of which must lie at the root of his desperate struggle against anything which he feels connotes domination. She must be generous with praise and acknowledgement of his worth, and give him the devoted care which he would so quickly deny needing.

While he prefers to provide the wherewithal for a good life, and to have his wife at home where he feels she belongs, he does expect her to keep house as neatly and systematically as if she were running a business establishment.

She also must keep herself attractive and well groomed.

He gives no special thought to these expectations, accepting as only natural the application of her talents to their homelife.

Like most Earth sign natives, he seems almost embarrassed at any show of sentiment, yet he will do many little helpful things to express his loving regard and will secretively buy her gifts which she would not be apt to purchase for herself. Despite his seemingly difficult nature, this innate thoughtfulness, his dependability and fortitude in the face of difficulties more than compensate for his stubborn traits. With one who understands him, there may be a lifetime of mutual contentment. He dislikes uncertainty—an atmosphere not in accord with his idea of domestic tranquillity. Sexually too she must not only be amenable but anticipate his unpredictable moods.

Lacking a warm communication his (sometimes) eager passions are stifled and he may then look for diversions elsewhere. Furthermore, should disharmony in the home seem to be irreversible, he would not long be satisfied (as are some men) with transitory, sex-oriented affairs, but would go in search of a permanent, more ego-enhancing attachment—one in which his libido and conscience can dwell together in peace.

GEMINI

I loved you but you opened not your heart to me
Nor lingered long
One moment you were here, the next were gone
Ecstatic nights that were
Are naught but memories now
Perhaps you never were
Content, but caught somehow
In wishful hopes—quixotic gallantry

Did you anticipate each unborn dawn
With quickened heart and further need of quest
While I partook of all your gentleness

So unaware
That if you loved, you loved reluctantly?
I should have guessed
For there is some wild, untamed part of you
That sought escape and which I did not dare
Explore or view
But though you left, and thus are lost to me
At evening's dusk, I listen for your step
And wait with indrawn breath and hushed expectancy.
I am bereft!

THE GEMINI MAN
May 22 through June 21 = Chief Ruler—Mercury
Decanative Co-Rulers = Venus and Uranus

Can Mercury's abundant offerings actually produce the many conflicting traits so often ascribed to its subjects?

Geminians are sensitive and empathetic—extremely interested in the history and environment of all races and peoples. Any issue of the day which reflects the needs of humanity, they study with concern and without bias; their preachments for justice and equal opportunity for all are urgently sincere. They can be impatient to the point of intolerance when confronted with prejudice in these matters—quickly vocal in denouncing unfair judgments by others.

A native of this sign is both imaginative and zealous whether in developing new ideas of his own or those of another. Moreover, though performing with greater facility and inspiration in carrying out his own designs, he can be equally enthusiastic when aiding someone else in an enterprise (especially if his warmer emotions are involved.)

All types of construction interest him but the interiors are especially fascinating.

Music frequently plays a prominent role, lending significance to his behavior and emphasis to his efforts, just as certain colors strongly affect his feelings and responses to erotic stimuli, and an author's words may inspire him to original thought and new objectives.

He has the necessary implements for natural accomplishment—initiative, awareness, brilliancy of mind, eagerness and active agility, but as a result of his affectionate regard for others, he is buffeted by both circumstance and people. Although he may be distracted from his purpose at times, his many talents and keen perception are readily available when he is driven to resolute attempts at performing the near impossible. It is through these strivings that rich rewards frequently come. If he seems satisfied with superficial knowledge of facts that should be important to him, this is often because he endeavors to cover an area of greater breadth than is readily discernible to others. He may for instance, scan four chapters of a book, seizing upon the kernels of truth which to him are most pertinent while another would read one chapter slowly enough to digest the many details.

Unquestionably, he often begins new projects rather than finish the tediously routine tasks of the current one. However, this is often due to percipience rather than weakness, since the Gemini native is quicker than most to recognize and admit that a project at hand has after all been a mistake or stands little chance of success. He therefore discards it and immediately replaces it with another (which might have been all the while competing in his mind for precedence.) Said to procrastinate, it is rather that his Mercurial interests are so varied and often so scattered that completion of a particular task may seem slow to one who may be waiting for him to produce results.

His unflagging ambitions undoubtedly derive from a compulsive need to achieve, yet his motivations are not selfish. Although his own esthetic tastes may dictate order and pleasant surroundings, he is remarkably adaptable and cooperative and is able to contend with many disadvantages and to do with few of the luxuries commonly desired.

Being visionary, and without pretences, he is slow to appreciate the power of affluence, status or possessions. Despite the intellectuality attributed to him, he often operates emotionally rather than through intuition, reasoning or logic.

He has little need of status symbols. It is usually through

family responsibility or consideration for a loved one that he
is led to work unceasingly and without complaint toward
those attainments which would otherwise seem unworthy of
the effort. Although normally amiable, he is subject to the
vagaries of his dual nature.

It is well known that this man can be restlessly discontented and easily depressed, yet just as unwaveringly optimistic. Though overly generous, if necessary he can be financially shrewd.

Quick moving and appearing tireless, he nevertheless
needs more than an average amount of sleep and rest to alleviate his nervous tensions. When overtired from prolonged
activity he can be satirical, impatient and abrupt even while
simultaneously being appalled at his behavior.

Usually conscientious and sincerely solicitous of his friends
or loved ones, at times he may completely fail to notice some
circumstance affecting their welfare or happiness. Even after
realizing and lamenting the omission, he may again abstract-
edly drift into temporary periods of disregard. This may
coincide with some very personal anxiety since there is no
greater evidence of his seeming inconsistency than in the
area of feminine relationships.

Here the Geminian is most assailable, his life pattern having taken on a will-of-the-wispish quality from his very early
years when he began following wherever Eros beckoned.

His first erotic episode is often with a sexually aggressive
woman, older in years or experience than he. Extremely
idealistic and anticipating a romantic affair, this Mercury-
ruled man is often hesitant about the choice of companion for
that first sharing of mutual pleasure. Thus, while he modestly delays in making a decision, he is taken unawares.
Conversely, his extreme sensuousness may lead him to very
early experiments and innumerable amours, each one
quickly following another.

If that first girl or woman is wise enough to weave a spell
of "mystical intrigue" about their liaisons, he may be entranced for life. However, if she should be at all obtuse as to
his finer instincts—the importance of his spiritual needs—in
all probability she will soon find that his interest has waned.

Since he cannot bear to think that his expectations were merely hopes, he begins that frantic search which never ends.

Once his romantic quest has led him down the "primrose path," he never falters and rarely returns, an unfortunate contradiction to his real nature, since of all Zodiacal natives the Geminian is without doubt the most persistent advocate of true and reciprocal love. Perhaps he is also the most yearningly needful of a union which offers it.

In any event, it is essential that someone special always be waiting near at hand. He prefers that she be gentle, serious and well informed but looks too for good humor, gay playfulness and adaptive qualities with which to meet his own fluctuating moods.

Yes, Mercury imposes unpredictability, but this provocative trait appeals to many women. Because he requires complete rapport and mental stimulation as well as physical, he is beset by the urge to make many changes.

Even though inherently active and enterprising, how can a man be settled and steady in any aspect of his life, when admiring girls are flitting like colorful butterflies in and out of his days and fantasies? Promiscuous? Never with intent. Each time he loves, he believes it is forever. He wants it to be. He can never quite believe that the fleeting games of amorous pretense which others often play are not sincere, or that his own tender passions may be attrited by repeatedly shattered illusions.

CANCER

A shell he found and treasured through the years
Significance for him is everywhere
I saw him lift a child and dry its tears
Remembering, mayhap, his own young fears
That strange foreboding which was always there

He asks not a reward for dragons slain
True empathy—compassion, in him lives

Solicitude for those he loves comes naturally
For them alone he struggles to attain
Success, prestige—a measure of acclaim
The shell he keeps but of his spirit gives.

THE CANCER MAN
June 22 through July 22 = Chief Ruler—The Moon
Decanative Co-Rulers = Mars and Neptune

Knowing the effects of the changing moods of the Moon itself upon all individuals, one cannot be surprised that occupying Cancer as it does, it leaves a native questioning his
own varying emotions.

There is also a great diversification among the natives
themselves. Some can be quite positive and decisive, immersed in innumerable projects and activities, seemingly
driven by inner demons to keep forever busy. Yet there are
those who desire neatness and order but prefer to supervise
rather than do the actual work required. Thus they are not
always eager for projects wherein the labor falls mostly to
them.

However, the Cancer man is obsessed with a sense of duty;
he can be relied upon to fulfill his obligations either in business or the social world. In fact, he often must protect himself from those who would take advantage of these qualities.

A well-planned home life is very important to him. His
deep devotion to parents or elderly family members is
unique, and while extremely careful of his own expenditures,
he will give unstintingly both materially and of his time and
energy when needed.

Though shrewdly economical, he is impelled to accumulate, continuously adding to his store of practical (though
frequently exotic) treasures. This is not so much due to the
esthetic pleasure derived from the possession of such objects
(as is true of the Cancer woman) but rather because acquisitions strengthen his feeling of security.

His abilities are many faceted, his business acumen so
noteworthy that in itself it provides the future security so
essential to his peace of mind. Yet his success is as probable
in the theater or the arts as in commerce.

Reserved and reticent but desiring approbation and a feeling of "belonging," he cheerfully welcomes new friendships and contacts, often leading an active social or religious life. Being somewhat impressed by the erudition of others as well as being interested in a wide variety of subjects, he keeps himself well informed on all current affairs.

He dislikes sudden changes and though uneasy in his need for diversion, he is never impulsive in satisfying his whims, planning well in advance for any exigencies. Jovial and optimistic at times, brooding and despondent at others, given both to idle fantasy and grim introspection, he finds it difficult to solve his problems of intimate portent.

Responding naturally to admiration and becoming as quickly deflated by criticism, giving himself to love and affection with sincerity and appreciation, yet ever mindful of slights or lack of understanding, he hesitates to form strong attachments. (Adding to his uncertainties is a sensitive discrimination)

Certainly he must be sure of unequivocal fealty from one for whom he cares. To please him, she must be willing to overlook his caution—to be tolerant and not overly demanding. He counts upon her to be thoroughly self-sufficient, with creditable talents and ambition of her own and to be correct and conservative in manner and dress. If initially lured into making an unwise choice, he may lose all rational perspective and begin to doubt the feminine sex itself rather than admit to his own lack of discernment.

With each aborted attempt to satisfy his longings for "that certain woman" he becomes a little less zealous, sometimes turning from his erotic searchings to lose himself in artistic or civic endeavors. However, these sublimating interludes are often beneficial, leading to success in a field to which he has previously given little thought or effort. The resulting boost to his self-confidence gives him courage and renewed faith in his masculine objectives. Even without remarkable accomplishment, the change of pace offers refreshing insight and the impetus to return to his pursuit of the illusive love object.

When he ultimately finds the one who fits his stern dictums and makes what he plans to be a permanent commitment, with the speed and directness of Lochinvar he boldly appropriates his lady love, bringing to the union a gentleness and understanding in remarkable contrast to his former more critical, exacting attitude.

Though in his mind the image of his home companion has always been one in which she is self-striving and independent, once he is sure of her love, he wants to protect her from the rest of the world. Toward this end he seeks to provide a beautiful abode. Who makes it attractive and inviting for his special comfort? The lady who was to have been out making progress on her own usually enjoys his contentment so much that she willingly obliges.

Though ever sexually aware, only in the event of the betrayal of his affections will he be unduly tempted to turn to others.

Liking the solidity and respectability of domestic life, he distrusts anything which might interfere with the perfection of its operation, fearing to involve himself in anything which might yield only temporary amusement.

LEO

There the fair damsels stand all in a row
Each waiting in vain for the others to go.
Which one will win? And which ones will lose?
How can they know whom a Leo will choose?

Too many maidens surround him each day
All seeking his favors, how many will stay?
Can he decide? Or will he be coy,
Scatter love's pleasures for all to enjoy?

THE LEO MAN
July 23 through August 21 = Chief Ruler—The Sun
Decanative Co-Rulers = Jupiter and Mars

Here is a man of strong and masterful demeanor—self-confident and visionary, idealistic and impressionable—a man of forthright opinions and refreshing candor wno is purposeful, direct and sure of his ability to influence others and thus gain his objectives. He is so forceful and convincing in manner that he can make one believe in any idea no matter how unreasonable it may appear.

He has scores of such ideas, some of them feasible even when seemingly impractical to those of lesser optimism.

From his early youth he maintains that while others are struggling with the actual details and necessary labor for the accomplishment of a project, it is the thinker, the planner and organizer, who reaps the sure rewards.

This is not to imply that the Leonian is lazy; his Sun has given him energy to spare, but to him it is sensible to avoid using it in unpleasant ways when he can discerningly direct the activities which will bring success.

This man was born to be a leader—to head the parade and carry away the prize. He never doubts it. It follows that he is superb in the field of entertainment or in any capacity where he is in the limelight, yet he is equally capable in professions such as law, medicine, politics, in promotional activities or in executive positions. (However, if he should desire a life of indolence with someone else furnishing the means, it is usually his for the taking. This Sun-favored individual is sought after for many obvious reasons.)

It should be mentioned, though, that there is another type of August Leo whose ego apparently has not been developed to this extent. There are divergent traits in all signs but this one presents an especially fine example of the "exception that proves the rule."

He is generous to a fault, exceptionally kind and solicitous of others. He is not often found in positions of great financial profit to himself, preferring to use his talents "away from the madding crowd"—sometimes hidden away in a library or office where his abilities are always useful. Though appearing to be self-effacing or subdued upon casual contact, his fires are merely banked. They still smolder. Seeming more flexible than the other natives, he has his own fixed convictions which are rarely changed by conflicting opinions.

While all of these men have a definite need for

appreciation—a constant audience—this is the one who actually requires it most, though he is less apt to attract it. Moreover, (quite surprisingly) if it is not forthcoming in his daily occupation, he may seek it in a variety of affairs just as his other Sun "brothers" do.

Whether domineering and persistently aggressive or deceptively unassuming, the Leonian sorely needs the esteem of women. Thus, flattery is the ally of any who hope to attract him. He basks in praise and responds to it as a plant does to water, and his lordly bearing only serves to emphasize his gentle but possessive ways which women admire.

His childhood homelife strongly affects him in later years, especially in determining his erotic patterns. The very sureness, the arrogant courage of the young Leo, although increasingly mitigated by an appealing friendliness as he grows older, often causes resentment in other male family members, resulting in misunderstanding and ego-deflating scenes which leave an unfortunate mark upon him. Being the source of all his strength and confidence, his ego is easily wounded; this can be catastrophic. If he has been allowed to develop in a natural way and there are enough compensations in other areas, the adulation and strong affection of one woman may ultimately be all he needs. She will have to be a woman of unusual attributes—chic in appearance, noticeably alert yet non-combative and of even temperament. She must be conversant with his many interests, share his views and listen to his schemes no matter how nebulous.

Still, she could have a career of her own if she chose, or even have a family background from which she derives some income—a financial arrangement whereby they would be afforded more luxury and status than would otherwise be possible. (The Leo man has great regard for the attainments and success of others.) Obviously, in such a case a great deal of diplomacy would be necessary.

He requires a household run with efficiency and without undue confusion—certainly without any physical effort on his part, although he might well provide the plans to facilitate the desired results.

If a woman who is versatile enough to fulfill his various

needs is not immediately found, he usually decides that quantity is better than quality—finds it less demanding and even more exciting.

In the coterie of eager applicants there is of course one who pleases him most or for a longer period of time. She understands that beneath that brave facade, there often lives a lonely, frightened man. She must accept him at his own projected evaluation and be willing to wait faithfully and uncomplainingly on the sidelines until he tires of the tumult.

Since he expects and thrives on commendation, if it is supplied with constancy and tact, he can be coaxed into domestic alliances. The duration of their union depends on her tolerance, but with this warmly affectionate man, even uncertain, ephemeral moments might be worth the price!

VIRGO

They draw upon his stalwart strength
But give not love
The feeble flames ignited by
His careful heart
In those he tends so dutifully
Protectively
Are all but drenched and out
Before they have a start
Because he hides the way he feels
Cannot impart
The warmth that prompts response
To all their needs—e'en love!

THE VIRGO MAN
August 22 through September 21 = Chief Ruler—Mercury
Decanative Co-Rulers = Saturn and Venus

Practicality marks this man's progress through life. He can be or do anything within the realm of his personal preferences, is apt to initiate industrious and frugal patterns very early and to retain them throughout his later years. His is energetic, painstaking and intelligent. When artistically inclined, his well known nervous vigor is translated into a fine attention to details and the perfecting of necessary skills to further his purpose, though at times, his innate modesty and shyness prevent his attempting things at which he could obviously be successful.

In the field of the theatre or television, his pleasing personality and gentle though urgent presence is strongly felt by all that view him, yet it is plain that he must be himself—that he has little talent for the delineation of traits foreign to his own nature.

This same honesty is seen in all aspects of his life, both public and personal. He is never imitative, devious or affected. Although greatly respected, his stern manner discourages casual intimacy, and he rarely bothers to strengthen ties which seem to him of little value, not wanting to feel obligated to anyone other than his family (sometimes resenting even these ties.) Though he feels a heavy weight of responsibility for their welfare, he nevertheless can be as incredibly critical of them as he often is of others.

At heart a kindly man, in trying so arduously to live within the framework of the ideal which he sets for himself, he seems to forget that humans are never flawless and that performance rarely equals one's intentions. (Counting so painfully upon perfection in those he loves, this very attitude can cause defeat!)

His insight is not infallible as he likes to think, and he can be deceived easily by another's false reporting. (Indeed, his naivete is remarkable!) When faced with undeniable proof of misplaced trust, he accepts it without complaint, just as he does the knowledge that his advice is seldom followed. He scorns recriminative reminders of another's past mistakes or failures.

Apparently the Virgo native renews his faith and replenishes his optimism with the rising sun each morning. No matter the conditions or his disappointments, he is prepared for the daily fray and hopefully expectant of better results.

No man can turn more directly from his true self, however,

if he allows anxieties and resentments to take over. This can sometimes lead to excessive indulgences or uncharacteristic aberrations, though usually in the form of food or drink rather than in sexual deviations. To one of his temperament, however, the dubious joys of "imbibing the grape" are often quite injurious when overdone.

Normally, the Mercury motivated man shows a natural restraint and integrity in all matters, due perhaps to his sense of order, his deference for ideas common to his locale, or to ancestral standards of behavior implanted in his childhood. Anything tinged with subterfuge or trickery annoys him. This description should not be construed as negating his strongly felt erotic drives though they are often carefully kept in check. Of an Earth sign, he can have exceedingly deep passions and unsatisfied longings, but his ingrained beliefs concerning "right" and "wrong," and his guilt at any avoidance of duty are ever present. He has a vast reservoir of strength and in adhering to self-regulating principles, is deterred from pursuing any questionable course of action.

Yet temptation is often his. Before effecting an actual marriage, he may have several affairs and to him they will all be serious, involving him completely. They will usually be terminated by the women since his empathy and conscientiousness would not allow him to desert them.

Despite these well meant ventures, very little of a true romantic flavor is apparent in his "love making." Almost invariably he succumbs to a person whose chief appeal lies in her need for his protective care—which he offers in great measure, asking in return only a well ordered existence. He requires loyalty if not noticeable ardor (though he would be pleased as well as surprised if affection were generously given, and could perhaps in time even reciprocate with less reserve.)

As for his own loyalty and devotion, had the ONE who said "Greater love hath no man than that he lay down his life for his friends" said instead "for his family," one could be fairly certain that HE had in mind the Virgo man, since once committed, he withholds nothing. It is said that he can live without sexual release for longer periods than any other man. If true, this could be because of stern self-discipline. In any case, he takes his marriage vows seriously.

Sadly, for all his sharp discernment in mundane matters (or those other than personal) he has the Mercury blindness when he loves. The woman of his choice may differ from him radically, both in habits and expectations. This quiet, hopeful man, so steady and reliable in his own peculiar way, is unable to transmit a warmth and spontaneity of delicate sentiment, and while most women would approve his natural faithfulness for the security thus engendered, he often finds it impossible in the restrictive, critical climate which he unwittingly creates, to count upon the fidelity and loving regard which he so richly deserves and so desperately needs.

LIBRA

Freighted with unearned guilt
With fears he does not understand, beset
Yet heeding not direction or advice
With careless feet he walks the corridors of time
Intent upon a course of gay abandonment

Tho there are hours when bitter and alone
Illusions spent but unrelinquished yet
Decrying now, excitements once he sought
And scorning roistering crowds, he locks himself within
A dark and gloomy tomb of self imprisonment

But Venus has compassion for her own
Allows him not to sicken with regret
He soon returns to laugh and love again
To fill his empty cup from Dionysian Springs
And find the cheer he craves in song and merriment.

THE LIBRA MAN
September 22 through October 22 = Chief Ruler—Venus
Decanative Co-Rulers = Uranus and Mercury

Much has been written about this man—most of it true but often incomplete.

He is like a quiet river, wending its gentle way through a meadow in which children play contentedly, but where, hidden and unseen, there are dark and dangerous caverns through which treacherous flood waters constantly seek escape. Thus the Libran's pertinacious loneliness and frustration ever vie for attention with his gayer moments.

Nourished by Venusian rays which encourages both love and beauty, he is provided with a suitable backdrop for the drama in which he is the central figure from his bassinet days onward. That bright, seductive smile that first delights his proud mother or anyone else within its range, continues to cast its spell throughout his lifetime.

Yet he, whom the Gods so richly favor, is not always a happy man. Although music permeates his very being (and frequently is utilized profitably), although he is inventive and artistic (normally using these talents to good account as well), is prophetic and perennially youthful both in spirit and appearance, he is still restless and impatient with only half submerged longings and anxieties—sometimes temperamental, impetuous, unforgiving and indolent—an unfathomed enigma even to himself!

However, his outward mien denies this. No man has greater charm! With disarming overtures and unfeigned friendliness, reaching out for warmth and affection, he indiscriminately wields his magic wherever he goes.

Men are drawn by his obvious sincerity and women of all ages are ensnared by his engaging manner.

If far horizons hold for him the same allure as that of capricious, untried mistresses, dictating frequent change of environment and occupation, it is because of an unreasoning belief that the fulfillment of his hopes lies just beyond the hill.

When he is moody and easily discouraged, it is because his ever-present, often illogical fantasies are so much a part of his every waking moment that their failure to materialize disconcerts him. These fantasies bring not pleasure but the poison of defeat. (Unlike Homer's Lotus Eaters, satisfied and complacent with the dream itself, he needs the evidence of accomplishment to still the urgency within.) His dreams promise affluence, "success," earned importance which would bring admiration and applause—but most of all a surcease to his fear of rejection.

The Libran can be opinionated through hasty, ill considered thinking, yet may vacillate with little apparent strength of conviction if withdrawal of friendship seems threatened.

His fondness of animals is unparalleled and though he usually is concerned and generous with people, he sometimes seems unaccountably indifferent, thus appearing to be thoughtlessly self centered. (Those who know him, however, understand that this attitude springs not from selfishness but from lack of awareness. Still, though he may manifest a deep sentiment for those closest to him, and want their approval, there are times when he offers genuine tenderness as cautiously and sparingly as if it were rare wine. In this too, one recognizes the paradox that best describes him. Needing affection, wanting the security of mutual rapport yet fearing—indeed, denying the obligation of true involvement, he withholds a part of himself, thus robbing his relationships of validity.

(This strangely tormented man reminds one of a small boy with a bag of candy, who generously distributes his goodies to all his friends, while from time to time, he peers surreptitiously inside at a particular, favorite morsel which he is saving and which he continues to clutch inside the bag, pressing it to his body as though in fear that it will vanish. Thus it is that the Libran retains and protects that one last vestige of himself which he never quite relinquishes.) Much as he may desire to do so, he can impart no emotional security to others since he has none of his own. Primarily wistful, ingratiating and appealing, a sudden, unexplainable change of feeling will cause him to swing rapidly from affectionate bantering to restrained inaccessability or unresponsiveness.

Intuitively, the Libran native most often chooses for his marriage companion, a woman who will be a mother substitute, giving him uncritical, tolerant regard and the bachelor's freedom he considers so essential. He prefers her to be modest and retiring—a woman he can respect and trust although he may enjoy in his leisure hours, one of more "earthy" or aggressive attributes.

(Some October men have such a fear of entangling obligations or perhaps of feminine preeminence, that they avoid women altogether.)

Oddly, now and then, a Libran is strictly faithful "in his fashion." Having rather antiquated, puritanical ideas of the accepted mode of conduct in wedlock, he hesitates to deviate sexually from his preconceived views. (He is though, blind to women's broader concept of loyalty in which unimportant erotic liaisons might be preferable to one in which he displays special interest or attentiveness. While typically, he is not of this chivalrous, old world category in which sex is abeyant (his sensual demands, even when of no great depth, are too urgent for that) it should not be deduced that he necessarily enjoys a Casanovian existence.

It may be that his superficial romantic episodes offer an escape from the disappointing realities in the other areas of his life. It may be that he never quite suppresses the feeling of guilt he retains each time. It could be that though these episodes satisfy his persistent, plaintive libidinous instincts, their evanescent, spurious quality prohibits the attainment of his real purpose. (One should not forget that this is a man of contradictions and that often he is motivated in his amours by that deep need to be admired and liked, which often leads him into unanticipated situations. Possibly too, his frenetic search for excitement and gay camaradarie is but the need for change and variety (the stilling of boredom) which prompts his other activities. (More likely, he is ever seeking his own true identity!)

Whatever the cause, even as he finds each venture only temporarily sustaining, undaunted, he compulsively continues his pattern of illusionary quest, bestowing his favors impartially and often with only assumed fervor yet with resultant eagerness of response.

A loving man, he, and a most lovable one, but since the scales of justice are the symbol of his sign, is it not ironic that his quest should be so often fruitless, leaving him continuously bewildered and without content?

Here is a thought, however! Perhaps it is only to the unimaginative observer that this seems sad. It is possible that this Venus inspired dreamer gleans more from life in the

search itself than do many who cling so fearfully, albeit so
heroically, to the dull, prosaic, more conventional pathways!

SCORPIO

'Twas meant that he be free
To run fleet footed o'er the sands—
To reach for moonbeams as
The ocean's waters lap his feet
And night birds softly sound
Their plaintive call in swift retreat—
To feel the gentle rain upon
His face in many lands
This is his dream; he seeks not fame
Nor wealth and its demands

Ah yes! 'twas meant that he be free
But passion's chains are strong
And conscience has a key that locks
The door to thoughts with wings
And love there is—and loyalty
With all the claims it brings

Thus doubts intrude and soon he feels
His yearnings to be wrong
And so conceals his longings for
The surf—the night bird's song
Renouncing all his precious dreams
For sober, mundane things.

THE SCORPIO MAN

October 23 through November 22 = Chief Ruler—Mars
Decanative Co-Rulers = Neptune and the Moon

The native of Scorpio is a man of rare self-containment
and composure. His talents are legion. He walks the earth
with quiet pride and confidence, knowing that he possesses
the ingenuity, the perseverance and the determination to

overcome all obstacles in accomplishing his certain purpose.

His incentives are of utmost value, since they dictate his goals, encouraging his struggle for their attainment.

His insatiable thirst for knowledge can lead to long periods of study and application to books on a variety of subjects; curiosity and interest in peoples of all origins can prompt a desire for extensive travel; filial or paternal responsibilities may motivate his ambitions, and sexual drives fire his abundant energies into paths of great financial gain.

He is self analytical and introspective, knowing well his faults as he knows his virtues; also, his cognition of the character, moods and emotions of others is remarkably accurate.

The Scorpio native's ideas on the issues of the day, the state of the world and the reasons thereof, may differ radically from those of the average person but while inwardly resisting conformity to a considerable degree, he fashions his days within the bounds of practical reasoning—not actually caring greatly about the opinion of others but understanding the value of tact and diplomacy. His reticence is in no way due to fear of facing his antagonist (indeed, he enjoys abstract controversy though preferring amicable, constructive discussions) but rather due to a courtesy which allows every man his own concepts, even though they may have been conceived in an unenlightened environment or background.

He understands that many persons need the support they have garnered from family or other early contacts to fortify their own weak and undeveloped beliefs and that to take it away would be to leave them completely defenseless.

Mars (though some say Pluto) makes the Scorpian inscrutable and secretive, not only for the sake of a peaceful atmosphere which is of vital importance, but because he must always have a separateness—an apartness through which he functions best. He has the ability to turn off all emotion, to hide behind a mask of impassivity so that one is never sure of his true feelings. (This serves him well when his surprising sympathy for others takes the form of service in surgery, medicine or psychiatry.)

No other sign provides a wider scope of possible rewarding activities combined with the attributes necessary for their performance. (Often, only a part of his numerous talents becomes known.)

He is effective in the use of words and ideas; color, form, and music have special meanings for him. Through these avenues come much of his pleasure as well as material success.

He is articulate, innovative, tenacious and quietly aggressive. He is provident though generous, vital and magnetic, exercising almost hypnotic power over others when he so wills.

True, there are some Scorpio natives who are overly suspicious, pessimistic, hostile, domineering and cynical, but these traits usually appear only in cases of childhood traumas or when the current environment is frustratingly restrictive. Once he has freed himself from the damaging entanglements and is able to direct his own destiny, his real self normally emerges.

He is though, an extremist. When he has no deeply felt obligations, he may enjoy a hermit's life and be so frugal as to deny himself many of the "creature comforts," or he may be stubbornly self-indulgent and intemperate in any way which pleases him.

In any case, this man needs room in the framework of his life style to be himself without undue pressure. He constantly carries with him a feeling of guilt—a conviction that he should accomplish more, no matter how successful he is in his particular field. Yet he longs to be free of all restraint—to roam the avenues and bypaths of life at will—to investigate the mysteries of the universe and peruse the thousands of volumes on library shelves in search of answers to the persistent questions which are his. From these secret longings spring the guilt that pervades the hours he spends in dutiful conformity with such apparent willingness.

Passionate and strongly interested in physical expression of affection, frequently marrying early, he remains in a sense, however, a man alone, cherishing his aloneness as well as the freedom and independence it bespeaks.

He has a secret place within himself where he hibernates

at times. This is at once a refuge and a liability, providing an enchanted haven—a quiet, restful place where he is free "and the world well lost," yet this need for frequent insularity sometimes provokes misunderstandings even with those he loves. However, these secret forays—moments or hours in lonely abstraction so jealously guarded and shared by no one, creates an aura of appealing mystery to many women.

Where his erotic passions are concerned, the Scorpian has often been maligned through hasty conclusions or by those accepting old theories without personal investigation. Although his amorous incantations never fail to mesmerize his subjects, he is not the seducer with Svengalian design so often pictured. Though jealous, possessive, virile and sensual (while he sometimes seems to behave quite cavalierly in his sexual demands and expectations) if his deeper affections become involved, he can display a gentle tenderness and quixotic gallantry rivaling that of the Knights of Old.

If he is seriously hurt by a woman, he accepts it stoically. There may be bitterness but outsiders never hear about it from him.

There is a "sweetness," a wondrous depth of comprehension in him—an ethereal essence of awareness and compassion which transcends all human pettiness. He is not easily beguiled by chicanery, however. Foolish ostentation and sycophantish strivings he scorns with a vehemence matched only by the reluctance with which he tolerates unjust prejudice rooted in ignorance.

If unmarried, his choice of companion is usually one for whom he has a strong attachment and who is suitable to his complex needs. Faithfulness to her and perhaps fear of secondary obligations deters him from indulging in other sexual exploits. However, as with all else, any rules concerning his intimate life are those of his own making. Seldom will he embark upon new adventures until the old have lost their spice and flavor.

Moreover, countering his customary prideful ways—as much to avoid the admission of failure in any area as because of any lingering fascination—or possibly out of loyalty, he may cling with seeming irrationality to a dying relationship, attempting desperately to fan the cooling embers of desire.

Only when he becomes convinced that he has been duped or manipulated or upon finally realizing that such compliant patterns of conduct are a threat to his belief in himself, will he transfer his interests to another.

SAGITTARIUS

Ostensibly he's always poised for flight
His eyes perceive what others fail to see
And thus he senses peril in delight
And knows that though he loves, he must be free

The arrow which he draws has no intent
Except to cause a moment's sweet rapport
'Tis dipped in passion's brew when it is sent
He loves, but loves his freedom even more!

THE SAGITTARIUS MAN
November 23 through December 22 = Chief Ruler—Jupiter
Decanative Co-Rulers = Mars and the Sun

This man of majestic bearing, iron will and incredible energy, is actuated by Jupiter, which brings him also astonishing good luck, innumerable opportunities for success and the adulation of many women, all of which he appears to welcome without surprise.

It is not luck alone, however, that sustains him. It is more probably his own initiative, enterprise and willingness to attempt anything, which begets his good fortune.

Action to him is synonymous with living, and because of his great vitality, he accomplishes much more in a given length of time than does the average person, persevering without hurry or confusion until a task is completed.

His boldness and tenacity sometimes leads to impetuous performance but if the first effort fails, new chances seem always to present themselves. Thus, it is little wonder that he retains his serenity in the presence of a defeat which he knows to be only temporary.

He is ingenuous, finding quicker, easier ways of execution in anything he does. It is as if he had been given "blue prints" at birth—a pre-knowledge of how things are done—information which others must obtain by study or experience. These qualities make for favorable recognition but though he is much sought after by those who become aware of his efficiency, often he prefers his own business or investments in areas which allow him freedom for his many other interests.

The Sagittarian keeps himself abreast of all topical affairs and avidly ascertains various viewpoints in philosophy, politics, and religion, participating in heated discussions which often become monologues as he pursues a subject beyond the ken of his adversary.

Though some natives are socially minded and seek the comradeship of both sexes, like travel and change of environment (especially when it keeps them out-of-doors), there are those who are reclusive to the point of eccentricity.

Whereas many men find pleasure in fishing and hunting expeditions with groups of fellow sportsmen, the strongly Jupiter minded man usually prefers being alone on outings, and although symbolically his sign is the Centaur, (half man-half horse—according to Greek mythology) and represents hunting sports, he actually is often so sensitive to the feelings of animals and birds that his only weapon is a camera.

He has a special affinity with canines, understanding their ways, respecting their pride, and offering them friendship. If this is not readily accepted, he effects a truce based on mutual trust.

With people, the Sagittarian is not always so tactful. Though willingly giving of his services when he sees the need, he resents those who are indolent and would take advantage of him.

Bombastic, forthright, scrupulously honest and bluntly outspoken, he sometimes embarrasses others with his observant, wry comments. Yet, he is so earnest and well meaning, that one easily forgives and forgets these negative qualities which are only seldom expressed.

Although unusually adept with the simile, he intensely dislikes coarseness and his penchant for joke telling and amusing stories takes the form of subtle infectuous humor only.

A cheerful, pleasant companion as a rule, his mood can quickly shift to irritability and petulance if he senses a thrust, however unintentional, at his pride.

This change is the more astounding because of its unexpectedness and can be as disconcerting as a sharp clap of thunder on a sunny day.

Seeking continuous activity as he does and possessing such boundless energy, he may fail to understand another's lack of endurance, mistaking genuine tiredness for laziness.

With all his diligence and preoccupation with the tasks the Sagittarian finds important, his consciousness of the women around him never wavers. He sees their movements, enjoys their "femaleness" and deliberately inhales their fragrance while his mind spins colorful fabrics of anticipation.

While his dreams are of sensuous pleasure, always touched with the seduction of romance, rarely do they include marriage. Although he is an ardent and thoughtful lover, he has no intention of limiting his experience to one person. In part, this is because of the novelty he finds in numbers; also, it is his fixed determination to remain free. His need for solitude precludes any desire for constant companionship, yet he will court and woo a woman with real finesse, bestowing upon her many personal material gifts and flattering attention.

Essentially truthful and ethical, he would deny any perfidiousness in his motivation, simply expecting the women he honors with his affection to be as happy and as free as he in their relationship.

A Jupiter ruled man likes his women attractively dressed and immaculately groomed, alluring to other men but circumspect in their responses while his own interest holds. They must be acutely knowledgeable concerning his aversion to anything "common" or crude. Inappropriate familiarity affronts him.

This is not to say that he shuns the intimacy of erotic embrace. This is life itself to him. His conquests have great romantic content and appeal and seem to him to be only natural. What he dislikes is any attempt to monopolize his time or person which he considers an outrageous intrusion.

Even when he has allowed himself to become greatly attached to one particular woman, he will be restive if she expects too much from him. He thinks of marriage as a smothering, confining institution for either sex.

Now and then, one who knows well the ways of men, corrals him for herself alone, but only in an atmosphere where he determines the action and is in command will there be any real joy in the union. He must not be "tethered." If she would keep him by her side, he must never be aware of such intention but feel forever free to range the vast distances and explore the bright vistas which only his searching eyes can see and which only one of his kaleidoscopic imagination can fully anticipate.

CAPRICORN

He suffereth much from Saturn's mournful rays
But will not claim defeat nor brook delays
He knows the Gods may will that he submit
But girds his loins to counter what is writ

He would not bow to grief if it befell
And insulates himself from love as well
The power he craves may come with this design
But disappointments too are in his sign!

THE CAPRICORN MAN
December 23 through January 21 = Chief Ruler—Saturn
Decanative Co-Rulers = Venus and Mercury

Saturn is an exacting teacher and thus the wary Capricornian learns early that he must hide his feelings and create suitable defenses.

If seemingly outgoing and aggressive, he is actually almost shyly introverted and extremely vulnerable to childhood environmental factors, needing persons about him at that time who are fully cognizant of his intellectual precociousness and his desperate need to achieve a feeling of self importance. Otherwise, fearing criticism or ridicule as intensely as he does, he must carefully build a wall of inaccessability between himself and the world and in so doing may effect a belligerence and antagonism foreign to his true inclination.

Saturn not only inflicts a morbid, melancholic attitude upon him but presents obstacles and time-consuming delays which can be overcome only with great difficulty. Thus, to succeed, a self-discipline and perseverance is required which counters the Capricornian longing for a more leisurely life style. Having been subdued and punished in the unpleasant process of adjustment, he usually becomes proudly self-sufficient—aware of his own worth and better able to cope with the lack of discernment in others.

He learns to yield outwardly with affable manner—to be diplomatic and benign—when seeking power or favor to use guile if it serves his purpose. Constantly though, he protects that inner core of precious individuality.

One might expect him to be of stern and gloomy visage but most Capricorn natives exude a pleasantness and calm which belies their inner turmoil.

His scholarly ways lead to extensive reading; he particularly revels in tales of ancient days and peoples and spends many hours with his books and notes, though he usually tempers this sedentary activity by participation in games and sports.

Frequently found in the theatre doing Shakespearian plays or others of serious import, he is more apt to write or direct rather than act in the production.

With his ability to be coldly objective and analytical, he serves well in positions where the "long view" is essential and unbiased opinions and decisions are sought. Law, politics, corporation management or instruction services appeal to him. Satirically witty and conversant on many subjects, his great popularity as a toastmaster and speech maker is surprising in that it seems out of keeping with his true nature. Further, the real man inside that misleading exterior, remains remote and detached, often enjoying his lonely pursuits more than the outside contacts. Conversely, while he so ably projects the man of self-reliance and dignified conservatism, the duality of his subconscious longings betrays him in its secret thirst for excitement. His brusqueness at times is due to a continuous striving toward that image of one who is concerned only with the serious realities of life. Impatient with stupidity and dullness, he is utterly bored with the necessity for creating a ficticious impression.

Undemonstrative in his affections, appearing cool and disinterested, one would never suspect that at an early age he was probably fighting with other little boys for the privilege of carrying a little girl's books, and walking her home from school. Although rarely promiscuous, he is never unaware of feminine enticements. Firmly possessive in his youth, he usually selects the prettiest or most intelligent girl on the campus and later on, the most popular one in his place of business.

As he grows older, though he may appear indifferent to women, they are still a challenge to him, and despite his reserve, there are many who recognize his true feelings and are the more admiring for his discretion. Hearing him express his views one might conclude that his ideas have a misogynic trend, but this is far from the truth. One can sense that the attitude is one of self-protection—no doubt assumed in the beginning as a means of evading marriage until he could find a woman of suitable ethics and temperament who would treat his own "virtues" with due respect and courtesy.

An adoring spouse is essential to his well being. Just as he needs understanding companions in his youth to support his uncertain self-evaluation, so too does he in later years require attachments which provide stability and reassurance as to his merit.

This Saturnine man will never reveal his needs. He has learned well the lesson of maintaining silence. To admit even to himself that he is not entirely self-sufficient would be a threat to his security.

He enjoys his home; the comforts, the solitude, the fact that it is his "castle," all combine to give him a feeling of satisfaction and completeness.

In all probability, he sees many women who attract him briefly. Certainly, his debonair manner attracts them! If he has not become too enmeshed in patterns that please him, he can stray into erotic situations which are difficult to control.

However, from prosaic necessity, he has buried deeply the self-image of his boyhood, although at heart he is still the hero on the great white charger, rescuing the damsel in distress. There may be wistful moments when a breeze bears for him faint Loreleian melodies; but for one of his established habits of conventional behavior to deliberately initiate actions which could have adverse results would seem to him extremely foolhardy.

AQUARIUS

The crested waves seem cold
He shuns the sea
And seeks the sun's bright warmth in desert air
Or kindles fires that burn eternally
In those he loves,
But doubting that they care
He rendezvous and soon forgets
That warmth is but a figment of the mind—
That coldness is a thing that one begets
When running wild, he leaves his love behind.

THE AQUARIUS MAN
January 22 through February 20 = Chief Ruler—Uranus
Decanative Co-Rulers = Mercury and Venus

While Uranus is now said to be the ruling planet of Aquarius, there are those who still link Saturn with the sign because it had been considered the ruler until Uranus was discovered.

The recurring moods of melancholia to which many of

these natives are subject would seem to invite some acceptance of this belief, but being an Air sign, Aquarius gives not only positivity and confidence but lightheartedness and vivacity as well. One thus influenced can adjust to circumstances very easily. Having such a variety of things to do and think about leaves him little time for self-pity or sadness.

Though his moods may range quickly from depressing anxiety to high spirits, the exuberance usually conquers and is more persistently predominant. This is true even at those times when he may shut himself away from friends and strangers alike, seeming bent upon a punishing review of (imagined) rejections and "hurts" (as Capricornians are wont to do and for which Saturn has always been blamed.)

Fortunately, in the case of the "water-bearer," restlessness and curiosity soon overcome his wish for self-inflicted isolation. He joins a merry or active group where conversation and laughter bring speedy forgetfulness of his recent miseries.

He makes friends easily but does not always retain them. Though sentimentally kind and thoughtful with members of his immediate family, he is distrustful of almost all others, keeping them at a distance or putting them on the defensive without reason, which often causes his friendships to die upon the vine of misunderstanding.

Not deeply interested in politics, he likes "electioneering" crowds—the pomp and ceremony, the dignitaries in their formal attire. To him, marching bands and gay parades represent democratic attitudes and altruistic purposes.

His convictions may often be narrow and stubbornly prejudiced, yet if he can be persuaded to reconsider a concept, no one could be more fair (though he finds it difficult to admit to his former intolerance.) Usually, he has simply not investigated the subject thoroughly, being peculiarly inattentive when others are offering views contrary to his.

There are few Aquarians who are not talented in music, mimicry or design though there are those who fail to develop latent talents along these lines. Many are in the theatre, designing costumes or sets, singing or acting.

Whatever the Uranus sponsored man wants, he has the capacity, the physical stamina and the determination to get.

While his mind is filled with fanciful pictures and revolutionary ideas which are not always possible to realize at the time, the ideas themselves frequently forecast future events which others are slow to accept, not having Uranian vision. He fanatically resents coersion, restriction or even criticism and must always follow the dictates of his own will. Therefore, he is better at planning a project than in following the lead of someone else. He may be indolent but only when he is uninterested. A man of enthusiasm and aggressiveness, he may waste his talents because he lacks great incentives and dislikes confinement and close application. Yet when all else fails, his deep appreciation of beauty in every form is ever present to spur him on, and his diligence is remarkable when he has a suitable goal. He can even settle down to routine tasks when necessary, and when he can chart his own course. (His hands seem to be imbued with the magic of creation and his fingers conspire with nature in their inspirational accomplishment.)

His is an intellectual rather than physical sign, yet his very existence is permeated with a desire for affection. He is eager to give of himself and is never happier than when administering to a loved one, but he lacks faith in his own worth or power to attract others. The slightest indication (real or imagined) of waning interest on the part of a woman companion will send him headlong into the arms of another. Perhaps this is just as well since it protects him from long bouts with gloomy despondency. (Outwardly, he appears to be blithely uncaring at the "defection.")

In marriage, like his Libran "brother," he needs someone who will allow him the freedom of bachelorhood while still keeping a cozy hearth for his return. (He might even be faithful if he could be sure of her sincerity.)

The mounting number of affairs in which he engages from adolescence on would suggest fickleness and little depth of feeling, yet he deplores and dreads inconstancy in others. Like Diogenes, he searches for truth, and like the Geminian, he seeks everlasting love. His own affections waver or seem but of fleeting importance out of fear and suspicion of feigned responses to his overtures. If a woman's emotions are not seriously involved or if desire is not mutual, the association will be brief.

Always he is in need of a lasting devotion and empathy, without which his chances for worldly success are greatly reduced. Love stimulates his creative activities and gives him faith in himself.

Sexual episodes are then commonplace but they leave him with many haunted hours—haunted with the ghosts of "It might have been" and "If only," because the Aquarian finally comes to know that if his search were not so frantic—if his repudiations were not so hasty and heedless, he might have recognized in some of his partners a kindred need for romantic integrity and permanence.

Fortunate (though rare) is he who finds a responsible, dependable mate who completely fulfills his hopes early in life. When he does, the picture is often one of unparalled felicity.

PISCES

'Tis all I ask, that you will dream with me
We'll search the world for treasures each new day
In fantasy, we'll plight our love at sea
Succumb to lure of countries far away

In Mother Goose's tub, we'll sail the Nile
Or hail a modern vessel on the Seine
We'll walk strange streets
Together all the while
And find at last our castles built in Spain!

THE PISCES MAN
February 21 through March 20 = Chief Ruler—Neptune
Decanative Co-Rulers = The Moon and Mars

The Neptunian influence pervades the imagination and concepts of the Pisces man, giving him originality of thought and action, accentuating his talents in music, art and writ-

ing and lending impetus and compensation for the skillful,
detailed work so frequently necessary in his varied undertakings. (Many world-wide enterprises owe their success to
his competence and dependability.)

His patience is phenomenal and his calm acceptance of the
inevitable arms him with weapons of defense against all
temporary personal difficulties. Though a man of intensity
and depth, through his consideration for others he rarely
displays his anger or frustration.

While stubborn about his beliefs, he seldom inflicts them
upon others. He learns easily and retains any knowledge
which interests him. He is reserved and possesses a self-
sufficiency which does not demand much in the way of
friendships.

Because he is modest, his talents are often overlooked. Indeed, they are even underestimated by the Piscean himself.
He is very impressionable, as are the other Water signs and
strongly affected by his surroundings and the people he
loves.

He is generous to a fault yet normally frugal regarding his
own wants. He plans for the future through fear of ever being a burden to others. Despite this thrift, he can still be
tempted into taking chances, especially upon the advice of
one with whom he shares mutual interests.

Observant, intuitive and even precognitive, through "wishful thinking" he may judge a person by the image that is deliberately presented for his benefit. Like Don Quixote in his
idealism, his loyalties are not easily shaken, and he will "tilt
at windmills" long after another man would have recognized
deceit and given up his defense of one who is faithless. His
very innocence (or optimism, perhaps) in regard to romantic
adventure often leads to disillusionment. The proper mate
would be invaluable to his peace of mind.

She should be totally honest with him—loving and perceptive, unquestionably his in every facet of her being and willing to share his dreams of far away places while spending
her hours in making him comfortable and proud in their own
home. If she were engaged in profitable outside work, this
must always be secondary to his ambitions and needs, else

he would lose his incentives. (He is unselfish but very possessive.)

If badly disappointed by one for whom he cares, he may follow the usual procedures of so many men (whatever their sign or solar influences)—the confidence restoring and exciting activity of associating with a variety of women for "fun and games" only.

The Piscean is a prideful man and many women can be needed to assuage his feelings of hurt or injured dignity if his faith has been betrayed. In addition, his philosophic bent, his independence, and his ingenuity in finding outlets for his erotic urges provide diversions and sustain him. Like his Water Sign "brother," the Cancerian, he often çalls on his latent talents. He may discover a gift for painting, write his first book, or become absorbed in some worthy cause. Out of his inherent sympathy for humanity, he often finds ways of encouraging greater understanding among alien groups. If his vocation is in medicine, as it is with many natives of his sign, through his experiences he may become involved in bettering living conditions for the underprivileged.

Never seeking notoriety, he is usually the one in the background who calls attention to the needs and provides practical solutions to problems, thus stimulating others who implement his ideas.

The Piscean determination to withhold approval of anything less than perfection for a serious alliance may keep him temporarily indifferent to women; yet, since he is in essence a warm and passionate man, his desires will not long be denied. Fortuitously too, the perfection he demands is not so much in the person as in the relationship.

Among the many women to whom he may be reluctantly drawn, there are sure to be those who arouse his curiosity beyond casual intimacies. When he least expects it, the idyll in the guise of simple sexual attraction may make itself known and although normally a somewhat diffident and restrained individual, once he has the assurance of genuine sincerity, he can be surprisingly gleeful and enthusiastic. He will then make plans for "permanence" very quickly.

If the Piscean is a possessive man, he is also conscientiously faithful. If he wanders into paths of infidelity during marriage, it is almost certain that his devotion has not been reciprocated and only after many futile attempts to maintain a happy household will he again take up the search for a woman upon whom he can safely bestow his allegiance and unwavering trust.

Chapter 3
The Zodiac

In the preceding chapter, characteristics and inclinations of the men in each of the twelve Zodiacal signs have been presented. However, there are divisional differences and those of varying element which should be explained since they are important in better understanding the subject of astrological theory.

Most individuals already have some knowledge of these precepts, but for those who do not, a quick briefing seems appropriate.

As the Sun appears to circle the Earth, following a course across the sky in which it passes through the rays of twelve constellations of stars, it creates the imaginary belt which the astrologers call the Zodiac. (Actually, the Earth circles the Sun.) Each constellation is a Zodiac sign; it is said to influence the lives of those born during the approximate thirty day period the Sun resides in it. Sun, Moon and planets Mercury, Venus, Mars, Jupiter, Saturn, Uranus, Neptune and Pluto are thought by most astrologers to rule the various signs, thus producing the potentials, attitudes and tendencies of humankind.

To avoid most technicalities yet provide the average reader with a general idea of this premise, the information herein concerns only the Sun signs. They are named Aries, Taurus, Gemini, Cancer, Leo, Virgo, Libra, Scorpio, Sagittarius, Capricorn, Aquarius and Pisces. Each of these has three approximately equal divisions called decanates or decans and two cusps composed of the first five days of each sign combined with the last five days of the preceding one.

The twelve signs are divided into groups of three, called triplicities or trigons—each group assigned to one of the four elements—Fire, Earth, Air or Water. Aries, Leo and Sagittarius are of the Fire element. Taurus, Virgo and Capricorn are Earth signs. Those of Gemini, Libra and Aquarius comprise the Air signs, while Cancer, Scorpio and Pisces form the Water triplicity.

Each sign not only has a planet as Chief Ruler, but its second and third decans also have co-Rulers—the second's being the Chief Ruler of the next following sign of like element and the third's being that of the second succeeding sign of the same element.

The following data contains the time span, ruler and element (triplicity) of each sign. It gives its three divisions (decans) and two cusps with with their respective co-Rulers and discusses the results of these Zodiacal influences.

(a) *The Signs, Their Elements, Decans, Cusps and Rulers.*

Aries (Fire) Chief Ruler, Mars—March 21 through April 20.

First Decan Ruler, Mars—March 21 through March 31.

Second Decan Rulers, Mars and the Sun—April 1 through April 10.

Third Decan Rulers, Mars and Jupiter—April 11 through April 20.

Aries-Taurus Cusp, April 16 through April 25—Mars, Jupiter and Venus, co-Rulers.

Taurus (Earth) Chief Ruler, Venus—April 21 through May 21.

First Decan Ruler, Venus—April 21 through April 30.

Second Decan Rulers, Venus and Mercury—May 1 through May 10.

Third Decan Rulers, Venus and Saturn—May 11 through May 21.

Taurus-Gemini Cusp, May 17 through May 26—Venus, Saturn and Mercury, co-Rulers.

Gemini (Air) Chief Ruler, Mercury—May 22 through June 21.

First Decan Ruler, Mercury—May 22 through May 31.

Second Decan Rulers, Mercury and Venus—June 1 through June 10.

Third Decan Rulers, Mercury and Uranus—June 11 through June 21.

Gemini-Cancer Cusp, June 17 through June 26—Mercury, Uranus and the Moon, co-Rulers.

Cancer (Water) Chief Ruler, the Moon—June 22 through July 22.

First Decan Ruler, the Moon—June 22 through July 1.

Second Decan Ruler, the Moon and Mars—July 2 through July 11.

Third Decan Rulers, Moon and Neptune—July 12 through July 22.

Cancer-Leo Cusp—July 18 through July 27—the Moon, Neptune and the Sun, co-Rulers.

Leo (Fire) Chief Ruler, the Sun—July 23 through August 21.

First Decan Ruler, the Sun—July 23 through August 1.

Second Decan Rulers, the Sun and Jupiter—August 2 through August 11.

Third Decan Rulers, the Sun and Mars—August 12 through August 21.

Leo-Virgo Cusp, August 17 through August 26—the Sun, Mars and Mercury, co-Rulers.

Virgo (Earth) Chief Ruler, Mercury—August 22 through September 21.

First Decan Ruler, Mercury—August 22 through August 31.

Second Decan Rulers, Mercury and Saturn—September 1 through September 10.

Third Decan Rulers, Mercury and Venus—September 11 through September 21.

Virgo-Libra Cusp, September 17 through September 26—Mercury and Venus (doubled), co-Rulers.

Libra (Air) Chief Ruler, Venus—September 22 through October 22.

First Decan Ruler, Venus—September 22 through October 1.

Second Decan Rulers, Venus and Uranus—October 2 through October 11.

Third Decan Rulers, Venus and Mercury—October 12 through October 22.

Libra-Scorpio Cusp, October 18 through October 27—Venus, Mercury and Mars, co-Rulers.

Scorpio (Water) Chief Ruler, Mars—October 23 through November 22.

First Decan Ruler, Mars—October 23 through November 1.

Second Decan Rulers, Mars and Neptune—November 2 through Novemer 11

Third Decan Rulers, Mars and the Moon—November 12 through November 22.

Scorpio-Sagittarius Cusp, November 18 through November 27—Mars, the Moon and Jupiter, co-Rulers.

Sagittarius (Fire) Chief Ruler, Jupiter—November 23 through December 22.

First Decan Ruler, Jupiter—November 23 through December 2.

Second Decan Rulers, Jupiter and Mars—December 3 through December 12.

Third Decan Rulers, Jupiter and the Sun—December 13 through December 22.

Sagittarius-Capricorn Cusp, December 18 through December 27—Jupiter, the Sun and Saturn, co-Rulers.

Capricorn (Earth) Chief Ruler, Saturn—December 23 through January 21.

First Decan Ruler, Saturn—December 23 through January 1.

Second Decan Rulers, Saturn and Venus—January 2 through January 11.

Third Decan Rulers, Saturn and Mercury—January 12 through January 21.

Capricorn-Aquarius Cusp, January 17 through January 26—Saturn, Mercury and Uranus, co-Rulers.

Aquarius (Air) Chief Ruler, Uranus—January 22 through February 20.

First Decan Ruler, Uranus—January 22 through January 31.

Second Decan Rulers, Uranus and Mercury—February 1 through February 10.

Third Decan Rulers, Uranus and Venus—February 11 through February 20.

Aquarius-Pisces Cusp, February 16 through February 25—Uranus, Venus and Neptune, co-Rulers.

Pisces (Water) Chief Ruler, Neptune—February 21 through March 20.

First Decan Ruler, Neptune—February 21 through March 1.

Second Decan Rulers, Neptune and the Moon—March 2 through March 11.

Third Decan Rulers, Neptune and Mars—March 12 through March 20.

Pisces-Aries Cusp, March 16 through March 25—Neptune and Mars (doubled), co-Rulers.

(b) *An Interpretation of Zodiacal Influences:*

To be noted is the fact that natives of the same element have much in common, particularly those of the second and third decans, due to the shared rulership.

The first five days of the first decan of each sign is governed by the sign's Chief Ruler, and to a lesser degree by that of the preceding sign's (and may even be affected by the co-Ruler of that sign's third decan.)

The second five days, being free of additives, has undiluted spectacular guidance from the Chief Ruler, which produces a person one might call the only "true native"—since all others have hybrid characteristics.

Influence of the latter two decans, of approximately ten days each, is based upon the relationship with the other two signs of the native's element. Thus, each is ruled not only by its own Chief Ruler but by a co-Ruler as well—the second by the next following sign—and therefore its Chief Ruler—of similar element, and the third decan by that of the following sign and ruler of like element.

The last five days of the third decan has the sign's Chief Ruler, a Decanative Ruler derived from its element triplicity and is swayed to a certain extent by the Chief Ruler of the next following sign.

In the two ten-day cuspal periods there is a mixture of infusion. The native retains the tendencies inherited from his natural sign, those from his decan Ruler (when it is the third) and in addition, has that which is transmitted to him by virtue of close proximity to the adjoining sign, which could intensify or modify, though in a minor way, that of the others. There is sometimes a variance even in the two five-day portions of the cusp, which, while being a part of the regular sign, (decan) and cusp, still have individual differences. However, the prevailing similarities of those within the ten-day span are very noticeable.

For further clarification, Aries' Chief Ruler is Mars. The last two decans are ruled by Sun and Jupiter, respectively. The first five days of the sign has Mars influence, Neptune from Pisces (and perhaps—only slightly apparent—extra

Mars infusion because of Pisces' third decan Ruler.) The balance of the first decan has only Mars but the second decan
has Mars (and Sun from Leo triplicity) while of the third decan, the first five days has Mars and Jupiter from Sagittarius relationship while the last five days has Mars, Jupiter
and Venus from cuspal alliance with Taurus.

To be sure, the influence of the Chief Ruler is always most
active and evident but while the traits caused by less dominant planetary urgings may not be so obvious to the casual observer nor even to the individual himself, they are apparent to those who look for them and often, because of their
nature, are of incalculable significance in the course of a person's life.

Beginning then with the Aries man: since Mars itself gives
energy, audacity and zeal, and Jupiter is only second to the
Sun in strength—both offering qualities which inspire progressive action—one rightly looks for practicality and ambition in business or vocation. Yet, it is not so easy to predict
the circumstances of his "love life."

Normally, from Mars' instructions, tending to be sensible,
he would leave most of his promiscuity behind when he
found a girl he could trust and safely marry, but when Sun
or Jupiter exerts undue influence, a different reaction may
be seen.

The Sun may bring fantasies of magnificent attainments
and grandeur, including the adulation that such success
could summon. It is only natural then, that the native so affected, should long to see the confirmation of his self-
evaluation in the eyes of women. (Perhaps he needs this
even more when reality denies him the fullness of his
dreams.)

This man of the second decan with the Sun as his co-Ruler,
could, like the Leonian (his triplicity "brother"), be greatly
tempted by those women who are clever enough to appear
extraordinarily admiring and appreciative of his "masculine
abilities." (A psychiatrist might find in him deep-seated fears
of failure which he has hidden from himself—hence the
satisfaction gained from blandishments which nourish his
ego. Still, if he has chosen his mate carefully, as many

Ariens do, she herself will wisely provide this, eliminating his further search. Actually, it is rarely for sexual novelty alone that the sun-influenced Arien has affairs, whether serious or trivial. He wants only affection and esteem and if this is generously forthcoming at home, he is happy to remain there.

There is a slightly varying picture when Jupiter and a likeness to Sagittarius is present. He expertly reaches out in many directions where the ability to see, understand and do are concerned. His interests encompass a wide range but though inherently kind and honorable, his almost fanatical determination to retain complete freedom of action may include associations with many women throughout his lifetime. It is not so much that this man needs their flattery as it is a symbol of his priceless independence. To his way of thinking, since he likes women and they so obviously like him, why not enjoy their charms? Unlike the Sagittarian, he may not be so frank about it (his Chief Ruler frowns upon such rashness).

Aside from these probable leanings of the Arien, those of the cusp must not be forgotten. With Neptune promptings he may be unusually talented in artistic areas; he may be industrious and even venturesome but still not attain the rewards that others of his sign do with greater ease.

Perceptive with regard to women, he may be an ardent lover and devoted husband, especially with Pisces decanative Mars added to his own. Yet here too, because of Neptune reserve combined with the Mars tendency toward fluctuating moods, he may fail to receive the special recognition which he cherishes.

The April native on the cusp of Taurus would certainly retain the proclivities common to those of his third decan but in addition, he has Venus initiating greater longing for affection and erotic experiences, while surprisingly also, a steady fidelity when his love is genuine.

The Taurean of the first five days whose Chief Ruler is Venus but who still may be nudged by Mars, from closeness to Aries (and even a bit by Jupiter—Aries third decan ruler) has very strong convictions regarding this fidelity, as does the "true" Taurean. In fact, most natives of the whole sign are so inclined even though Venus provokes desire for physical pleasures. The same steadfast consistency and good judgment which he displays in his efforts to accumulate worldly goods, he maintains in the more intimate aspects of his life.

In his second decan, with Mercury as his co-Ruler, the subject is also marked with firm integrity but is sometimes too critical and over-expectant of others. Thus, he seems to disavow the warmth of affection even though innately kind and considerate. Disliking frivolity, he applies himself assiduously to matters which he deems of greater importance and appears to ignore the needs of the heart and the satisfactions of mutual attunement—avoiding the simple, loving gestures which mean so much to women. (His intentions are so worthy that he is often forgiven this attitude by one who loves him.)

He of the third decan, with Saturn as co-Ruler, is even more frequently accused of preoccupation with interests not enjoyed by those around him. Despite this apparent indifference, he too is usually accepted for the selfless motives that are reflected in his strivings for family security.

The Taurean on the Gemini cusp, although again having Mercury added, which gives him fifteen days of its influence (decanative and cuspal) may, himself, in this instance be eager for indications that his affections have ample response. During this five days with Mercury joining his Venus and Saturn, he may be less careful of money even though he spends it more effectively than the Geminian usually does. He too (like the Arien with Neptune influence) may not be suitably rewarded for all his toil and effort, in this case because he can be distracted by his warmer emotions from following his personal goals. (This applies even more to those of the first five days of Gemini). However, his increased adaptability, optimism and versatility often provide more opportunities for the use of his talents than he would otherwise have.

In this Gemini portion of the cusp, the Taurean influence has a stabilizing effect which is quite evident and just as

Mercury in the first five days offers the courage to attempt new ways when old ones fail, Venus here, provides invincibility and the determination to see things through regardless of the obstacles. (There may be many, due to even slight influence from Saturn, third decan ruler of Taurus). It also adds to the withdrawn nature of the Geminian an honest compassion and greater warmth. This man, though, is constantly searching for a soul-satisfying alliance and while ready to give of himself in love and devotion, often asks for more in return than he can logically expect from his partner.

Those of the next five days of Gemini with Mercury as the sole Ruler are often exceedingly changeable, being unable to remain constant in their decisions regarding either employment or "love" interests. To cover their uncertainties, they seek to appear adamantly and stubbornly positive in their general attitudes. If their mates are patient, such a man may overcome these tendencies by learning new habits and gaining a better understanding of himself.

Venus in the second decan, giving appreciation of music and greater sociability adds also increasing zest to courtship maneuvers. There is more energy and endurance. Both the need of accomplishment and a liking for the appurtenances of "gracious living" are spurs of motivation. Although coolly self-contained, like the Libran to whom he is decanatively related, he has a love of pleasure and likes the excitement created by fascinating occupations and associations with interesting people. (Yet, also like the Libran, he is never quite at ease.) It should be noted that Venus is co-Ruler of 15 days of the sign—five from Taurus proximity and ten from decanative structure.

Uranus in the third decan does not lessen the desire for change and variety. Indeed, it often adds considerable unconventionality and with it there is a self-assertion and independence which, while boding well for the furtherance of the native's career, is often a detriment to permanent sexual unions.

In the last five days of the Gemini sign, the Moon's rays are also felt. This lends the native more desire to seek close relationships but affects very little the distrust of his ability to attract the genuine regard of the opposite sex even though he has the necessary will for all other accomplishments.

In the next five day period of the Gemini-Cancer cusp, Mercury often seems still stronger than the moon in that Cancer's leaning toward dissatisfied introspection and debilitating depression is mitigated. However, restlessness is a problem in both signs as well as shifting moods of optimism and foreboding. It perhaps also is aggravated by Uranus (Gemini's third decan Ruler). The effervescence of Gemini may be helpful and the continuously changing interests could provide diversions in both leisure hours and those of business. Pursuit of women is indicated, but it is not always of serious intent.

The "true" Cancerian is completely suffused with Moon derived doubts concerning women. Thus he justifies his hesitancy in forming permanent attachments, keeping himself so busy with other matters that he seems oblivious to their overtures.

In the second decan, Mars gives the native practical aggressiveness and insistent sexual urgings. More sentimental than those of the first decan (even though he hides it) his parental ties are always of prime importance. This attitude is sometimes misunderstood which may account for the numerous early affairs which are without much validity.

In this third decan, Neptune joins with the moon to intensify his humanitarian and artistic qualities. This combination often makes possible a quicker choice of mate.

He of the sign's last five days, with support from the Sun, is more audacious, more apt to attempt new enterprises and more adroit in his erotic maneuvers. Self-esteem overcomes any inclination toward diffidence and his natural conservatism is modified to some extent.

On the other hand, the Leo native of this cusp is given sound ethical standards of behavior by Moon influence and his need of the flattering attentions of women is tempered by his fondness for a pleasant home atmosphere. Marital ties bring closer unity.

The "true" Leonian has utter belief in himself and his ideas. No woman could ever change him. He is as much a king in his personal life as is the lion of the forest.

His second decanative period is favorable for attainment of all he desires. Jupiter aid makes him more knowledgeable both in business and in love relationships, but although women persistently flock around him, real affectionate interest on his part may be absent.

In his third decan, Mars prompts even greater ambition and directed activity as well as more substantial romantic alliances.

In the case of the Leo-Virgo cuspal resident with Sun and Mercury both ruling, Leo's attributes of sponteneity and resourcefulness combined with those of the sobriety and seriousness which attend the Virgo personality, can prove very fortunate. The man born at this particular time has both self-confidence and prudence. He is not only inventive and practical but has genuine willingness of performance and with it the tenacity to develop the latent artistic talents which many of this group possess. (Since the Leonian is more adept in sexual matters than the staid Virgoan, there is here a compromise which usually presages success with the ladies, even though there is usually adherence to marriage vows. Leo's decanative Mars suggests this in the first five days of the sign and Mercury, Chief Ruler of Virgo, in the second.)

As a matter of fact, the same could be said of the busy "true" Virgoan and also of the subject of Saturn influence in the second decan—a man notable for his trustworthiness. (Saturn, coupled with Mercury, while insuring more patience, an interest in both mental pursuits and sports, does little for the native in demonstrations of affection but his allegiance is rarely questioned.)

Venus though, of the third decan, even when not strong enough to bridge the spiritual distances between the native and his loved ones, does create a better understanding of their needs.

He of the last five days, on the Virgo-Libra cusp, is especially vulnerable where his family is concerned, but having extra Venus influence (decanative and cuspal) is also more interested in women. The men of these two adjoining signs could hardly be of more opposite viewpoints, hence the native of this cusp often swings between two attitudes, sometimes seeming narrow in his convictions but under changing circumstances being anxious that justice triumph.

In the early segment of the cusp, preoccupation of the Virgoan with unimportant details is lessened by the Libran indifference to such trivial matters and there is a broader interest in the artistic and musical. In the latter half, the subject has dexterity for creative pursuits and also a determination of accomplishment often lacking in the "true" Libran.

However, no Libra native is ever lacking in his attraction to and for the opposite sex. Since Venus is the ruling planet, the whole sign affords both talent and allure. (Love of erotic pleasure is here more pronounced than it is in Taurus.)

In the second decan, Uranus provides additional energy and urges a steadier application to the native's vocation. There are few serious affairs and marriage may not materialize. If it does, it may not be of a rewarding nature to either partner.

In the third decan, Mercury, while causing restlessness and boredom, gives great versatility, providing also an extraordinary harmony with women. This can be a gateway to much happiness in marriage but sometimes is the ingredient which destroys the very nucleus of its meaning. (Fifteen days of Mercury influence in Libra—five cuspal, ten decanative).

When Libra and Scorpio are combined, with Venus and Mars ruling, this generally gives a blend of resourcefulness, self-awareness and courage. If there is egotism, it is alleviated by intended kindness and a desire to be agreeable. There is both spirited self-interest and a friendly wish to please. Scorpio's unflagging perseverance added to Libra's offerings of imagination and "search for glory" often leads to unusual prestige or positions of great prominence. Erotically, this man is gentle, romantic and subtle yet at times startingly detached and evasive, presenting a contradiction of traits that apparently is very appealing to many women.

In the first five days of Scorpio, while having his sign's more accurate knowledge of the feminine psyche than the Libran normally needs or bothers to explore, it is perhaps that bit of decanative Mercury from Libra which causes the native to be chary of strong attachments just as is also the ambitious and literate "true" Scorpion who, finding less time for sexual adventure, keeps it light and of little significance.

In his second decan, with Neptune subduing his more aggressive traits, but allowing him to follow a lucrative and purposeful course through life, his attitude toward women alters considerably. Though independently geared, his affections and loyalties are securely anchored. There is an unexpected warm responsiveness of manner which is devastating to women, yet he reserves his intimate moments for the one he loves.

In his third decan, with the Moon's emotional additive, there is need of more rest and frequent solitude to counter the activity of his varied occupations, sometimes making him appear antisocial. His perceptiveness is not diminished nor is his devotion to his family. Too, his faithfulness to a love concept remains intact.

In the early cuspal portion of Scorpio and Sagittarius, the former personality is still dominant. Mars prevails but Jupiter casts its shadow. However, these planets are antagonistic and this can create a constant conflict within the subject. He often procrastinates, then feels compelled to overwork in compensation. The sporatic nature of his efforts is his only handicap. He is purely self-generated and his persistence coupled with inherent ability opens many doors leading to success. If somewhat arbitrary in his judgments, his keen perception lends honesty to his philosophical ideas as well as to his close relationships.

In the second five day cuspal period that infinitesimal Moon influence from Scorpio's last decan keeps the native extremely conscientious. Here, self-interest is united with a deep sense of responsibility, which while augering "love" affairs of various intensities, promises contancy while they endure.

The "true" Sagittarian is more unpredictable—disliking rules, laws, confinements of any kind. Women he likes in extravagant measure but he fears and often rejects marriage.

In his second decan, he has Mars' dignity and fire from

Arien likeness. (15 days of Mars in Sagittarius). Added to
Jupiter resourcefulness, there is the initiation of plans for
the future and possibly reluctant acceptance of a conventional home life.

In the third decan, the Sagittarian's practical capabilities
are present, but again he has a lack of seriousness toward
women. The sun brings him a liking for variety and freedom
but does not necessarily appease his hungers.

The cusp of Sagittarius and Capricorn is one bearing fortunate omens since the gloom of Saturn is often nullified by
the lively, cheerful influences of Jupiter (and the sun). There
is little difference between the two five-day periods. The native tends to be good natured but candid and forthright.
Erudite and articulate as is the "true" Capricorn, he is also
as able as the Sagittarian in action. Versatile and intellectual, he has many fields of endeavor from which to choose.
Having more energy than is usually common to Capricorn,
he is often more active and so is restless when not continuously occupied with engrossing projects. All those of the first
Capricornian decan enjoy a serene home life; they are not so
eager for variety in feminine companionships and often effect
a domestic arrangement satisfying to their lonely natures.

In his second decan, though he busily seeks fame and
notoriety, Venus adds more fervency to his passions and
more interest in beauty to an otherwise reticent nature. His
pessimism is lessened and he is inspired to cast a more in-
quisitive eye at feminine enticements.

In his third decan, though inwardly tense and often sensuously "earthy," he is self-controlled—seemingly impassive
and though often more romantically inclined, is very careful
of his image, devoting his time and energies to the serious
and lucrative aspects of existence.

A mixture of Uranus with the Saturn influence benefits a
resident immeasurably. He is self-reliant with definite opinions of his own and is usually unmindful of suggestions
made by others. Yet, he of the first five cuspal days, disliking conflict and confusion and having a need of surroundings
conducive to study and contemplation, normally brightens
his manner with a wry sense of humor. Combined with a

wide range of interests, this makes possible many opportunities in business or profession. Idealism and independence are combined here but this does not necessarily produce happiness. However, this man's sober mien belies a surprising sentimentality probably contributed by Capricorn's Mercury. Sometimes it wins over skepticism and he finds someone who enjoys sharing the quiet nest so important to him. (Many natives of the last five days prefer to remain single.)

The "true" Aquarian can rightly be said to be as forceful and independent as anyone in the world and he too may evade the limitations implied in close relationships. Uranus has a powerful influence upon its subjects, inflicting abrupt changes and a wilfulness which is often inimical to compatible unions.

Yet, in the second decan, while the subject retains his self-sufficiency, Mercury provides more interest in humanity and its ills—a bending of the will to meet emergencies (as well as more attention given to essential activities.) There is a greater desire for companionship and more interest in his intimate intrigues.

In the third decan, with the coaxing of Venus, he may be lackadaisical but his friendly attitude compensates for his combative tendencies even though his inability to compromise may be a hindrance to his erotic adventures.

In the cuspal area (Aquarius-Pisces) Neptune's amiability blends well with the power and decisiveness of Uranus. The man of the whole area, so blessed by Neptune but enforced by Uranus, (yet gentled by Venus,) ruler of the Aquarian third decan, has a multitude of ingenious ideas plus the will to execute them. He is visionary and altruistic with incomparable charm and an appreciation of spiritual values. This combination is very useful.

While the "true" native of Pisces is detached and reserved, he is much sought after for his dependability, his intuition and originality. He has a liking for woman yet is not always trustful. Usually, fearful of a trap which may involve him too deeply, while leaving the emotions of his partner untouched, he has a number of casual alliances before settling down to serious commitments.

In his second decan, with the Moon's cooperation, he may
be more cordial and congenial in his social contacts as well
as with his business associates but lack the perspicuity in
his judgments of women which could save him from the pitfalls of unhappy marriage. Still, his liking for a safe harbor
makes him prefer the uncertainties of marital life to that of
tempetuous conquests or those affairs of only passing interest.

In his third decan, Mars gives the native opportunities and
drive for developing his competitive skills or artistic talents,
but adds to his natural secretiveness. While he may seem
more unresponsive and there may be no abatement of caution, he does have more faith in the feminine sex.

As was shown earlier in the cusp with Aries, he is ambitious and reliable but may not be properly rewarded for these
qualities. This applies particularly to the first five days.
(Pisces has 15 days of Mars influence. The extra amount
here, with maybe a "whisper" from Jupiter, can bring him
rich success and happiness too, if he will quell his threatening moods and strive for equanimity.)

(c) *Interesting Sidelights About the Various Zodiacal
Signs:*

Certain general characteristics are reputed common to
each triplicity. Fire Signs are said to be indications of ambition, temper and passion; Earth Signs point to great strength
of purpose, strong dedication, meticulous efforts and a lack of
demonstrative emotion; Air Signs are thought to show intuition, changeability and a tendency to be erotically unpredictable, while Water Signs are credited with producing deep,
self-contained emotion, strong sensuality and indomitable
pride. Certainly, these traits may be found in anyone, yet
here there is noticeable emphasis and a correspondence of
particular leanings in natives of like elements. Sometimes
the decanative or cuspal modifications are so outstanding
that these tendencies are less discernable. Then, too, while
there are many similarities there are also subtle but marked
differences.

To elaborate further, Aries, the head sign of Fire Triplicity, offers a definite sense of direction and unusual foresight,

but the Leo native does not so much plan ahead as work on projects which the current circumstances provide.

Through his enthusiasm, he inspires others to join his ventures. On the other hand, the Sagittarius resident recognizes the need for planning—as Aries does—but may not formulate it in his early years. He appears though, to have a pre-knowledge with which to utilize his talents when he does get into the whirl of activity natural to him. In other words, natives of this triplicity all attain about the same results yet they approach their objectives somewhat differently. Where women are concerned, their attitudes differ considerably, the Arien seeking a wise marriage while the other two are less willing to relinquish their bachelor's freedom.

In regard to the three Earth Signs—Taurus, Virgo and Capricorn of which Triplicity Taurus is the Head, all of them are reliable and seriously involved in accomplishment. The Taurian is a bit more obdurate than the other two though genial of manner. He is innately conscious of the need for financial gain in order to attain his goals. Virgo, as well, clings steadily to his principles and is conspicuous for his hard work or application to business, but he lacks something of the Taurean warmth so holds women's interest less easily. This aloofness also applies to Capricorn—a tendency which affects his own dealings with women. Money-wise, he is as thrifty as his Trigon "brothers."

One sees quite a similarity between the Fire Signs and those of Earth, but there is a great disparity between these two and those of the Air and Water elements, the latter two of which have some traits in common.

Gemini is the Head of the Air Triplicity with Libra and Aquarius following. None of them have early definite plans for the future although their imagination and continuous strivings often bring startlingly favorable rewards. Gemini is hampered by the fact that his affections take precedence over all else. Libra, similarly involved—not so much giving as attracting affection—is thus more free for progressive action. Aquarius is less constricted than either of them in the areas of heart interests and although he too lacks direction, he has more sturdy strength to support the fearlessness which is his.

While it is true that the Air and Water Sign subjects resemble one another to some degree, especially in their fluctuating emotions, those of the latter category give more thought to the future than do the others. Although erotic pleasure is in the minds of all, Cancer, the Head of the Water Sign Trigon and the other members, Scorpio and Pisces, are more strongly urged toward accomplishment because of a practical concern for future needs and emergencies.

Everyone desires approval; personal pride, human dignity and love needs are the incentives, yet goals and methods of attainment differ. Fire and Earth natives operate through pride of self, while those of Air and Water do as their emotions dictate since they are driven (and bound) by them. When considering the similarities caused by like element, it is well to remember the variances that exist because of each planetary influence to which an individual is subjected.

The pattern offered by the Sun is positive, prideful and idealistic, by the Moon one of practicality even though moodiness is present. Mercury gives intuition, logic and adaptiveness, while Venus exudes sentimentality, restlessness and determination. Mars provides energy, courage and aggressive action; Jupiter kindness and discernment in spite of some fanaticism. Saturn's ways are melancholic, skeptical and assertive; those of Uranus eccentric, unpredictable and forceful; of Neptune, subtle, psychic, reserved and selfless. Pluto is everchanging and morbid. There are other words which apply to each planet, but those mentioned are most evident in its subjects.

One matter that also should be discussed is the fact that those of different signs, although ruled by the same planet, may differ greatly in their traits. This is especially true of Aries and Scorpio, Taurus and Libra, Gemini and Virgo. For example, (reviewing), Aries and Scorpio both have Mars as Chief Ruler, yet while each has much emotional infusion, Aries manifests his in sudden, sharp outbursts of surface impatience, while Scorpio's feelings run hurtfully deep and he seeks desperately to conceal them.

In love also, Scorpio is constant and self-sacrificing even when disappointed, while Aries more easily turns to someone offering sympathy or comfort, even if with a sense of guilt which he tries to subdue. He is sentimental without involving too much of himself. Of the Fire element, restless and aware of women's charm, his pride may seek assuagement through their responses though paradoxically, he often sublimates his eroticism in deference to the opinions of his peers and to retain a self-image with which he can peacefully live.

Scorpio, a Water Sign, though in need of more sexual expression, usually is interested in only one woman at a time—is bound by his loyalty, his tenderer instincts and his sense of duty which is greater than he cares to admit. These ties become secondary in importance only when he is vastly involved in his vocation.

Today, it is believed by some that Pluto co-rules both Aries and Scorpio. Pluto is said to exert an influence to upset old traditions and ideas and this is rather typical of the Scorpio man's views. He does tend to see much that should be changed in our culture and often is quite pessimistic, feeling that mankind has so ravished the earth that our species can but die out because of its stupidity, greed and selfishness. Contrarily, the Aries man, while especially capable in establishing new methods and procedures which might facilitate desirable changes, is apt to cling rather doggedly to traditional ideas, customs and mores of past generations. These differences in two natives both with Mars, the same planet, ruling, mark two personalities much alike in other ways. The fact that one is of the Fire element and the other of Water is no doubt significant.

Taurus and Libra are two natives of different elements (Earth and Air) both with the same Chief Ruler, Venus, but who also display these natural differences. Both are sensuous and strongly attracted to the opposite sex but Libra scatters his erotic energies. He feels compelled toward all women— wanting their attention and response—perhaps because he has not a conviction of self value and thus the feeling of personal security which is the Taurean's.

As with Scorpio, the Earth Sign native concentrates most of his sexual verve upon one recipient at a time and is devoted to his choice. He is more stable than Libra but much less demonstrative and so has not the same power of seduction. Women have to know him more completely to be aware of his charm while Libra has a radiance that permeates his whole being and is reflected in every gesture and cadance of his voice. (One must add, however, that his feelings usually have not the depth nor constancy of those of Taurus.) Both are greatly gifted but Taurus applies himself with greater fervor toward accomplishment (he has to!) while Libra rather expects the Gods to toss success into his lap and is often actually so favored.

Two other natives of similar rulership are Gemini and Virgo and here it seems very strange that Virgo, of the Earth Triplicity, being so dependably stable, nevertheless displays a lesser depth of feeling than does Gemini, an Air Sign, said to be fickle and changeable. Indeed, Virgo can more easily forego sexual companionship than those of any other sign while Gemini is not content without that special person for whom (at the moment) he constantly yearns, though not altogether from sexual desire. (He has as little emotional security as has his Air Sign "brother" Libra and in case his partner's interest should cool even imperceptibly, he may turn to someone else in his need for mutual rapport.)

Virgo is more patient under these circumstances, hoping for a revival of understanding and consequent reconciliation. Both Gemini and Virgo are critical, neither forgets the wounds to his heart and pride. One difference in these two natives is that it never occurs to the Virgoan that he might be wrong or that he perceives only one aspect of a situation, while the Geminian always realizes that he is being intolerant and is disturbed by his unfairness.

These few examples are cited as reminders of intermingling influences prevalent throughout the varying signs.

Another noteworthy point is that of top ranking men—and particularly of women who become well known either in business or as entertainers, there seems to be a great preponderance of Mars endowed individuals. These include those in whose sign Mars is the Chief Ruler and those of the respective decans and cusps so involved also. Mars energy and pertinacity apparently serve well here. However, each planet and each element provides its own special attributes. *Wherever there is a disadvantage, much is given in the way of compensation!*

When one decides that the delineation of those of his own sign does not apply to him, he should remember the variances—the factors of genetic, geographical and environmental background. Yet he should analyze his motivations and his reactions to people and events. If he is honest, he will admit to the underlying tendencies—often hidden but never completely obscured by his efforts or his rationalizations. He should be sure that his self-image is the true one—that his picture of others is not one distorted by his need to feel important. He should utilize the talents and the abilities which are his alone in the appropriate framework of his potential. (In so doing, it is never necessary to resort to methods of belittlement and denigration of others.) Every man has at birth the tools for the realization of his practical dreams; he can accomplish almost anything if he is willing to pay the price and understands this when he is young enough to prepare for doing so. Only laziness, inertia, negative attitudes and the over-indulgences of the body can defeat the spirit. Obviously, this does not mean that there is equal opportunity for all humans but many a person creates his own shackles. There are *always* ways of improving oneself and of enlarging the area of resulting progress.

There is a difference too, between dreams and fantasies. The latter are for the lethargic who would rather imagine or pretend that they are capable than make the effort to be so. Dreams can be formulated from the sturdy fabric of realistic possibility—sculptured to fit the pattern of one's own nature and correlated with a life style with which he can be contented. For this purpose, not every individual's needs are the same.

(d) *Wrong Impressions Based Upon Inadequate Information:*

It is true that one should not discard the theory of there being general tendencies inherent in each Zodiacal Sign because he himself cannot perceive they apply to him. By the same token, he should never attempt to pass judgment upon another, based solely upon information he gathers from a discussion of the subject by those not versed in patterns of propensity and behavior. Multiple influences have a great bearing upon the resulting picture and *no general description can fully describe any one person.*

It is easy to obtain erroneous ideas if one becomes impressed by certain words or phrases heard too often without making an effort to learn also of the opposing characteristics which could ameliorate if not completely invalidate those which he more readily remembers.

Aries, for instance, is said to be "hot headed" and impatient, yet his concern for others—his natural friendliness—compensates for these less desirable tendencies.

Stubborn is a word often applied to the Taurus man, yet when this very trait is translated into a determination to accomplish or to overcome an obstacle on the way to achievement, it becomes admirable.

The Gemini man is accused of being changeable and without purpose, but when he has the proper incentive and an environment in which he is appreciated, neither fault is obvious.

Unstable and emotional are words often used in reference to the Cancer man, although his humane efforts for others, his ethics and high standard of conduct are so noticeable that one usually sees only these finer qualities which dominate his life.

The Leo man may appear to be vain and overly prideful, yet his great generosity, his optimism and his apparent self-confidence inspire that trust which he seeks.

The Virgo man may seem so aloofly self-satisfied that he depresses those of warmer natures, but his dependability and kindness to those for whom he feels responsible refutes the assumption of indifference.

One hears that the Libra man wants excitement or constant pleasure, but how many are cognizant of his innate sentimentality or desire to please?

It is rumored that Scorpio is sensuously erotic, and yet his outstanding moral values and extreme sense of duty are even more pronounced.

Freedom loving is the first thought one has regarding the Sagittarius man although he is intelligent, articulate and hard working, all of which almost denies this restive state.

The wary Capricornian is often seen as one of stern fiber—cold and unresponsive. This false impression though is only what he hopes to convey as he keeps his personal life uncluttered with non-essentials and pursues whatever goals that appeal to him.

The Aquarius native is known to be unpredictable and obstinate, but he gives of himself so unstintingly that few people recognize any objectionable inclinations.

The amateur astrologer invariably speaks of the Pisces man's patience. His is the only one of the signs to which those with little knowledge first attribute a commendable characteristic. Probably that is because of his penchant for accepting the inevitable with good humor and fortitude. Without question, these fine qualities as well as many others are his, but they may hide an underlying resentment, since he is well aware of frequently being unfairly taken for granted. Also, his sensuality, as great as that of Scorpio's, often goes unnoticed.

Thus, it is seen that in all men there are contradictory forces at work, but if one is aware of leanings which are displeasing to himself or to others, he can either turn them into assets instead of liabilities or may employ his other qualities to greater advantage.

Each man creates a self image with which he can be most comfortable and in which he is more or less able to believe. This, he tries to project and manifest to the world although the mask he wears may be more self-deceptive than it is effectual in impressing his associates. However, that which in the beginning is only a facade of pretense, may with practice, eventually become the true image.

It is unfortunate that with so much knowledge available of the human species, there are still so many misconceptions among individuals—and so little real understanding—between sexes.

Chapter 4

Stumbling Blocks

Oh there was a little girl
Who had nary a pretty curl
Yet her mommy said it didn't really matter

If she'd mind her P's and Q's
Any male she'd ever choose
Would come running with his head upon a platter

Still she worried now and then
Might he have some special yen
Maybe like her best if she were thin—or fatter?

Well, as girls are wont to do
She soon learned a trick or two
And found out as mother said it didn't matter

Men were softies when she smiled
Turned to putty when beguiled
And came running with their heads upon a platter

But the years can take their toll
Younger sirens play her role
And it matters not if they are thin or fatter

Tho' she keeps her hair in curl
There is always some bright girl
Who collects her husband's head upon a platter!

The young are often ill advised or are too easily influenced by the behavior of others. They have not yet learned that appearances can be very deceiving. The girl who is just beginning to discover the power of her youthful charms may not have the wisdom to conserve them. If at all personable, she will be opportuned for favors before she is hardly aware of their significance.

Frequently she believes that all she has to do to "get her man" is to project the impression that she is "sexy." Most of her peers prescribe this. Movies, plays and books also lend credence to it. She may think that ingratiation and coquetry will bring her all that she desires from men. However, exploitation is dangerous; she may be the one who is eventually exploited. If she marries, it will not take her long to find that this is an over-simplification. Offering sex as a bribe or withholding it for one's advantage can create many problems. It is essential for a man to feel wanted and to retain his pride.

Any girl can arouse a man sexually, before marriage or afterward. (That is no great accomplishment.) One woman's passionate overtures are not much different from another's; yet such enticements are insufficient when her motives are serious. If this is all she has to give, the union can never be one of strength. From a wife, men also want warmth of true affection, approval, commendation and constant reassurance of her loyalty. (Many need "mothering" although they would deny it—the kind of "mothering" that is uncritical and fosters confidence.)

A good marriage is never founded on sex alone even though a man often uses this criteria in his argument for pre-marital intimacy. The back seat of a car, a motel room or even his or her "pad" is not the place to find out about compatibility. One can be thus attracted to one's lover, but the fascination may have little to do with genuine love.

Too often, in the days just preceding marriage, the girl is more concerned with thoughts of the beautiful wedding gown, the bridesmaids, the rituals of the ceremony, the crystal, linens and silver than she is with the groom himself. She may even be one of the innocents, not having known the raptures of eroticism until this man introduced her to experimentation. Therefore, she may mistake her feelings of ardor for love. This is a period of her life when she is eager, vibrantly alive, and longing to give of her fire and passion.

Unfortunately, these euphoric days are soon gone and replaced by trials of friction and adjustment. It must be obvious that no two persons are alike, yet many couples are bewildered, or deeply angered, when they find that their ways are diverse and their thinking in complete opposition.

(In courting days, they are preoccupied with the deliciousness of touch and feeling. They probably enjoy each other's "love making" however unimaginative it is (although they may have some secret doubts). They are convinced that somehow, once the vows are read, everything will fall into a pattern of rightness and fulfillment. Then comes reality.

Their sex life can improve a bit as time passes, but they may be surprised to learn that even this is not perfect. For example, the girl may now be so irked and embarrassed by some of her husband's idiosyncrasies that she cannot relax enough to respond to his gauche connubial gestures. The man may be so appalled at what he considers her laziness, her lack of housekeeping accomplishments, that he too may lose much of his amorousness and astonish her by apparently being more enthralled by T.V. programs than he is by her.

The chances are probably one hundred to one that even today's young man actually knows very little about either his partner's physical anatomy or the aesthetic concept which had originally been hers in regard to these contacts. He may even think that sexual intercourse is just a step further than self pleasuring, and any indication that his lack of discernment leaves her unappeased is apt to puzzle and anger him. (She may be deluded into accepting his views of the situation. It is true that she may need to be informed about receptivity and cooperation; there is information which could be useful to both, but often the ones who most need this fail to seek it, or else they read books which are written for shock and sales value rather than accuracy.) Sex, then, is not always the glorious messenger of communication which some have been led to anticipate. Usually, a great deal of patience is needed and a definite sense of purpose, for the young girl to find contentment in the several areas of her new domestic life. At the outset, she will find that her husband's immediate, personal wants must always come first, that she should be flexible, able to correlate her own needs with his. (She has usually failed to notice the endless concessions which her mother has always made.)

First of all, a young woman should ask herself if she actually desires marriage. (Might it be that Schopenhauer's idea that marriage attrites love is true?) If she plans it as a vocation, is she equipped for its demands? (Why is it that for this most conspicuous phase of the average woman's life, she often comes into it with so little proficiency?) It is often no wonder that her young mate is so disappointed that he keeps referring to his mother's cooking. (One reason, by the way, that many wives bear a grudge against their husband's mothers and try so desperately to alienate them.) However, any young man will have known of his girl's lack of such skills because of inexperience and therefore should allow her time to learn. To be noted is the fact that neither of them thinks of her new role as one requiring preparation! (How many brides know even the rudiments of housekeeping, cooking, serving, entertaining, shopping and laundering?) Before marriage she should know whether this is to be her prime occupation. If she prefers to have a remunerative position as well, can she do justice to both? Will the man of her choice do his share of the household tasks? Will be spend a proportunate part of his time to match that which she must expend there, with the recognition that the chores should be shared, thus resisting the temptation to feel "put upon?"

Will *he* have the strength, the emotional fortitude or the capacity for this double duty? If he is not so consituted is she capable of organizing the whole procedure so that she can handle it and also her other employment without feeling martyred and causing him to feel reproved or uncomfortable? If not, can she earn enough to hire help and still retain enough profit to compensate for her outside activities?

If his earnings, his professional advancement or his state of health depends upon quiet, unhurried, restful times at home, is she willing to forego her own job opportunities or other personal projects in order to provide such an atmosphere?

How much does she actually know about him? Is he as ambitious as she? As resourceful? As determined? Does he have good judgment? Can he be relied upon in emergencies? Will she be content with the amount of prestige his work offers? Their life style?

Are there religious, political or racial differences? What of his usual manner and disposition? Is he overly aggressive and opinionated? Or considerate, genial and perceptive? (Would she rather he be less forceful and consequently attain less financially? Does he dominate others? Sacrifice his own wishes for the sake of peace or to be liked by those about him? (Which traits does she most admire?)

Is he easily offended? Does he harbor a grudge? Try to "get even?" Does he have "temper tantrums" or sulky moods? Does he nag at her until in frustration she retorts with anger, at which he accuses her of causing his ill humor?

Is he neat and orderly? Does this coincide with her own tendencies? Does he like order but expect others to maintain it? Does he do his part of any project at hand or make excuses and wait for someone else to do it?

In driving, does he always blame the other person for his difficulties? Or is he courteous to other drivers and thoughtful of those in his car as to air or speed? (It is surprising how a man's actions in a car reflect his attitude under other stress.)

Is he extremely careful with money? Yet less so in expenditures which bring him personal pleasure?

If he is fond of sports in which she does not join, how much of his free time will he spend upon them?

Is he jealous of her family members or resentful of her women friends, critical of her looks, manners or background?

Does he boast about old sweethearts? Is he overly affectionate with girls in their group or those with whom he works? After a few drinks at a party does he become indiscreetly amorous? Or ignore her while staying constantly with the men? Is he ever openly unfaithful? If so, is he afterwards regretful or sullenly defensive?

Does he inquire about her convictions? Encourage her creative talents?

Have they similar tastes as to music, movies or plays? Is their entertainment designed to please himself or her?

When they have a "date" is it spent only in "making love" or do his plans also include visiting with friends or frequenting places of amusement?

Are his "dates" with her often broken? Are the reasons

justified? Is she sure of his truthfulness?

A man's treatment of his parents can give a girl a rational conception of what his eventual ways toward her will be. Does he condemn them for his own failures or lack of business acumen? She should think a bit about his family members. True, she is not marrying them, but her husband should not be expected to disassociate himself from them because of marriage.

Then, there is the question of children. Do they agree upon such matters as the number to have, whether to adopt or to conceive? Are they selfless enough to place the children's welfare before their whims or customary pastimes? Sufficiently mature to cope with the responsibilities of parenthood? Devoid of the jealousies or envy which can warp and stifle a child's potentialities? Will the husband's income support and educate a growing family or must she supplement this with one of her own? In this case can commendable arrangements be made for their care?

Progeny should never be had to relieve the boredom of the mother, to free her from unpleasant work away from home or to "save a dying marriage." (This latter attempt is never successful. The greater problems which then arise tend only to promote more discord than was already theirs.)

Unquestionably the wife should be in control of the situation as to her pregnancy. Will she take the pill? Or wear a diaphragm? Would her husband have a vasectomy if this seemed to better serve their purpose? (There is rarely an excuse for his refusal now that there are "sperm banks" which make possible his having children later on if he so desires.)

All these factors could have a real bearing upon any marital alliance. Also, when becoming seriously interested in a specific man, a girl should acquaint herself with his habitual erotic responses, as well as his abilities and aspirations, but first she should understand the motives that prompt her decision to marry at all.

Does she want a home because she is in love or could it be just to get away from her own family domain? Is it because others of her acquaintance have taken the traditional step? Is she lonely? Is it for financial support? Oscar Wilde opined that the tragedy of getting what one wanted was often as great as that of *not* getting it! Thoughtful deliberation is surely indicated in any decision which could so effect her whole future! Why is she intrigued by this particular individual? Can he provide her with the emotional security which every woman needs? When "the honeymoon is over," will she still be as starry eyed and enthusiastically avid for his "love making?" If she has any doubts at all, she should reconsider. There are other countries to explore, other peoples to know, further knowledge to be had (and presently the means to acquire it!) There are professions and jobs offering limitless opportunities which were never before available to women! She might even meet a prospective husband better suited to her if she is not too hasty!

As she ruminates, it would be wise to think about the descriptions herein of different men, comparing their ways and inclinations. It is a ridiculous fallacy that she can love only one. If she admires and likes a man, there is every probability that she would also love him, if given the proper chance.

The pitfalls of unwise marriage are not the only ones the immature individual faces. When she has preconceived ideas pertaining to the use of girlish wiles in obtaining her objectives, the unhappy results may be two-fold. It is true that some men are susceptible; on a job, she may be promoted more quickly or receive extra financial remuneration (for a time) if her manner is temptingly promising, but eventually she will be expected to fulfill those promises. Is she prepared for this?

In any event, it should be realized that competition will be hers and that as her freshness vanishes, her appeal will also dwindle. Does she really want to barter her wares? If this is her choice, surely her self respect should demand some selectivity. If she is so naive that she counts upon flattery, a few seductive smiles and a surreptitious kiss now and then to purchase advancements or luxuries, she will be cruelly disappointed. The recipient may come running with his head upon a platter, but he will be fumbling at his zipper as he runs!

Chapter 5

Differing Concepts

There would not be such a continuing disparity in women's and men's ideas if the women themselves had not originally encouraged the myth of male superiority and meekly accepted the concept of men's greater sexual urges. Actually, many men are not so concerned with sex for its own sake as for that sense of power they attain through this channel.

As for their penchant for changing partners as old fires lose their brilliance, planet guidance may be the deciding factor there, just as it is in determining most attitudes. If they seem obsessed with their sexual victories, this preoccupation is often prompted by a general assumption that he who manages well in this area, must be quite a fellow in others. Still, those who dedicate themselves conspicuously to their careers and in so doing become highly successful in their special fields, often either have too little time or less inclination than others to waste their energies in brief superficial affairs. Could it be also that as men of conscience, their spectacular application to work springs from a fear of the wayward tendencies which they suspect and denounce within themselves? Are they driven in their ambitious pursuits by a conviction that (as Voltaire said) "all people are good except those who are idle?"

A man such as this may have a mistress, sometimes in this case more as a status symbol than from sexual desire. (Adler and Jung and many of their followers did not agree with Freud that sex is the chief motivation of humans but rather that a *will to power* is the urgent force behind all action. If this be true and the ego needs are paramount, they are still often fulfilled by some men through their sexual drives.)

While it may be the men who do not find prideful satisfaction in their vocations who are more apt to seek compensating pleasures through erotic diversions, it is likely that the influences from their respective Zodiacal signs are largely responsible for the basic variances. However, the differences in the men themselves are as nothing compared with those between men and women.

A man may love as completely as a woman does, yet he is initially attracted by her physical endowments and even later on, in loving her, is so inextricably bound by his need to possess her sexually that he is never able in his own mind to separate this from his devotion to her as a person.

A woman, on the other hand, first responds to some indefinable quality which she believes she senses in the man and it is only after he has touched her that she consciously reacts to him erotically. Even when he is unable to fully awaken her in this regard she may willingly give her life into his keeping and spend the rest of it in his service. (It is unfortunate that what she sees in him is often a reflection of her own needs; she endows him with the attributes which these needs invoke.)

Since one could rightly say that a man's erotic impulses and the sexual patterns he establishes can affect the entire course of his life, it would be logical to suppose that a woman's passions would produce the same results, but this would rarely be accurate since she is primarily actuated by the men with whom she has important relationships.

Furthermore, her drummer's call is one demanding sacrifice and service. Love, while named the "tender passion," is not composed of gentleness and warmth alone. Its strength must bear uncertainty, discouragement and doubt, its patience light the way along dark paths of stressful living and endure the vicissitudes of time.

While women of varying Zodiacal signs react diversely to amorous involvement, their attitudes are still dissimilar to men's. As custodians of the human race, their instincts prompt matings only of serious intent, which Desmond Morris calls "bonding" since only those of this nature have been found practical for the rearing of children. (Some of today's communal experiments may eventually refute this.)

Perhaps it is from this very instinct that a woman's search for genuine commitment is born because while many men can indulge in casual contacts bearing no connotation of interest in their partners, other than a moment's physical gratification, women as a rule want more meaningful reasons for such intimacies. Few of them, even today, enjoy the brief meetings in which they share such pleasures unless they have allowed themselves to believe that something more substantial, more tangible will be forged from the union. (Many in trying to adjust to the changing mores, must contend with inner conflicts.)

While men's motives derive mainly from sexual stimuli, a woman's every action betrays her longing *to be needed.* (Is it surprising that her subjugation has been so complete?) Although she may be attracted by a smile or a softly spoken word, she may react favorably to a disarming boyishness because subconsciously she recognizes a man in search of "mothering," and this may stir in her a maternal response, arousing that ever prevailing willingness to serve.

Often her craving for affection is so great that she blinds herself to that inner voice of warning. She may be intrigued by a certain man for reasons not apparent to herself and may succumb to a romantic association if her husband or lover is failing to provide the attention which allows for spiritual enrichment, pride and dignity. Also, as has been noted elsewhere, a very well meaning and otherwise dependable husband often retains preconceived ideas of sexual communion and having chosen for a wife a gentle, quiet girl whom he mistakenly identifies with a former "mother image" imagines her to be almost sexless in her needs. In both instances, she can be denied her individual fulfillment.

No matter her age, her marital status or the inappropriateness of the attraction, she may become implicated with someone who can only do her irreparable harm.

Just as a very young woman may be misled by her senses, mistaking her first sexual awakening for love, and bewitched

by the romantic aspects which she fancies exist, so too, a discontented wife may be enticed by a man of strong physical
appeal (though convinced that there is more than this to
their rapport) which could even lead to a breakup of her
marriage although she may not have weighed well the consequences which often attend such situations nor have
bothered to learn whether there is the remotest chance of
sustained interest between them.

It is not only the young who makes mistakes. An older
woman can be fallible also. Often it is she who, through
loneliness or fear of a continuing life without love, rushes
into the most ill advised alliances, maybe even seeking marriage with a man who is obviously a poor risk, or with one
whom she plans to change. (If he has habits, ideas or man-
nerisms which she finds distasteful, she is sure that for her,
he will effect different ways.)

He may be a lazy man with no intention of supporting her
or even himself, expecting financial gain or income from her.

He can be a person with interests and tastes quite dissimilar to hers, from a vastly different background—religious,
political, social, racial or educational. He is often aggressively outgoing, a true extrovert, enjoying lively friends and
constant sociability albeit she is somewhat reclusive, and
his presence is enough for her. Or these descriptions might
be reversed, she preferring outside festivities although he
favors long evenings and weekends alone with her. Either of
them may like to frequent bars or have a dependence upon
alcohol, while the other is disturbed by misgivings about his
own ability to control its use.

Many a woman expects a man to show a sensitivity of
which he is entirely lacking. For instance: the Don Juans,
the Lotherios, and those of "gay" propensities who plan to
circumvent their homosexual leanings through marriage.
Some men remain bachelors in spirit and action even after
marriage; many are compulsively drawn to younger and
younger women as they themselves advance in years. When
over-hasty, she may consider none of these differences nor
the possible results of this incompatibility.

It is almost always humiliation or a wish to prove her own
worthiness, rather than erotic impulses which sends a wo-

man into the arms of another when her husband or lover is a philanderer, but it is a longing too, for a rewarding relationship (although usually she will not find it there). Being unhappy, she persuades herself that this man has the qualifications she had earlier looked for in her mate. (Ironically, for the same reasons some other dissatisfied wife may turn to the one from whom she flees. Often overlooked is the fact that the most beguiling of men may spend very little of that charm in keeping "the home fires burning.")

Incredibly, there was a time when most men revered women, an era when, as David Suskind has said "the good girls said no." However, that prompted the men to "protect" the ones they loved by seeking out others for relaxation and pleasure. Helen Gurley Brown asserts that today a husband has affairs only when he has become disenchanted with a wife who is inadequate or unresponsive. While this could be true in some cases, surely most women have long since discovered that this is often merely the excuse with which he assuages his conscience or gives to his secret paramour. In reality, no woman can be provocative, intelligent or "sexy" enough to hold a man's sole interest constantly and indefinitely. No matter how wistfully eager, or how diligent her efforts, she can never be sure of his fidelity unless his innate character traits dictate it. Bacon said that bad husbands often have good wives, a truism which should read that "the better the women, the poorer judgment they may have concerning men." This is evidenced not only in their choice of husbands but in other involvements wherein their motives are usually incomprehensible even to themselves.

Freud once admitted that he knew very little about women, which one would readily deduce because of his placing so much emphasis upon erotic drives without stressing the motivational differences between the sexes.

It is questionable whether any male psychologist or psychiatrist has a true picture of women's real emotions since automatically feeling that he would see their problems only from a limited viewpoint, and being careful of the impression thus invoked, they are apt unintentionally if not purposely to color their accounts by either minimizing their own faults or exaggerating their companion's. (Also, a great number of them would never consult a male counselor.)

It is not men alone who enjoy flattery. Everyone enjoys it and "heart hungry" women most of all! One must understand their blind enthrallment under specified circumstances to have the empathy with which to perceive their extraordinary credulity, but there are thousands of them who fall into traps which though seemingly set by insensitive men, may have been initially created by the women themselves through their individual needs and their self-deception. One can be positive though that those needs are very, very rarely entirely sexual. How often is it the difficult child that a mother seems to love best? Similarly, she reacts to a man who inspires in her an urge to protect and care for him. It has nothing to do with eroticism at the time. Her definition of love is never known to those who speak of a lonely woman as "just needing a man." When in a state of infatuation, she sees first that which stirs the heart, later in a secondary stage, this may include erotic response.

Not always does a man take advantage of such a woman but if she is amenable he may see no reason to resist the temptation.

Women can be extremely logical in every other phase of their lives but be shockingly imperceptive as to the recipients of their affections. Having been steeped in the idea of men's preeminence, they not only give generously of themselves and are unsparing with both praise and affection, but often go overboard in these efforts to please, becoming entangled in relationships which can only bring them eventual regret, while the men remain unscathed. How can there not be unhappiness where there is such one-sided giving?

Chapter 6

Illusion

The young wife who becomes a "swinger" at her husband's behest, often has regrets almost immediately. For a while, both of them may enjoy the freedom and exhilaration of having extra-marital liaisons but usually it is she who begins to yearn for an association in which there are real values and mutual commitments. She may allow herself to become pregnant with the hope of bringing this about but almost invariably, the situation is immediately worsened by bickering and recriminations. Often the husband disclaims all responsibility (as well he might, since she herself may not be certain whose sperm has served her purpose.)

Yet, what could she have expected to gain when she embarked upon the original experimentation? Could her anticipation have been anything but "wishful thinking?" Sometimes, such a young woman is a product of a home where the parents were overstrict and now she may be only trying to prove her right to independence, although there are also parents who have so shocked their children with their own conduct that while the motives differ, the results are the same. More often, the girl is following the age-old pattern of concurring with her husband's whims in order to retain his presence or his love.

However, it must be plain to almost anyone that where there is no greater stability in a relationship than is manifested here, it is not even worthy of the effort toward continuation. Does it never occur to her until too late that her husband almost certainly will find a partner in whom he will be more than casually interested?

It is ignoring all knowledge of human nature to assume that two persons with any depth of feeling for each other, could spend amorous hours with other individuals and then return home to lie side by side in peace and harmonious comfort. Each would be filled with thoughts—even longings or prurient memories of those persons with whom they had been consorting. They would also be exceedingly curious, indubitably jealous and resentful of their spouses' recent activities and partners. If there is none of this, the couple themselves could have had little true affection between them. It is not apparent why they would have prolonged such a travesty called marriage.

What if she wants to end this pattern of erotic adventures which may have seemed so worldly and fascinating in the beginning? Even if both of them agreed to do so, could they build then a fabric of communication in which there were trust and complete satisfaction? It is doubtful!

Single women also have problems. When lonely they sometimes seek companionship at clubs, bars, or resorts, all of which are fine breeding grounds for promiscuity. Unfortunately, most of the men who frequent these spots are either secretly married or confirmed bachelors, and while many women may find even more entertainment here than do the men with whom they share these matings, they are but advertising their deep and desperate needs and the fact that they have so little other recourse. Can either partner forget this to the extent of feeling at ease with one another? The man is often a bit disdainful and the girl self-conscious, and whether or not an alliance of any kind develops, the woman's plight is degrading and humiliating! No matter how much she rationalizes her status by vocally asserting her liberated ideas, it is still she who eventually sheds tears of remorse and bitterness.

Too, there is the elderly widow who is often beset with trouble which for obvious reasons are rarely disclosed. She has to be tragically lonely—this woman—to allow herself to be beguiled by a young, unscrupulous man who has only his own monetary benefits in mind, but if she is even moderately wealthy, there are those who may prey upon her through her own emotions and need of human interest. Even the aging, often confused woman living on small retirement funds is not exempt from the overtures of the self-seeking individual who has a number of such women on his list and would rather spend a few hours each month beguiling her with endearments and "fond" gestures than exert himself in profitable legitimate labor.

Sometimes these affectionate pretenses for which her heart is athirst is all he offers. This man is almost more dangerous than the one who entices her sexually. It would be difficult for most young people to understand a physical relationship between age and youth, especially when it is the woman who is of advanced years, but there are men who will not hesitate to use this device.

A widow in her sixties or seventies may have had very little wooing in her lifetime. Her late husband normally would have been a product of an era when men knew only a few arousal tricks and these were often omitted soon after marriage. She also may have resented their purely physical aspect and now be astonished at the seeming awareness displayed by this young man of today, and amazed at her own culminant response. Although her glands may have been long quiescent from years of deprivation, they could betray her now. Ridiculous? Pitiful!

Paradoxically, the woman most likely to become involved here though, is she who has known real fulfillment in her marriage relationship. Because of her greater loss, she is the more vulnerable to any gentleness shown her by the opposite sex. She it is who suffers most when that terrible moment of reckoning is hers and she has to face the fact of her blind stupidity or deliberate self delusion. Only when she finally realizes that her "friend" will always have an "emergency" which requires his "borrowing" money from her every time he calls, does she accept the truth. One can only guess at her chagrin. If she were not left in a miasma of self denigration and shame, one might almost forgive the man's culpability in view of her renewed youth and the surcease to her loneliness.

As her pain subsides, if she can see the occurrence in its true proportions as a woman of her mature years should be able to do, her trauma may not be so great as that of the young woman, sincerely in love, often for the first time, who learns that their affair has been much more serious to her than to her partner. Similar cases are so numerous that they should be considered classical.

> There's something plaintive in the air
> Unreadiness and dread is there
> A wistful questioning of Spring
> The birds seem restless as they sing
> Or, is it I who cannot bear
> Relinquishing the passing time
> That offered hope tho' hastening on?
>
> Perhaps it is; this Spring portends
> But dull routine and untried friends
> My anguished heart, refusing change
> Still hesitates, still finds it strange
> That love should fade as winter ends
> Ah yes! the lonely mood is mine—
> The dark despair, *for you have gone!*

Sex may not necessarily be beautiful, but love is. Even a girl who cares for a man of unthinking behavior can attest to that! It is always beautiful even though it is sometimes painful. She thrives upon the delicious manna found in her "never-never land!"

While she is in love, even a picnic spot is paradise. To her, the music from a carrousel is like a rhapsody voiced by a thousand angels in joyous celebration; the woods become an enchanted forest where The Little Folk dance in happy camaraderie, but when love has flown, the caliope sends forth a jarring discord of funereal sound. If the eyes of her imagination should search the coves for frolicking sprites, there would be only emptiness and the hush of desolation.

A woman in love is beauty itself. Her giving is without reservation because she loves whole-heartedly in a self-forgetting way inexperienced by men. Such a girl may meet a man with whom she is entranced—a man of seeming integrity as well as availability. They establish a "meaningful relationship" that seems to be uniquely theirs, surpassing all those that ever were before or could ever be again. Even the moments away from him are sparked with tender musing, and she is filled with a quickened eagerness to be in his arms again.

The days slip away and then inevitably at some unpredictable hour, they meet another girl on the street or at a party, to which they may even have been reluctant to go. A glance is exchanged—perhaps he reaches out and with casual touch betrays that ever-present need to "stake his claim."

It may appear as an insignificant gesture. Indeed, he himself may be aware only of a momentary urge or slight curiosity, but the spell is broken! It is irreparably shattered and the effect upon his companion's spirits is as devastating as a physical blow.

(He may be her first sweetheart, playing the games of love until the "right" girl comes along, or he may be honest in his belief that like himself, this girl had wanted only a temporary "arrangement;" he might possibly be the husband of another woman, waiting long hours at home, wondering where he is, but the scene is the same throughout the world, only the actors change.)

He will go on with little feeling of guilt, to other dalliances. How can he understand her torture? He himself has never felt the glorious raptures which were hers so he could not be cognizant of the ravishing loss of pride or the self-denunciation she endures at the memory of her innocent trust.

In comparison, the chimerical imaginings of the woman in love with her married "boss" seem even more foolish and immature (although she may be 17 or 50), and there is little variation in this theme, either. Her attitude toward him is one of worshipful awe. To her, he is a rare mixture of Prince Charming, Sir Galahad and God; he can do no wrong.

There are many opportunities for clandestine meetings in a private office and more probability that the woman will allow herself to become helplessly ensnared, but even if they are both employed by an organization where there are others working in their vicinity, only a bit of ingenuity is required for them to find times and ways for being alone together.

If she is his private secretary, one can imagine her dusting his desk lovingly, perhaps holding briefly in her hands the framed photograph of his wife and children. She sees the faintly wistful look in the wife's eyes, but sees too the slightly sardonic smile which the camera cannot hide and which she interprets as complacent satisfaction.

She would have been told that his wife is coldly practical, that real feeling no longer exists between her and the husband who has "given her everything," devoting long hours to the ordeal of earning a living, establishing a beautiful home for her and providing many advantages for his family.

He perhaps tells the smitten girl all the things she wants to hear: That she is warm and far more exciting than his wife had ever been, that if he had only met her first, they could have spent their days and years together in shared contentment; she is sensible and understanding and he knows she would never have expected from him such strenuous application to work as has been his!

He explains ruefully, though, that he cannot yet bring himself to leave the mother of his children. Besides, he is sure she would never give him a divorce. Yet, things could change, especially when the children are older. Meantime, (this is so typical that it seems incredible that any girl could be so bewitched she would not perceive the truth!) she can console him and make his life worthwhile. Before he knew her, he had come to feel that nothing really mattered but now that he has her, everything is different!

She would do anything for him. She loses all interest in outside activities. Her men friends no longer appeal to her. They seem insipid and shallow. To their detriment, she compares them all with him. She seldom even sees or talks with women friends, preferring to spend her evenings in trying out new hair styles, giving herself fragrant shampoos, exotic manicures and pedicures, lying in the tub of scented water night after night, all in preparation for the moments when she can again be with him. She lives only for this!

He sees the light and the hope in her eyes and because of it feels as Godly as she believes him to be. Not always does he approach her sexually. The boost to his ego which her admiration gives him could be all he seeks. He may though maintain a room or apartment nearby his place of business where they spend a few stolen hours now and then. These are utter bliss for her and a mixture of carnal pleasure and ego stimulation for him. He may not grant her even that dignity and face-saving consideration. Instead (in frustration or retaliative anger at his wife) he may use her nearness as an excuse for quick moments of sexual release for himself—moments that could but lack all subtlety and be of no pleasure to her except that they offer an intimate way for her to serve him.

In any case, he enjoys most the feeling of mastery and power which her adoration engenders. Usually he has no thought of having betrayed either his wife or this girl who may spend many precious years in futile waiting or resigned acceptance.

She who is so engrossed with him during their working hours together, would hardly recognize the man he is on weekends. Here he is a picture of contented domesticity. His friends think of him as a fine husband and father.

The wife undoubtedly suspects his disloyalty. Women have built-in antennas which apprise them of these episodes and affairs and normally know just how casual or serious they are. She may have a secret sympathy for the girl, finding her own lot more desirable than that of one who wastes her bright earnestness and warm enthusiasms in unrequited longings and unrealistic hopes. Could she be responsible for his perfidious conduct? Certainly there are as many kinds of women as there are of men; some of them do drive their husbands unmercifully in their desire for prestige but almost without exception, this type of man has exaggerated his difficulties in the home, and misrepresented his relations with his wife. The evidence of success, the embellishments for the ego may be more important to him than the accompanying life style is to her.

As every girl should have been taught before she was ten years old, a man who tries to seduce her always has a wife who "does not understand" him! In this instance, she no doubt knows him so well that she has long ago made peace with herself about his sexual or amorous infractions, knowing that his greed for admiration is insatiable. They may have had good years together, despite the lessening physical attraction between them and their many other differences. She may still retain a protective love for him.

Her reactions to his sly maneuvering largely depend upon her Zodiacal sign. (Women of different signs vary in their ability or desire to adjust to circumstances beyond their control.) She may settle for expediency; she may leave him, if this better suits her purpose, in which case, the chances are still minimal that he will marry his "love stricken" playmate; usually he chooses someone from his own social group. (One dislikes thinking of the girl in her abandonment.)

Yes, there is the woman who uses her husband's inconstancy in ways beneficial to herself but there are far many more who make adjustments, convinced that the future will bring back the days of their more mutual empathies.

In presenting the foregoing instances, these particular ones have been chosen because of their amazing duplication. It is hoped that in seeing the dilemmas of others who give of themselves under such inauspicious circumstances, there may be those of similar predicaments who will gain a clearer perspective of their own.

Are those who play such masochistic roles as well as the countless others who so often give their love without seeming reward, really as tragic as they appear? Or are there compensating factors inherent in the bittersweet moments which they cherish so desperately?

It would be foolish to state any firm convictions arrived at from the Zodiacal signs alone as to which women might more readily lend themselves to such situations. Under certain conditions or at a special time in her life, almost any one of them might be captivated by a particular man or follow her instincts to respond when called upon.

Some women are more gullible and therefore much more vulnerable than others. Those of the Capricorn-Aquarius, Taurus-Gemini, and Leo-Virgo cusps are apt to be, as are those in the last decans of Virgo, Libra and Aquarius. The genes of each and her early environment are partially influential, yet there is within her a unique Zodical entity and *those* persuasive urges which play a major part in her day by day reactions must be taken into account. They can be used to her benefit instead of her detriment *only* if she understands them and their significance.

Women should learn to pay heed to that inner self, being wary of the inconsistencies and utilizing the strength of their most favorable traits to overcome the weaknesses, so that they will not be misguided by the programmed feminine propensity to please men at any cost to themselves. Due to today's permissive mores, there are new temptations and experiments to be considered, while old ones still maintain. Women must now be wiser and more foresighted in every facet of their lives.

Those who become embroiled in situations which they later deplore, should not reproach themselves too harshly. Although true that what one has written upon the pages of Life is irrevocable as reminded by Omar Khayyam in his Rubaiyat—"The moving finger writes and having writ, moves on Nor all your Piety nor Wit, Shall lure it back to cancel half a Line, Nor all your Tears wash out a Word of it"—the future always holds opportunities of redeeming quality. Why waste the hours in sorrow or lamentuous litany when unwritten pages beckon with quickening promise?

Not every one has the same options but there are none who with planning and courage cannot establish better routines, develop unused talents and bring about more viable conditions in their immediate surroundings!

Whatever her Zodiacal sign, each woman has latent abilities perculiarly her own which she may have ignored, and with the greater wisdom gleaned from past mistakes, she can go on to meet more profitably, whatever lies ahead!

Chapter 7

Women's Inclinations Based Upon the Zodiacal Signs— Including Compatibility with Men of Various Signs

THE ARIES WOMAN

The Arien is an excellent example of the woman who will not accept defeat. Groups with a just Cause need women like her to head their organizations. No one, not even a skeptical man could deny her fitness.

She is physically vital, mentally well balanced, consistent in her thinking. She is creative, ambitious, strong willed, eager for the responsibilities and challenges offered through her directing skill. Her perception of a project or subject without needing lengthy explanations from others and her constant search for newer and better ways of performance add to her productivity in any undertaking.

Efficient in business enterprises, she is also outstanding in theatrical fields. An astonishing number of our best known and admired women entertainers are Aries natives. Their depth of concentration—their singleness of purpose (an almost masculine self-orientation) insures the achievement of their goals.

If the Aries woman *wants* a home and family obligations, she can create a beautiful orderly background where she presides with graciousness and ease. Her children would be well cared for and properly educated. Also, her other varied interests would prevent her giving them an over amount of attention, a fact which would allow them a greater self-reliance.

She would be an asset to any ambitious, progressive husband, her astuteness and enthusiasm fortifying and inspiring him in his own efforts toward accomplishment. A man who evinced signs of financial success would more quickly interest her, but she would be also receptive to one of modest means if he had commendable personal attributes in such fields as painting, sculpting, science or music. In this case, she might even devise lucrative ways of supplementing his income, so that their way of life would include affluence and breadth.

The Aries woman is inflamable and quick tempered, with aspirations understandably high, yet she is sensually vibrant and only a deeply ardent and attentive man can hope to retain her affections.

With suitable cooperation, she can cope for a time with situations not to her liking, but she is too intolerant of indolence to waste a lifetime with one of aimlessness or lack of drive. Neither will she condone unfaithfulness. To a woman as proud as she this would be unbearable, an utter rejection of herself as a person.

Her own loyalties are reasonably strong. When of the second decan with the Sun encouraging gay moods and flirtatious episodes, she might be amenable to overtures otherwise refused. When of Jupiter's influence she appears always to be touched with an impatience to be off on some urgent errand. (Loving her, could a man be sure, if having dreamed of frightening loss he reached out for reassurance, that his seeking arms would find her there? Not necessarily, unless he was a man she respected and admired and in whom she placed implicit trust.)

Who then, will that person be, who could make her happy? The *Aries*, Mars directed man? Undoubtedly he is as ambitious and capable as any she could find. Also he has his objectives clearly defined early in life. They both appreciate the appearance and the reality of cultured living. She could be proud of his attainments just as he would be gratified by hers as long as they did not interfere with his; both are passionate and possessive.

Would his penchant for warmth one moment and coldness

the next, disturb her? It is conceiveable that having similar tendencies, she would understand this changeability of which he himself is often barely aware, but if he is of Sun affiliation, would his need for attention be fulfilled by her or would she resent it? If he was of the third decan, might not his Jupiter clash with her Mars? (Or visa versa?) Both planets are strongly dominant. Would the Aries man find intolerable her unrelenting ways which could possibly match his own? These questions deserve consideration if marriage is the goal of the Aries woman.

If she is very young and thinks of her youthful sign affinity only in terms of a fun-filled phase of the moment, her purpose may be well served. He would be an agreeable companion, escort her to places of mutual interest, follow her lead or her dictates in sexual matters and if dissatisfied with this, without too much argument would go on to someone more innured to his way of thinking.

If the Aries girl is older, perhaps with a meaningful job of her own, she should weigh with shrewd honesty any serious relationship with this man. Is she willing to give up her own ambitious designs in deference to his? Is it marriage he wants with her?

Indubitably, she has the necessary qualifications to fit into his life, if this she desires wholeheartedly, but it should not be forgotten that her disposition is very like his and her needs for self-agrandizement may even exceed his. There can usually be only one person heading an Arien household and that person is never the woman! It is questionable whether an Aries native could submerge her forceful nature and adjust with any real satisfaction to a union in which she is of secondary importance.

In case of a "love affair," these two might know such temporary bliss that it would take precedence over all else. It would be intense and overwhelming but perhaps shortlived. It could even lead to marriage but not certainly to permanence.

If he is married, however, and this is a clandestine association, it is doomed from the start. The Aries man dislikes tarnishing his image or taking a chance of destroying the

marriage structure he has erected so carefully, and if he is a
true Arien, his conscience will not long excuse his infidelity.

Apparently, then, this Mars ordained woman must be careful in deciding upon the wisdom of choosing a mate of her
own sign.

What of the *Taurus* man? What can she expect in relation
to him? Of course his money wisdom would please her. His
steadiness and tenacity would be assets, but his slow caution
might arouse her impatience, and his jealousy and obdurance
could prove disasterous over a long period of time. She would
accept as presumptuousness any mandate he might issue
concerning her conduct. Marriage here would require self-
discipline from one of them. Which one would or could provide it?

A young woman would be impressed by his business acumen. An older woman might find him desirable as a lover,
but not too many Taurus men are looking for secret intrigues unless they have marriage partners by whom they
feel they have been belittled or neglected, and an Aries woman is too discerning to spend her time "holding the hand"
of a man who, because of fancied wrongs, has developed a
grievance against a worthy spouse. As his wife, she would
need to be quick with cajolery and the sympathetic understanding he requires (while being loath to give) and without
which he may tend to stray.

While both are sporadic in their amorous impulses, the
Arien does crave affection and yearns to hear words which express it. The Taurean, though indicating his love in many
material ways, is sometimes hesitant in saying the words a
woman longs to hear, a failure which can deflate her ego
immeasureably. In the last two-thirds of the sign, if the
Venus influence is quite strong, it may overcome the reserve
of Mercury and Saturn which tends to lessen his attentiveness and thus be a hindrance to an otherwise exciting and
stimulating companionship.

Mercury's presence should encourage the Aries woman to
consider a *Gemini* mate, even though in loving her, he might
express his feelings too fully and continuously for her liking.
(She admires men of formidable strength and could construe
the Geminian's natural solicitude as weakness.) Conversely,

there is the fact of his frequent mental absorption—his reading, writing, or contemplation. This could irk a person whose primary interests lay always in progressive activity.

However, the greatest problems here would accrue from her own compulsive leadership which could dampen his enthusiasms and diminish his ability of performance. Simultaneously his unorganized pursuits (even if successful) could outrage her sense of order and planning. Thus, the warmth so necessary for satisfying continuity in Gemini relationships is usually lacking in this union.

Fun times in youth are always possible but for the Aries girl thinking of the future, there is little to be gained here. The natives of Venus influence might divert her for a time and those akin to Aquarius in the last ten days of the sign would command her respect because of their greater gregariousness and exceptional stamina, but the very *effectiveness* of this woman is inhibiting to a Gemini man, thus making it almost impossible for him to function in a way important to their happiness. Even as lovers, these two are usually incompatible. They may come together in moments of deep physical attraction but there is nothing cohesive about their contacts.

The *Cancer* man with his thrift, his proud but engaging manner, his love of home and possessions, should at least arouse the speculative interest of the Aries woman. While often even more emotional than the Gemini man, he is not so quickly swayed by feminine pressures nor so devastated by their criticisms. In fact, he can be quite resolute in handling the reins of the household and while resenting this, the Aries woman would secretly admire his fortitude.

Still, his tendency to ignore certain unpleasant situations in the hope that they will be solved without his intervention bears no semblance to the Aries proneness to settle problems promptly; she could find his reluctance defeating to her impetuosity.

Another disparity in their natures lies in their manner of dealing with their emotions. Both have periods of depressing moodiness but while the Arien finds outlets and counteracting distractions to keep his in hand, the Cancerian reflects his in each aspect of daily living. Too, while his element is Water, he can be as fiery as an Arien if stirred or excited. Aries natives also tire of sameness while Cancerians hold fast to familiar patterns.

Under the spell of romanticism, these two might be deluded by their mutual interests in a home but one should remember that Aries is sometimes ready to condemn and Cancer is not easily mollified.

Could she conquer her own combativeness in deference to his security needs? If his decanative planet is Mars, he could better "hold his own" with her's but this could present other greater problems. If Neptune sponsored, he no doubt would possess many sentimental needs beyond her ken.

For some reason, the Aries woman seems to make a more determined attempt at understanding a *Leo* man. (She is of triplicity likeness.) Being of her element, Fire, he is very quick to anger but she apparently accepts this inclination as perfectly normal. Although she may take umbrage at the arrogance she reads into the Leonian's frequent vehemence, more often she is pained by his dislike of physical effort.

However, despite this latter trait, he may still attain desirable heights of prestige, in which case, she should not be sparing in offering needed praise. Certainly, if he loiters overlong in the pleasure of other women's admiration, (which he is wont to do) she will reject with disdain his passionate "love making" which she would otherwise cherish.

This Fire sign combination does sometimes hold possibilities when the woman has a fruitful occupation and is preoccupied with its performance and rewards so that her husband or lover is secondary in her thoughts or needs.

Though the Aries woman aspires to a proper home setting, mirroring intelligent planning and good taste, she is known to make compromises when furthering her own special career, or even to support a Leo native, either in or out of marriage, in the style he chooses. She can be very happy in the process if he but affects an image which she can glamorize to herself and to her friends. He may not be anxious for marriage, with his natural Sun influence, especially when Jupiter adds reluctance. However, like the Arien, he of the third decan may have urges which take a conventional form. With a greater community of ideas and tendencies, this latter combination is sometimes very favorable although he may prefer that she remain at home, using her talents in the encouragement of his.

In the case of the *Virgo* man, marriage would be the basic consideration, since he could rarely be led into any situation which he thought unusual or questionable, but his cool, critical manner would be antagonizing to the Arien woman as much as her impulsive, arbitrary ways would baffle and affront him. Needless to say, there is little chance here of an amour. While applauding her professional ambitions, and enjoying her company, nevertheless he would be unsettled by any arrangement other than that of the traditional wife-home-husband routines.

The chance for happiness in marriage is also very remote. To feel or show affection, the Virgoan needs to protect and shelter others. (An exception is the immature Mercurian who himself requires sheltering but the Aries nature is not geared for such empathy and forbearance.)

Even though the Virgo native of Saturn influence might have more insight concerning their marital difficulties, this would seldom serve to resolve them, and if of Taurean similarity, while Venus could offer provocative inducements, her constant liveliness and exciteability would usually be too over-powering for him.

With *Libra,* the Enchanter, however, these qualities of hers make a fine impression and his warm effervescent manner strikes a spark of instant response in her. While their attitudes toward life in general are as widely varient as the sunshine and rain, their natures in being loving, ardent and generous as well as prideful, sensitive and quick tempered are identical, thus they find great delight in being together.

This is another example in which the Aries woman willingly provides the luxuries in a marriage or a trysting place; she often assumes responsibility for their financial needs while he prepares for a profession, is working out musical scores or is busy in some other artistic field.

Under these conditions, she somehow finds it possible to

subdue her masterful leanings, accepting his amorous attentions with all the overt coyness of a first sweetheart. Yes,
the Aries woman with her fine intuition, senses that she
could never hold a Libran's affections if she betrayed her
positive tendencies. She does, however, demand fidelity and
unless he refrains from his natural dallying, he will soon be
looking for another "angel."

Both of them might seek extra-marital affairs; he, because
it is an ingrained erotic pattern; she, from injured pride and
to prove indifference.

This often happens when he is in the second part of his
sign with a likeness to Aquarius. If of the last decan he
might quell his liking for variety but would lose for her some
of his charm if he became too placating and amenable.

Such compromising qualities, she could rarely expect in
the *Scorpio* man. He is one that the Aries woman might love
devotedly if she were caught off guard in the lure of his passionate magnetism and could submissively tolerate his
dominance.

Yet, both of them are ruled by Mars and at their first
casual meeting, she usually recognizes an antagonist and
rightly guesses that he must always be the leader and the
head of any mutual project. Usually, she would rebel at this,
even though there was a strong sexual affinity. Although he
matches her in desire for financial attainments, the clashes
resulting from this combination can make prohibitive any
close relationship.

There is a greater inclination to make an effort toward adjustment if the Scorpio native has Neptune lending a hand.
Yet, her changeability under displeasure, and the unpredictability of her passions could seem like a rebuff to one of his
sentient feelings. Emulating Cancer in the last one-third of
his sign is of very little help. Aries and Scorpio could but be
in conflict.

All the more surprising is the Arien alliance with the
Sagittarius man. His need for freedom is as great as hers.
Jupiter's gift is one of strength and vitality which equals
hers from Mars, resulting in situations in which their
mutual combativeness and tenacious determination often

reach a stalemate. Yet, this twosome sometimes finds considerable felicity. They seem to understand and respect one another's imperiousness, their amicability not being necessarily contingent upon agreements. There are few arguments concerning life patterns. Often, each follows his own bent as to career and money making. When the Sagittarius man seeks quietude in the woods or other out-of-the-way places for lonely vacations in order to reflect and revitalize his forces for the strenuous activities in which he usually engages, the Aries woman apparently duplicates this through her own devices in his absence—thus a tranquilizing balance is established. Their union does not always include marriage, but he has a strong tendency to remain more faithful to her than to most others. This is particularly true of those on the Scorpio-Sagittarius cusp or those of the second decan, both of whom have Mars influence. With Leo similarity in the third decan, there is some possibility of permanency.

As to the *Capricornian*, this man may feel the way she likes a man to feel toward her, but he seldom shows it! She can respect his abilities and intellectual traits, but with her fire and energy, would she have the sufferance to devote herself to his ideas of comfort and quiet living? Possibly they might make a satisfactory commitment to each other if he would agree that she continue her vocational pursuits. (They must still reconcile their common need to rule.)

Almost certainly, he could be trusted regarding other women, but would this compensate for the necessity of negating the expression of her views and her forthright attitudes? If he were of the second or third decans, the same problems would here attend that beset an Aries union with Virgo or Taurus. Added to these would be Saturn's pessimistic interference.

What then of the *Aquarius* man? One remembers that Venus and Mercury impose their effects upon this sign as they do upon Capricorn. Too, there is the Uranian aggressiveness which can be a threat even to that of Mars. She could be overwhelmed in any matter of authority. She might judge him to be quite dilatory. (He is active enough in any area which interests him.) To her feminine eye he could seem inconsistent or careless while he might find her overbearing. Here again is the clash of two strong personalities and it is doubtful whether either would make a serious attempt at conciliation.

Allied with this man, she could be the one to indulge in affairs (out of frustration and stubbornness). Still, with Mercury or Venus reducing his Uranian forcefulness, she would be less vexed with him. If he is gentled by Mercury, her irritability might be appeased yet her interest would more surely be held by the erotic incentives provided by Venus in his third decan.

Finally, there is the *Pisces* man and one wonders whether with his modest, subdued manner he would initially impress the high-spirited Aries woman enough for her to make a true appraisal of either his ample proficiencies or his romantic nature. The Arien, seeking the very qualities which are here unrevealed, may easily overlook the possibilities of a prosperous life style and a warm, human relationship. Too, good natured as the Piscean is, he still will not be completely dominated by a woman. This applies particularly to one of partial Mars control. Fire and Water do not often find the tranquility together in which the Piscean is comfortable. Usually, disdaining outright combat, he finds a more appreciative companion. Since the Moon of Cancer and Mars of Scorpio offer little hope for compatibility, one cannot expect that their lesser influence in Pisces would suffice as an aid here.

It could be hoped, perhaps that the Piscean of Mars temperament would be better equipped to match the Arien in aggressiveness, yet his Neptunian placidity and ethereal concepts precludes any certainty.

Thinking back over the various men with whom the Aries woman might find happiness, it is seen that it is she, herself, who must subjugate her talents most often or restrain her tendency toward commanding attitudes. Those of her own element, Fire: Aries, Leo and Sagittarius are imbued with the same urgent need to be first that impells her. Those of the Earth Signs: Taurus, Virgo and Capricorn are equally unalterable. Of the Air Signs, Gemini, Libra and Aquarius, only the first two will be influenced by the dictates of another and then only briefly through their affections (which would mean the loss of their native competence.) The third, Aquarius, will immediately rebel against an authoritative manner. And finally, of the Water Signs: Pisces, Cancer and Scorpio, even when amiable of behavior and conscientiously considerate, they are unwilling to accept the imposition of others, particularly of women.

What then, should the proud Aries woman do for fulfillment? It seems fairly obvious that through her own efforts she is destined to be a leader and an organizer (not only of women's causes). How could she be content without utilizing her various capabilities? She should have a career or profession where her talents have proper scope and where she is given increasingly favorable opportunities for development and self-expression.

If she be greatly endowed with tenderness, compassion, maternalism—the qualities so necessary to a happy family life, she often must be willing to suppress the strong urges of her basic self, to deny the very essence of her psyche! No self-deprecating woman, she, yet if she thinks it worthwhile, it is not beyond the realm of possibility.

All women in the past have been guided by learned tenets to give of themselves and to make sacrifices for those they love. Some subordinate themselves more easily than others. For the Arien, it has never been easy. She may give joyously in personal relationships but she has within her other energies and aptitudes seething to be called into meaningful action and direction.

She can have it all, if she so desires—a well-planned home life and a prestigious place in the "Scheme of Things." One fact to be remembered: men do not take kindly (either in public domains or in private) to preemptory, officious ways. Can the Arien restrict herself to being diplomatic—using subtly persuasive methods when appropriate? The will, the energy and the ability are hers, for any way of life she chooses.

TAURUS—April 21 through May 21

THE TAURUS WOMAN

A tower of strength, the Taurean, both in her home and in shared responsibilities elsewhere—an opportunist in recognizing ways of turning effort and ideas into money. Because she frequently lacks the spontaneity of the Aries woman, she often is not credited with the equal imagination and fervor which are hers. Above all, she is dependable and practical, capable of "seeing things through," whether in business, a profession or her personal life. Indisputably, these endowments make possible her free choice as to her niche in the world.

She can easily deal with the requirements of family life. If "a man's home is his castle," a woman's is very often her workshop and this the Taurus woman likes. If she has help in keeping it clean and well organized, so much the better. This leaves her with energy and the necessary time to make it a place of beauty as well as comfort. She often enjoys, though, the active aspects of running the house efficiently and therefore, unlike the Arien, may prefer making a career of her domestic life, forgetting or disregarding the latent longings for other compensations.

Yet, the Taurus woman, like the Arien, can easily manage two jobs simultaneously, that of wife and mother and an interesting, profitable one outside. Being an Earth sign native, she is usually physically fit, having the strength and exceptional drive as well as the calm amiability to serve her in either capacity.

Often she is a writer, working in advertising or educational fields. Like the Capricornian, she is fascinated by the lore of ancient days and all historical facts, yet appreciates too, the more ethereal qualities of poetry. Shrewd and instinctively foresighted, she is excellent managerial material and moreover, has the good judgment which is necessary in such positions. However, one finds that the very proficiency and self-confidence of this woman are sometimes irritating to men.

Although she appears to be more genial than are the others of her Earth Trigon and is affectionate and sympathetic toward those she loves, when meeting with resistance to her plans or ideas, she can become quite unyielding, an attitude not readily acceptable by those who happen to fall under her direction.

In a husband, she looks for one who is destined for success through intelligence, initiative and unceasing perseverance, taking it for granted that he will be as enterprising as she in order to acquire the power and the pleasures of eminence.

Who, then, can answer the needs of one of her nature and still retain his pride and equanimity?

Could it be the *Aries* man with ambition and drive so similar to her own? Would her cautious, methodical ways be a hindrance to a man of his vast enthusiasms? Would he be able to demonstrate his special financial prowess? Certainly he is not one to relinquish his position of leadership nor would he long tolerate moods of ill humor or resentment which she sometimes displays when angered.

As mentioned earlier, he could take genuine pride in a mate's noteworthy talents, never down-grading her abilities or her creative efforts. Their variety of mutual interests, their urgent passions, would contribute to a cooperative marriage. He would not be apt to seek extra-marital affairs unless their association became detrimental to the pride of one or both.

However, if an early April Arien with Sun engendered susceptibility to the allurements of other women should show noticeable restiveness, she would be quick to grant his release. (If he were of Jupiter thinking, she may not have been able to get him to the alter at all!)

Significant as these problems are, the *Taurus* man presents those of equal seriousness. There is no need to review his characteristics—only to remind one that they are like her own except for the intensification attendant where the native is male. Taureans are strong willed and intractable, while being reliably logical and kind.

Obviously, any helpful compromises here must be initiated and quietly accomplished by the woman. If either is of the

second decan, there will be more complexities because of
habits of censure and if Saturn from the third period adds
gloominess, only their strong physical attraction to each
other can assuage the irritants. If an alliance is formed,
probably neither would defect unless their ego needs were
completely overlooked at home.

This could be true, also, if the Taurean chooses a *Gemini*
man, yet there are great differences of temperament here.

As before discussed, Earth and Air Sign subjects vary considerably in their outlook. Even so, favorable speculations
could be made concerning a union between these two. She
could indeed provide a steadying influence upon one of his
visionary nature but would this be destructive to his inspirational endeavors, nullify his eagerness or weaken his incentives?

He would be happy in surroundings pleasing to her and in
a home where tidyness in all things was the common practice, even though he does not believe in making a "fetish" of
such things, but would his haphazard application to the projects at hand seem to her to have a mercurial instability?

While she is tuned earthily to love-making, he is searching
for fulfillment of the whole self as happens in his illusionary
fancies so there is marked divergence in their needs. With
Venus leanings in early June, he could better understand
her complacent ways, though his interest in other women,
however transitory, could arouse her fierce jealousy. Uranus
in his third decan gives a stubbornness to combat her own,
but this very likeness lessens their chances of felicity.

In spite of this, if the Taurus woman is unselfishly in love
with this man, when she does not attempt to manipulate
him, is careful not to offend his inner delicacy of feeling, a
satisfactory relationship can sometimes be achieved; otherwise, he will be prone to continue his quest elsewhere.

Although there can be similar contingencies when a
Taurus woman is allied with a *Cancer* man, his craving for a
rewarding companionship and a well-ordered household
should overcome any hesitance on the part of either. Both
are thrifty and aspiring, with like beliefs in the propriety
and safety of marriage.

She should never underrate his emotional reactions and needs, however, nor fail to comprehend his inclination to retire into moody silences when harried. This could be exasperating to one as frank and outspoken as the Taurean. If though, she is primarily interested in her connubial life, this is a man with whom she could pleasureably share it.

Without question, it is within her power to cope with any dissuading factors, although it may be a full-time assignment! Still, she can be very compassionate and though not always evidenced as such, her loves are deep and enduring. With personal help from Mars or Neptune, in his second and third decans respectively, their mutual passions would give emphasis to a "togetherness" which both seek. Jealousy could be a problem but seldom is well founded in this case.

What if she meets and is mesmerized by a *Leo* native? Need she be reminded that the lion is the king in his jungle? Or that he is not always jovially playful? Would she realize that he must be constantly immersed in schemes? Howbeit, these never-ending schemes do very often come to pass and when he reaches for the seeming impossible, he often is amply rewarded. He would then be delighted to provide that solid background and that important bank account which pleases her. If his own grandiose plans did not materialize, he would probably not object if she sought a career of her own. She could brighten their lair with such colorful, tasteful tokens of success that he might forget the flirtatious temptations of other women.

Jupiter influence in early August could deter him from marriage plans, but if the honest Taurean can bring herself to use the devious ways of some "sister" sirens, she can perhaps hold his wavering interest.

The native with Mars additive might intrigue her even more since his ideas of both money making and marriage coincide so well with hers. The Leo man's love making could lend a sparkle to her unmistakeably more prosiac ways.

In the *Virgo* man, the Taurean would not be apt to find this warmth. Furthermore, although they are both of the Earth Triplicity and therefore alike in being sturdy, sensible and industrious, it does not necessarily follow that they appeal to one another. Her strength of purpose might be admired by him, but her latent admiration of the beautiful and her surprising desire for clothing, home furnishings and other trappings of pleasureable living could be counter to his more spartan ideas.

Fault-finding attitudes are common to both, yet neither can accept suggestions from others, a fact especially noticeable in those with Saturnian influence (her third decan and his second). Even in romantic areas there is a disparity. Though to some, she may seem over-controlled, Venus is her Chief Ruler, and therefore her passions foster an expectancy of response which Virgo's diffidence could but chill unless he himself has Venus intervening. This could be true of the third decan native or of one on the cusp of Libra. In that case, this twosome might be drawn closely together and could resolve their other differences without too much difficulty.

Obviously, then, the Taurus woman and the *Libra* man himself would be a favorable combination. Two Venus-ruled natives should enjoy their sex life together, even though his random romantic moments might sometimes occur at inopportune times for her. All other aspects of her life must be in satisfactory order before she can enjoy her sensuous interludes. Another obstacle to their bliss could be his laissez-faire approach to practical matters—an attitude which could be bewildering to one of her sterner self-disciplined fiber.

Still, the Taurean can regulate the situation if anyone can! She would be able to go her own way as to gainful occupation although this mate would be able to accomplish more if remaining the revered provider while she spent her hours in making him comfortable and nurturing his self-esteem. In whatever way she decides to manage their life together, it must be done with perceptive care. Even if they are successful in joint ventures, she must see to it that he gets the credit and the praise or he will be robbed of all intitiative. Can the efficient Taurus woman curb her own tendencies and actions to this extent?

The Libran with Uranus rays could seem quite unorthodox to one of her staid ways just as the native with nudges from

Mercury might be accused of flightiness, yet with their mutual ruler Venus interceding, these disadvantages could be overcome. Perhaps not so easily could the Taurus woman adjust to the Mars inflexible nature of the *Scorpio* man. Yet, though both are stubborn when angered and their jealousies noteable, there are some fortuitous aspects.

Her more unpredictable erotic instincts could be greatly enlivened by this man's imaginative overtures. Her sense of fitness and appropriateness would be appeased, since his conscientious ambitions match hers. However, she must inhibit her own strengths and abilities in deference to his. Her outside interests must be few. At home all noise and confusion must be confined to the hours when he is away. This is a frustrating procedure for a woman so persistently occupied with household tasks, but the domestic picture he enjoys is one where duties are done with ease and dispatch and little effort. This he expects rather than admires since it compliments the dexterity with which he feels that his own activities should be performed. This bit of fiction and the conformity to his home-woman-image, she may find most rewarding, feeling no regrets for the loss of personal opportunities.

A Scorpio native also, with Neptunian altruism and compassion, is surprisingly amenable to his mate's needs and ideas, and if he, with the Moon's adaptibility can cope with his jealousies, this too could make further probable a good partnership. Unless a Scorpio cuspal native, the *Sagittarius* man presents problems of adjustment. He has the "know how" in many areas and is so constantly busy working at it that he often gives only superficial attention to the women in his life. They are very important to him, yet he keeps them in a separate compartment marked "diversion." The Taurean could find him too much engrossed in his work, his philosophies and his quest for information, to suit her possessive liking.

The Sagittarian is progressive enough and diligent to a fault—she could not deny him that—but he is as cautiously elusive in the protection of his freedom as is the canny coyote on the western desert trails. He is a gallant, casual lover and a thoughtful friend, even when skeptical of their sincerity. He has no objection to women being in business or holding political offices, but these views are abstract; he does not intend them to effect him personally.

With Mars aid in the second decan (just as on the Scorpio cusp) there would be greater inducements toward compatibility and since the Taurean finds the Leo native so fascinating, if the Sagittarian is of the third decan, with enough Sun influence to provide similarity to Leo, there could be a mutuality of magnetic response to bind them. Otherwise, the conventional Taurus woman would no doubt look around before committing herself.

When doing so, she might do well to consider the *Capricorn* man. His sly witticisms and knowledgeable pronouncements, delivered with such detached indifference, often captures her unwilling admiration. She senses too, that beneath that benign exterior, there are hidden depths of feeling that few people ever perceive, even though his Saturnian melancholic tone may trouble her Venus need for warmer communication than he offers.

With him, she would be free to follow her own dictates as to outside occupations and interests as long as their home life was restfully seclusive and he spared from household concerns. As a rule, neither has any worries about erotic competition elsewhere. Both being of the Earth trigon, they have a sameness of outlooks, yet she could possibly be drawn more to the man of Venus attributes in the second decan. He of Mercury bent offers an assurance of honest effort admirable to Taurean precepts, but his more austere manner could strike a note of discord.

When of the Aquarian cusp, his somber qualities are somewhat brightened as is true with those of the *Aquarian*. He though is usually too determined in his self-assertiveness and too lacking in conformity for the Taurus woman with her own firmness and highly developed sense of propriety. His seeming inconsistencies in planning and life style could offend her more careful methods, and the feeling of constraint which she would inflict upon him would result in repercussions detrimental to both. Actually, an ingrained positivity is all they have in common and neither their Mercury nor Venus decans render much alleviation to an inauspicious situation unless in the latter case, Venus influence is greater than Uranus or the Aquarian is of Piscean cuspal origin in which the Neptunian flexibility could help, as it does for the *Pisces* man.

If the Taurus woman, who after all is a romanticist at heart, is looking for a mate who would allow her full reign in managing her personal affairs but still offer her affectionate regard and steadfast loyalty, she will find him in the loving Piscean. Their artistic tastes are in harmony, their ideas of thrift, identical, their love of home and family of bonding nature and their emotional attraction for one another constant. This man of rare attributes does insist upon faithfulness, but the Taurus woman is usually willing to comply. The Moon influence of his second decan intensifies home interests and Mars of the third, while producing more resistance to any competition on her part, still adds amorous spice to this favorable union.

Retracing the various male potentialities for the Taurus woman's needs, one decides that there is no certainty of Aries or Sagittarius of the Fire Signs being especially agreeable spouses; Leo might be acceptable. She would be tempted, although disliking his entrancement by other women. Of her own element, the Taurean and the Capricornian are better suited as her mates than the Virgoan. The Geminian of the Air Signs, particularly if on the Taurus cusp, could perhaps qualify yet there would be dissatisfactions with both the Libran and the Aquarian. In the former instance, these sometimes are resolved. All three signs of the Water Trigon could be compatible if she remembered their tendencies and acted accordingly.

Yes, she is a strong, purposeful woman, the Taurean, but withal, one who is innately knowledgeable, reasonable and discerning. Not so impatiently quick tempered as the Taurus man, more able to guard her tongue (having found that it was she who suffered most when self-restraint faltered) she can thus make those adjustments required in any area.

No matter the level of society she inhabits, the particular

group in which she moves will be enriched or improved by her presence. Though a woman who will always place her family first on her agenda, when following a career, she will be equally diligent in its progress. In the past, many a Taurean has chosen the single role of homemaker, in which she indubitably shines, but with the many current alternatives, she may prefer using that fine mind in more lucrative ways. There are many opportunities open to one with her talents.

GEMINI—May 22 through June 21

THE GEMINI WOMAN

The Gemini personality is one of strange contradictions, formulated both from illusionary assumptions and earthy realism. Even more than the male, the Mercury governed woman manifests this duality from hour to hour, in the many changing phases of her life. Her belief in the good intentions of others reflects her own sincerity or lack of ulterior motives, and her feeling that no person or group of persons should have power over others derives from compassion and a strong sense of justice. She is appalled by all violence, anything that could be remotely termed persecution or cruelty and cannot comfortably abide the slights she sees even inadvertently inflicted upon one human by another in the ordinary process of daily living. She is quite psychic in knowing another's thoughts or in anticipation of things to come. Being mystically inclined, that which pertains to the occult or the transcendency of mind over physical experience deeply interests her, yet she is incredibly logical when the situation demands.

Although softly, modestly feminine, the Gemini woman is firmly, staunchly almost masculine in some of her thinking. In truth, no trait can be said to be solely of one sex or the other, yet until very recently, the subtler, gentler qualities were ascribed to women while those of strength and tenacity were attributed to men. In this context, the Gemini woman can be said to be masculine in her reaction to difficulties or circumstances requiring her direction or intervention, while in her personal relationships she retains her inherent womanliness. She dislikes menial tasks which take their toll in loss of energies and time that could be spent in creative or profitable effort. This does not imply that she shirks such duties. On the contrary, she may be deludingly conscientious in taking on duties of others thus robbing them of their initiative, strength, and satisfaction in the mistaken belief that her help is essential. Actually, the impulse springs from her own need to make herself indispensable in a relationship in which she often feels insecure.

Through her affections, she gives of herself unstintingly, persuading her reluctant inclinations into the necessary activities of homemaking. She despises all but that which directly brings comfort to those she loves. Never are tasks done singly. She will not be found gazing pensively into a pan as she stirs the contents; at hand will be another chore which is completed simultaneously as she hurries from one to the other.

Fastidious, though scorning ostentation, she would rather write a sonnet or compose a musical score than work at attaining the perfection of housekeeping which she admires. She would rather paint a room than clean it and would find more pleasure in designing a house than keeping it in the "show place" condition which her instincts demand. Just as she seeks perfection in the home, so too does she function in business, where her reasoning, her easy adaptability, and her intuition make for success in many areas.

Organization and direction are well within the scope of her able action. Artistry is innate, music and rhythm so inherently a part of her that they beg for repeated expression. Facility in acting and all forms of theatrical work is hers yet often her sensitivity and awareness of the reaction of others inhibits her performance and negates her spontaneity. She savors words and phrases as others savor food.

The Geminian's amorous passions are strong but not aroused by careless or casual approaches. When she reads her first love story, she identifies with the young, unawakened maiden whose ardent and adoring lover teaches her rapture with a gentle, cherishing tenderness. According to the author, such rapport as theirs continues "forever after." This fantasy, the Geminian believes and never quite abandons. It permeates her very existence and lives upon its own beckoning promise. From this naivete is fashioned her concept of all romance, and that which others call her fickleness or unreliability she knows to be a frantic, unsatisfied searching for the man in the story.

No woman, whatever her sign or background has a greater need to give in love and devotion, yet her defenses are fragile and her protection against perfidy negligible. She is not easily defeated in life's general struggles, but is completely annihilated by disloyalty or rejection. Those to whom she gives herself her heart ever remembers. Changeable, variable she may be, but once loving deeply, she can never forget! Yet, due to her strange nature, her contradictions and insecurities, her amours are many and are without permanence. She is forever hoping for tender, protective solicitude.

Despite these inconsistencies she is not weak. So sincere that she appears over conciliatory to some, she has within her a surprising strength and incredible tolerance and it is perhaps these qualities that are sensed by those who draw upon her maternalism for their own needs.

Thus the Mercury endowed woman frequently appeals to men who are plagued with vague mistrust of themselves and who, in doubting their own worth, are unable to provide the complete understanding she so greatly prizes and without which she is extremely vulnerable.

Only those Geminians of the last ten day cycle are fortified to some extent by the imperviousness supplied by Uranus. They can more easily follow their own bent without fearing the abrogation of happiness. Often, they relish the freedom possible in associations without matrimonial bonds.

Few men there are who can fulfill the unrealistic standards of behavior which this woman's erotic innocence suggests. What man then, could best justify her dreams?

Could it be the *Aries* man? He has many qualities which she would admire. His steadiness and his way of life would be pleasing to her and in satisfying his own restlessness in pleasureable activities and travel, he would perhaps appease hers as well.

Both are impulsive and given to being over generous and thrifty by turns. Would their respective expenditures be in opposition? The Arien is careful of money but not to the disadvantage of those he loves. The Gemini woman has not so much concern about material things as she has regarding a communication of spirit and a harmonious atmosphere. Could the Arien curb his sharp impatience so that it would not weigh too heavily upon her easily deflated ego? If he found in her his true wife-image, he would no doubt make the effort. If he were aware of the depth of her needs and would offer her the tenderness that one of her delicate sensibilities finds imperative in "love making," there could be a very special kind of happiness here.

If, however, his Sun guide in the second decan gave his eye even a glimmer of interest in another female, the thrust of hurt would deplete her passions and injure the structure of her child-like imaginings.

Obviously, with Jupiter in his third decan, even prescribing variety in such interests, a union would be ill fated from the start unless through the prompting and dominance of his regular ruler, Mars, he held fast to a closer relationship.

Could the *Taurus* man better fulfill her expectations? Probably not. Since she is ever seeking a mate with extremely sentimental and devoted ways, his often brusque and abrupt manner could but seem clumsily devoid of the feeling she so implicitly requires in intimate contacts. (Taurus men often could provide this if she but gave them the opportunity. Sometimes, their brusqueness hides surprising warmth and gentleness.)

His intellect she could appreciate, his probable faithfulness be very tempting, and since Venus offers a natural love of muted colors, symetrical forms and even poetic rhythm at times, all of which are her natural tools, this would seem to portend a mutually pleasing combination.

Yet even if she could be persuaded that the Taurus native were the one for her, she might soon find that her own quick, restless mind-oriented nature disturbed his phlegmatic, stolid approach to conservative living. She could seem very flighty and irresponsible to him. Especially, he of Virgo resemblance might be so affected, even though his Mercury would encourage a greater quickness and activity to match her own. Too, he could not be expected to refrain from reproachful suggestions which she is so ill equipped to accept.

The Taurean of the last ten days, with Saturn's sober cynicism could suppress or even quench the flickering flame of her ever changing enthusiasms.

What then of the Gemini man?

Would he not be the ideal person to understand the Gemini woman? Would not their needs be the same? Their mutual aesthetic instincts be of optimal importance?

This is all possible. There are many such couples who even learn to synchronize their swinging moods. Their life style can be adequately fulfilling since they can attain whatever their combined aspirations dispose. They may not follow the pattern prescribed by sapient forethought, their aim be peculiarly their own and one not impressive to others but this should not disturb them.

Although naturally capricious, two Gemini partners would very well know that seeds of sexual attraction fall only upon fallow ground and that to germinate and produce the bright blossoms of love, there must be a day-by-day loyalty and consideration which begets trust and confidence. If one or both have the Venus gift of physical magnetism though, their pleasures are enhanced. While both sexes of this sign lean toward mental pursuits, they are nevertheless stimulated by novelty and variety; with their versatile imaginations, they can supply this for each other.

Regrettably, when both are Uranus impelled, this influence makes less viable a happy union.

What of the *Cancer* man as a favorable companion? If he could accept the Gemini elusiveness, her investigation of the new and exciting, his home loving traits might strike a spark of appreciation which would be a basis for compatibility. These two have much in common in their familial conscientiousness and charitable interests as well as in their liking for beautiful objects and surroundings, but the diversity in their handling of finances could prove discordant. Both are emotional and analytical which calls for real discretion and tact. The Geminian needs brightness and cheerfulness about her to support her spirits and the Cancer native has a brooding stillness when annoyed which could be depressing.

He of Scorpio likeness with his urgent physical approach might seem over anxious while often Neptune's addative, though being auspicious to the man himself, could serve as a disheartening deterrent to her more sprightly ways.

(These are conditions for the individual to weigh. Often when couples accept one another's differences, they come to actually enjoy them.)

The *Leo* native, strong and vigorous with the Sun and perhaps even more so with Jupiter or Mars in the respective decans, could well satisfy the Geminian's needs for perpetual enthusiasm but alas, this man is so trapped in the vision of his own anticipated accomplishments, that little else penetrates his bemused preoccupation with "deals," fortuitous opportunities or gainful manipulations, thus all the Gemini interests may be unheeded.

This is one union in which she could go her merry way without question, perhaps even without notice, a possibility too deleterious for her to entertain.

The Leo man of the second decan could be off at all hours on unexplained personal exploits from which she is excluded and while he of the third decan, if somewhat like the Arien, might offer more substantial material benefits and be just as resourceful, he could also be more demanding.

In *Virgo*, a man of Earth element, one finds a lack of perception regarding the Mercurial Geminian even though his own sign is ruled by the same planet. Here, however, there is more realistic thinking, a steadier performance and while the two would agree as to discriminating fastidiousness and often see eye to eye as to work habits as well as artistic endeavors, his sober restraint would reduce her exuberance and make more difficult her approval of his routine "love making."

With Saturn's dampening influence, there could be no doubt of this and with Taurus-like pertinacity prevailing in the third decan, this also could only be confirmed despite the Venus presence which, while giving more warmth, here provides insufficient tolerance in disputable areas.

In *Libra,* however, Venus is at its best in fostering charm and gentleness of manner and thus this man attracts the gullible Gemini woman on sight. Both of Air Signs and alike in many of their tastes and tendencies, they can experience a true rapport when in each other's company. Both are music lovers and also share an interest in other art forms.

The native of the second Libran decan, however, is often overpowering to the Geminian. Being less conformative, he may also follow his practice of sexual quest outside the nuptial bed, in which case, from chagrin and disappointment, she may retaliate with like measures. Her own Mercury affinity offers more empathy but the same danger of wavering affections exists.

In *Scorpio* one sees the idealogy and keen mental acrobatics which so enthrall Gemini women, many of whom have succumbed to the attraction only to find themselves at odds with this man's fearlessly peremptory ways. She is at once beguiled and discomfited by his compelling eroticism, yet their many common interests in a variety of world affairs and people prompts a constancy and continued admiration for each other. Also, one must not forget that her passions are incandescent too; their difference lies in the fact that her responses depend upon the intangible mystical significance which she reads into any love relationship.

Scorpio's second decan with its Neptunian modesty, grants a closeness to the Gemini ethereality. His gentle tactics never fail to arouse responsive feeling.

In the third, the native with his Mars affined with the Moon, while promising a staunch integrity of affection, could be too emotional for the Geminian's taut nerves. With her intuitive warnings, she would be ever on the alert for his darkening moods, unless his self-control were well developed as it may be of those in the third decan but not always in the second.

As to the *Sagittarius* man, combative and wayward though he often is, he can provoke a certain unwilling respect in the Gemini woman. Perhaps his frankness seems refreshing to one who grows tired of surreptitious philandering. With this man, she often appears to be able to sublimate her deeper hungers in gratitude for his honesty. Usually she finds contentment in her work outside the home, sometimes, (it must be said) with other lovers, keeping these associations on a light and casual level as are those of her Sagittarius partner.

Is she happy in such an arrangement, this woman with her luminous dreams and earlier expectations? Who can tell? The Gemini woman can be as secretive as anyone if the circumstance demands. She adjusts well and is sometimes a dissembler, even to herself. If this is what fate has ordained and the edict is irrefutable, she also might be resigned.

If he is Mars effected with Scorpio nearness or of Aries' type, there might be a stronger fidelity in both, but if of Leo tendencies, the Sagittarian would be even more inclined toward the lure of variety, a situation she might not actually condone without compensating affairs of her own.

In the *Capricornian* she could expect allegiance, but his reasons for it would give her little satisfaction. Only too well would she realize that his abstinence from other involvements would stem not from the depth of his love for her but from immersion in his intellectual reveries and the preservation of his public image. Despite their joint absorption in books and music, his qualities of inconsonance and the long, uneventful hours at home, would be incalcubly stifling to her need of a more romantic or exciting atmosphere, nor could she usually find alleviation from dullness through his outside participation in sports.

If he could quell his own misgivings, he of the second decan with Venus help might bring himself to use conciliatory gestures at times, thus lessening the divisive elements which would otherwise defeat their chances of contentment; moroseness of the native with Virgo leanings would be too stressful unless Aquarius cuspal residence added Uranus lightheartedness.

Notwithstanding the directness of the *Aquarius* man, he

and the Gemini woman often find many mutual concerns which negates for her the threat of this trait. They share the desire to be helpful to others and frequently join in projects with this activity in view.

Of course, he is as changeable as she and is in constant search for pleasureable adventure. As long as this does not lead him into faithless sojourns, all is generally well.

He, with Mercury presiding, would have less confidence in her response to his feelings so could be more diffident. Still, there is a greater similarity here to the Geminian herself; this is often helpful.

Venus in the third portion, annuls some of the Aquarian's fear of commitment and makes for stronger amorous attachments, while still allowing a certain amount of freedom, important to both. (This is especially true when the Geminian has Venus in her own sign.)

With the *Pisces* man, this latter condition could rarely endure. Neptune gives him a wistful longing for much attention and although he would be solicitous concerning her welfare, his self-assurance could well be endangered if she did not channel most of her time in his direction.

Although loving and kind, the moody preoccupation of the Moon affected subject could fail to encourage her ardor, while conversely, in the third decan with Mars bringing him more boldness, he could appear too eager.

With how many men then could the Gemini woman find felicity?

Of the Fire Signs, there is a possibility of a union with Aries or Sagittarius, but in both much depends upon the natives' decans and the untoward influences sometimes derived from planetary combinations.

Those of the Earth Signs are problematical, not only from the Gemini viewpoint but from that of the men themselves.

Of the Air Signs, her own and that of Libra offer the greatest probability of alliance though extensive compromises are indicated even here, due to the insecurities inherent in both signs. With the Aquarian, there could be a mutuality of tastes and ideas, but with him the Gemini woman would often feel on the defensive.

Concerning the Water Signs, one remembers that she is often attracted to all three but is reminded also that there is much emotionalism and moodiness to be taken into account, as well as Scorpio's dominance, and that it is essential to know whether these various men would contend with her vagaries as it is to speculate upon her desire to mate with them.

No matter how she works out her love life, which is as important to her as the air she breathes, this woman obviously needs other diversions and an occupation which nourishes her ego. The danger is that through her affections in early life, she will be carried away on divergent paths before preparing for the responsibilities and performances in fields that later hold her intense and knowledgeable interest. Although wifehood and motherhood are of utmost significance in her life, her dualism can never be satisfied without rewarding achievements in other areas, so she must learn to compartmentalize her thoughts and energies.

A composite of many women, however, with relentless, conflicting forces within vying for supremacy, she finds it difficult to identify with any fixed pattern of self. That thin veneer of easy going geniality with which she greets the world gives little evidence of the indomitable will to accomplish, the real determination, the preciously guarded optimism or the sharp insight which are hers.

Unfortunately perspicuity sometimes fails her in her judgment of people; she tends to see them through the eyes of her own ethics and compassion.

The Gemini woman must be ever aware that though logical in other aspects of her life, she is fallible both in her need to be liked and in her rationalization of other people's actions. The innate, though often subliminal maternalism with which she encircles all those toward whom she feels protective, can be misinterpreted as an indication of weakness.

Although it may always be a compulsive motivation, if she is to attain her goals, she must be prepared for contact, even competition, with some who are unprincipled and ruthless, and acknowledging this fact she must use suitable and effective weapons for defensive vantage, since the very substance of her existence depends upon her ability to do so.

CANCER—June 22 through July 22

THE CANCER WOMAN

Enjoying her friends and many outside activities, the Cancer woman is still primarily devoted to her home and family. Her greatest satisfaction lies in making the home as comfortable and restful as it is attractive and inviting to those she welcomes into it with such gracious hospitality.

Of impeccable taste, she demonstrates it in every phase of her life, surrounding herself with possessions of intrinsic beauty, both man-made and those provided by nature.

Lovely china, silverware and linens, as well as unusual antiques find real appreciation here; heirlooms are treasured as a link to the past and for their aesthetic value.

Almost invariably, she creates beautiful apparel and decorative objects for the home. Hers is a spic and span house (particularly if Neptune in the third decan gives compulsive habits of meticulous cleanliness. It is well if she has someone else to do the more tiresome tasks since her capabilities in more rewarding areas are numerous.)

Although she is usually adept at "from scratch" cooking, it is probable that with subtle experimentation, she has found newer, quicker methods in which to obtain the same fine results. She herself enjoys good food and she serves it enticingly displayed to both her family and guests.

One could have no safer confidante than she. Entrusted with intimate or personal information, under no circumstances would she reveal it. Many seek her friendship, but she prefers the companionship of those who share her interests and hobbies, the trend of which is very often humanitarian, including projects for the benefit of the ill, the aged or those less fortunate than she in possession of worldly goods.

The penchant for accumulation and the practice of thrift are of early origin, perpetuated through fear of later difficulties.

While capable of holding enviable positions elsewhere, and often doing so, she can generally be content in the roles of homemaker, wife and mother, yet often shares with her husband the management of a service or business. If it happens that he owns a shop and her time is mostly taken up with housekeeping and child care, it is almost certain that she still keeps the books and types the correspondence. Well read and conversant on many subjects, she is frequently found employed in libraries and class rooms but one sees here a continuation of the mother image, which she so typically represents.

Warmly maternal, her instinctive knowledge of children and their ways prompts a tactful firmness in her relationship with them. Although tolerant and understanding, she refrains from any tendency she feels might lead to weakness and vacillation in youthful development.

Disciplining herself as she does to allow her own children independence, she is, however, intensely possessive in her personal "love life."

Aware of ways in which to capture and hold a man's interest and erotic awareness, she usually finds also the loyalty which she deems important. Not loving lightly, she carefully enfolds her dear one in a downy blanket of adoring admiration and binds him to her with delicate strands of passionate yearning, a soothing loving imprisonment artfully conceived and one from which any man would be foolish to try to escape. (Few do!)

The Mars aggressiveness inherited in her second decan is seldom prominant enough in the Moon-governed woman to cause marital difficulties; it only increases for her partner the delight in their sex life (as is true also if she has Neptunian influence in the third.)

Yet, with some men, understandably, there can be problems.

With the *Aries* man, for instance, who is ruled by Mars, she does not always find contentment. Water and Fire sub-

jects are antagonists. His restiveness often tends to make her
feel incompetent and this is disastrous to her regular good
humor although she is amiability itself when a pleasant, unhurried atmosphere prevails. Also, both natives of Leo and
Sagittarius likeness would feel constricted by her desire for
closeness, while she would be adversely affected by the impressions they make upon other women.

The *Taurus* nature is one which the Cancer woman often
finds consonant with her own. (One wonders about this.) His
thrift and practicality are assets from her viewpoint, but the
Aries man too has these traits as well as being faithful, and
yet in his case this is usually not enough to compensate for
those not to her liking. The difference in her feelings toward
the two may lie in the Venus sponsoring of Taurus. This apparently provides her with more self-assurance since it
makes for a more affectionate bond.

It is readily seen however, that if from Mercury influence
he had Virgo traits, his lack of sentimentality would be a
hindrance, just as the gloom and reticence of Saturnian origin in the later third of the sign could dampen her easily
deflated spirits.

With a man of *Gemini* personality, Cancer might cheerfully cohabitate unless she found him over-exciteable and his
seeming lack of stability disturbing. Her own stability sometimes needs fortifying.

He of Venus warmth in the second decan would attract her
physically could she but cope with his constant need of outside contacts (often feminine).

However, the unexpected crises caused by Uranus in those
of the third decan might discourage unity.

With her own affinity, another *Cancer* subject, there could
be real joy, providing that between them they did not generate too much emotionalism or moodiness. There could be
jealousies to overcome with a man of the Mars group and
with one of Neptune's influence, and a need to respect each
other's silences. Yet, all three decans promise the fidelity she
takes for granted.

Surprisingly, the sometimes inconstant *Leo* native offers
much that pleases the Cancer woman. His congeniality coun-

ters to some extent her more retiring tendencies. Although she might be frightened at times by his seeming lack of diligence, she would revel in the fruition of any of his schemes.

The Leo man whose mentor is Jupiter might cause her to doubt the genuineness of his affection but the Mars directed native of the later decan would be more seriously involved and more apt to supply financial safety as well.

Unfortunately, the *Virgoan* with all his dependable traits does not appeal to the Cancer woman. Her susceptibility to glumness which she often must overcome in herself, is detriment here. If this could be circumvented, their mutual desire for a solid domestic life and backlog of substantial savings could bode a promising union.

He of Saturn imposition could probably not entice her, but he with Venus likeness to Taurus should be considered.

The *Libran,* with his need of loving care would thrive on that offered by the Cancerian if her mental depressions did not rival his, but rarely would she contend with his bachelor's ways.

Uranus in his second decan could not be depended upon to soothe her anxieties but Mercury in his third might do so if she could adjust to his lack of caution in financial matters. Indeed, the vivaciousness of the Libran's attitude could be exactly what she needs. Of course, there is no guarantee that Venus with her beckoning pleasurers would not cause grief.

Scorpio? He may be the proper mate for the Moon maiden! She can no doubt accept his masterfulness without misgiving, appreciating his artful "love making" and his amused tolerance of her moods. If Neptune has bequeathed him gentleness, so much the better and if the Moon has provided that extra "edge" by guiding him as well as her, their romantic idyl could become permanent. An exception exists where her nativity is of the second decan, ruled by his guiding planet Mars. She would then need to remember that he must be the leader.

Sagittarius so greatly differs in temperament from the Cancerian that she could hardly be tempted to try for connubial experience. Normally, it would be useless to do so although she might have a brief and wondrous affair with him.

However, this woman usually thinks in terms of lasting attachments. If he were on Scorpio's cusp or even in the second decan of his own sign, there would be a greater possibility of a serious alliance because of Mars bringing at least a tentative faithfulness.

He of proud Leonine demeanor with his Sun lending radiance and joviality could bring an answering sparkle to her eyes but she wants affectionate protection, not competition from other women! No, the wary Cancerian would probably not consider the Sagittarian.

As might be expected, Saturn's taciturnity usually prevents her initially becoming interested in the *Capricorn* man. Yet these two actually have much in common, if she would but look beneath the surface of his casual ways. Both have a liking for the printed page and the lore of past history. Both primarily seek loyalty and a simple though pleasant home life. A Capricorn-Aquarius cuspal native might provide her best prospect for contentment.

If of Venus genre, he could attract her physically. (She is amenable at time to both Taurus and Libra because of Venus rulership.)

The Mercury attuned native might also win her attention with his solemn reliability and their marriage could even be beneficial for both, with her offerings of comforting faith and admiration and his provision of the financial means she wants. (Each has much to give which the other seeks.)

As for a Cancerian *Aquarian* combination, there is little promise of complete rapport. Their only real mutual understanding is often through their compassion for the elderly or sick. Still, bonds have been formed of more fragile material than this! Such a couple could be drawn together through some charitable project or even during the more personal care of someone with whom both are involved.

On the other hand, it is not likely that this man would furnish the steady accountability the Cancerian admires. There is a danger also of his being too outspoken for one of her sensitivity.

If Mercury lends a hand though, this tendency could be nullified and thus a better relationship established.

If Venus plays a part, that could be very favorable indeed, considering the Cancerian's erotic tastes. All in all, a good man to keep in mind!

As for the *Piscean,* there is real compatibility in all parts of this sign. It has already been noted that a Neptunian influence pleases this woman, that he of her own Moon guidance is looked upon with favor and that a union with one who is Mars instructed portends real agreement.

To summarize: Of the Fire Sign men, it was found that in Leo there is a possibility of a pleasurable association. She might prefer those of Mars persuasion with Aries likeness even though the Aries man himself is thought to be somewhat dominative. The Cancer woman is so loving that one has to be reminded that she is often also quite spirited and perhaps subconsciously resents a man who is too obviously in control. The Aries-Taurus Cuspal native, if somewhat gentled by Venus is often acceptable. The Sagittarian could appeal to her senses but would avoid her because of her possessiveness.

Of the Earth Signs, the Taurian could be selected by her but neither Virgo nor Capricorn seem capable of making her happy. Exceptions are when one of either sign is of the decan with Venus as personal sponsor, or a Virgo-Libra cusp native. If Venus were strongly activated in these instances, the difficulties might be overcome. As mentioned, he of Capricorn-Aquarius residence should be remembered.

Of the Air Signs, The Geminian offers the greatest chance for a comfortable, meaningful alliance, although she could feel deep love for the Libran if he were willing to be domesticated. Just possibly, he of the third Libra decan, of Gemini similarity would be so grateful for the Cancerian's warm concern that like a newborn kitten, purring contentedly at its mother's lavish administrations, he would forget all else. With the "true" Aquarian, more obstacles prevail, but decan or cuspal distinctions (Mercury or Venus intervention) could change this.

Those of the Cancer woman's own Water element offer more congeniality and security than do any of the others. Yes, with Pisces, Cancer or Scorpio natives, she could be very happy.

As has been said, here is a woman who can often be satisfied without outside occupations other than those of charitable or similar undertakings. Unlike those of the Air Signs who think of household tasks as dull drudgery, she may see them only as loving actions. Her womanliness requires that she serve others. It is in this way that she finds peace and a feeling of well being.

Nevertheless, with the changing times, she may become restless and deviate from former patterns. Certainly, with her fine talents, there are corollary achievements possible if she is so inclined. Her artistic ability, her natural aptitude for languages and constant desire for travel, the unusual communication she has with children and the deep regard for the welfare of others all bespeak a dependability that is widely needed and indicated a fitness for specialized work in. many fields.

She has but to decide what paths to take. She does, though, find her felicity mostly with extremely independent men, many of whom might prefer that her goals be reached in the furtherance of their own careers. No woman is better suited, or more apt to find sufficient rewards through this choice.

LEO—July 23 through August 21

THE LEO WOMAN

If the Leonian appears haughty and inaccessible, her regal manner may only hide a reserve difficult for her to overcome. Normally, though, she learns to simulate the assurance and vivacity her pride subscribes. If her confidence is fed by needed approval, the patina of bright pertness and self-sufficiency becomes as real to her as it seems to others.

If she marries early, she may be very domestic, baking delicious pies and cooking gourmet meals at all hours, sending her daughters off to school in dresses which are the envy of all their friends, and keeping a house which reflects her own tidy person. If employing some one else to maintain this cleanly order, she directs and organizes the procedures—perhaps also provides the necessary monetary outlay for this purpose, preferring to use her time and strength in occupations where there is greater appreciation and financial recompense.

In the face of adversity or whenever she deems it important, she can put her shoulder to the wheel with a willingness and an urgency unmatched by many women, yet usually seeks to do so through the activities of a career, not alone for financial reasons but also that she may feel completely independent.

With her children, she is apt to be alternately firm and extremely lenient, her heart suggesting pampering, her mind cautioning discipline.

As is the Leo man, she is sometimes overpowering and authoritative but can be quietly persuasive when necessary, counting upon the magical effect she has upon others to produce the results for which she plans. Also, as in his case, there is one type of Leo who is so warm hearted and sincere, modest and unassuming that one cannot believe the two personalities to be akin. Either a Cancer or a Virgo cusp can promote this honest warmth and friendliness, yet even here there is a fierce independence beneath her benign manner. She can be submissive to a husband when it is required but it fills her with frustration which is damaging to her incentives. Deep within the gentlest Leo is a compulsion to lead.

The Sun blessed woman may follow many courses but usually is involved in something pertaining to showmanship, glitter or design. She may operate a business, often a beauty, health or dress shop where she funnels her stout energies into avenues of creative beauty, attempting to make other women as attractive as she herself wants to be (and generally is). She is well known in the theatre where her sparkling effervescence quickens many a heart beat. Even in this latter profession she will probably have chosen the motif for her own clothing, her dressing room and much of the scenery! There is little chance of her failing to use her abilities to good purpose, whatever her background or opportunities.

Men she can always have as her mood determines, but for

marriage, she should choose one of honorable position or assets which make possible his offering her substantial benefits or more glamour or exciting experiences than she can obtain through her own resources. Only with such a person could she comfortably sublate her own self expression and preeminence or still the urge for achievement which would bring her the praise and admiration which is nectar to her insatiable hungers.

If her birthday is in early August, she may be slower to seek marriage (if at all) but, if of Mars extraction, she will no doubt prefer it.

Could it be the *Aries* man toward whom she would turn? Though of a Fire Sign like herself, sometimes impatient, unpredictable and given to quick angers, he can also be warmly tender and affectionate which would greatly appeal to one of her passionate nature. Moreover, they would agree as to prestige and money.

Could she forego engaging in the flirtatious commitments which fortify her ego? Or resist being audaciously managerial with him, or with others in his presence?

There is some doubt, if he has inherited Sun influence and partakes of these Leonine traits himself, whether he would tolerate the same from her. With the strength and (sometimes) arrogance of Jupiter infusion, any great hope for an agreeable relationship is negated.

If she looks to the *Taurus* man, what would she find? There is the same strong physical attraction and coinciding ambition found in Aries, but the Taurean refuses also to be coerced (most certainly by a woman) and he might interpret her decisive ways as an attempt to rule him. Also, he is extremely jealous, so one wonders about the outcome of such a combination.

Neither cusp offers mitigating factors, but he of the second decan with Virgoan patience and curiosity might possibly be aroused by the fire of this unusual woman and even forgive any amorous forays if they were not too frequent or embarrassingly obvious. She should be ever mindful of that natural jealousy and not press her luck too far.

In his third decan, if he is overly imbued in Saturnian

suspicion and finds his own ego deflated, there would be considerable friction.

The *Geminian,* of course, is too sensitive for Leo's impetuous domination. Though often enthralled by her popularity and her possible interest in sexual excursions, he would have to take the lead in erotic matters or be submerged in doubt of his own capacities. Could she care enough to stifle her own attitudes in order to intensify the importance of his?

Venus intrusion whispers of clandestine pleasures and could provide some entertaining moments for both, yet the leadership qualities of most Sun influenced women are too powerful to be long kept in abeyance.

He of the third decan would glory in these temporary romantic liaisons but would disdain competing with her in any lengthy association.

The Leo-*Cancer* combination is one that astrologers reluctantly recommend since the Fire and Water elements would seem to foretell trouble, Yet in truth, one does sometimes find this duo living in harmony. They have many similar tastes but there is the question of how the possessive Cancer husband might react to the Leo aptness toward inconstancy—even her appreciative response to flattering overtures. Perhaps she can control her urges if satisfied by the genuine love and warmth the Cancerian has to give. This could be more probable in his first and second decan than in his third. (Neptune is patient but the subject's gentleness may evaporate under the pressures that could here arise.)

Just as was shown concerning Aries' second decan native of Sun influence (the fact would be even more applicable here) a *Leo* man would not be likely to adjust well to a woman with his same positive traits. He would distrust her seductive manner no matter how innocent, resent the authority she might assume and refuse to share with her the spot-light of attention so essential to both.

The Jupiter guided native might make no attempt to understand her and he of added Mars pride could only be condescendingly amused at a woman having such temerity.

Could she then interest the *Virgoan?* Yes, strangely, this

man with his modesty and integrity is often so filled with
wonder at the Leo woman's exuberance and ambition that he
is moved to endure her very diversant ways. (She is probably
happier than he!)

If of his Leo cusp, however, an alliance would rarely be
feasible nor for one indigenous to the Saturn invaded portion
of his sign.

Venus in the third provides the same chance as is shown
with the true Virgoan.

Since Venus rules the *Libra* native, the Leonian is instinctively drawn to him. Without exception all women like the
cajolery he is so adept at using and it is ambrosia to this
woman's self-esteem.

He enjoys his share of the same treatment and usually Leo
is too unheeding to provide it. Also, alas, she wants that
proverbial "gold" in the present—not at the end of some
rainbow! Leo "dreams" the same as Libra but is more impatient for quick results. This is particularly true of the Leo
woman who is often more practical than the Leo man. More
than any other, this trait is responsible for difficulties with
those in all Libra decans.

The Libran himself could also have criticisms to make, not
being able to cope with an overly forceful woman nor one
who would not recognize his ego needs because of her own.
In brief contacts, though, he often finds her quite physically
compelling and many ecstatic interludes have been blissfully
savored by this twosome!

It is advisable with *Scorpio*, even more than with his triplicity "brother," Cancer, for the Leo woman to deliberate a
bit before rushing into a serious union. There is little doubt
concerning her interest but unless she confined her arbitrary
ways to the household (and this mostly in his absence) there
could be little rapproachment between them. One of the
Scorpio nature is not prone to offer undue adulation to anyone.

If he were of the second decan with Neptunian optimism,
there could be some effort made toward amicability, but
neither he nor the Moon subject would be as fruitful in their
occupations if allied with most Leo women.

Very often the *Sagittarius* man makes a fine impression upon the Sun ruled woman. She likes his industry and is tolerant of his bluntness which is comparable to hers. Secretly, she also delights in his insistence upon the retention of his freedom since she has longings of identical nature. (Both are Fire Signs.)

If he is of the first or second decan, there is evidence that the association can last.

The native of the third decan (of even greater likeness to herself) may hesitate over-long in making up his mind.

With the *Capricorn* man, once again, the fact of Saturn's moroseness must be reprised, since it could be debilitating to this lively woman. High spirits are an integral part of a Leo woman's charm, so it is well that she senses danger here. Certainly, she would admire his mental abilities, but although he might return the compliment, she could offend his ideas of propriety. The Capricornian wants a settled life, uninterrupted by the gaiety Leo requires.

He would be indignant concerning her audacious intrigues and having no liking for officiousness in any woman, would resent it in her, although the native of either the second or third decan would be more apt to succumb to her manipulations than would he of the first.

Uniting *Aquarius* with Leo proves more fortunate when the Leo native is the man. In the present instance, the situation being reversed, it may still be a favorable alignment, although both natives are incurably implacable and not given to making apologetic gestures to anyone. Yet, despite their vigorous confidence and constant mobility, both are generous and often extremely self-sacrificing.

This is sometimes the bond that welds them together. The first and third decan offer the greatest possibility here. Mercury in his second, if of any great influence when competing with Uranus, makes for less acceptance of the dominance which the Sun provokes in its subjects. (These two could blow horns and ring doorbells together but the fun would end there for the Gemini-like man.)

With the *Pisces* man also, this woman would need definite tact and finesse which she could inadvertently forget. The strain of attempting to correlate their divergent natures usually is too much for both.

Only with one of the second decan, with the Moon's intervention, would a union not be burdensome.

Checking back, it is seen that the Leo woman may have many problems in alliances of real seriousness, although many men admire and are attracted to her.

Of the Fire Sign men, there is a slight possibility of congeniality with Aries and Sagittarius; very little with her own sign, Leo.

With the Earth Signs, constant negotiations would be necessary, although there is much mutual liking, especially with the Virgoan who might prove a willing partner.

The Air Sign men too are often interested but long lasting relationships are rare. With Libra or Aquarius she might hope to establish a rewarding contact but the chances are negligible for permanence.

The Water Signs seem more significant in this regard, Cancer offering the greatest indication of understanding, and of Scorpio and Pisces, those cusps relating to Cancer's Moon influence also seem most favorable.

It seems very sad with all her bright, flambuoyant eagerness and spritely manner that many men should pass her by for those women of lesser obvious merit, when this need not be so. It only tends to be when she is unaware of a seeming stridency. If she finds a mate with whom she could be happy, all that is necessary is for her to tone down her own aggressive qualities. She has so much to offer if she will only quell her need to make all the decisions.

Although there are those of imposing, dazzling talents who must learn to minimize their aggressions for the sake of love, there is also that certain type of Leo woman mentioned earlier, unobtrusive but often just as capable, loyal almost beyond reason and contending with all sorts of unpleasant conditions for the sake of her family; she it is who most often appeals to men.

Yet, too often she is unmarried and found in school rooms, dressmaking shops or with a palette and easel, turning out beautiful work for which some one else may be getting the credit. (She is likely of the Leo-Virgo cusp.) Or of her second decan, with Jupiter edging in, she may be off on a ship, as director of some special cruise or guiding groups of tourists to famous spots all over the world. Regrettably, though, without some obstreperousness, she may be only working in some travel agency, wistfully thumbing through the literature of distant ports.

Not to be unnoticed are the Leo women who, through fear of male dominance, will not compete with them in any way. Usually, they have sublimated their erotic urges early in life and although still liking and seeking the attention of men, still remain "cold" and relatively unresponsive in sexual contacts. If this woman marries, the union is often one of short duration, with the man soon turning to outside affairs both for sexual and ego reasons. If she remarries, it will likely be to a man with such inherent self-confidence that he can afford to encourage the freedom of self-expression which she needs.

In a career, the average Leonian knows no limitations. Any business establishment or enterprise needing a poised, sure feminine personality "fronting" for them, would be fortunate to have her services. A leader she was born to be!

Can one conceive of a woman of her drive and talent being satisfied with "make believe" victories? Those confined to the square feet of a home, however great the size?

Could she be content in fostering the success of her husband even in environments where she was socially active with entertaining, parties, shopping and the correspondence attendant to this life style? Or, under other circumstances, devoting herself to the usual household duties, having no more competitive outlet than baking a better loaf of bread than her neighbors? One has only to ask any woman of her sign!

VIRGO—August 22 through September 21

THE VIRGO WOMAN

The Virgo woman is found wherever dependability, neatness and diligence are primary requirements. She is imperturbably efficient in anything she does, being methodical, orderly and almost too meticulous concerning all details, which thus gives her an advantage over co-workers who are bored with monotony and repetition.

Her standards are high; she tends to burden herself with unnecessary work which her conscience will not allow her to renounce. She is thrifty and foresighted—incapable of understanding those whose imaginations are attuned to visionary plans. She is the one to whom these folk turn when their enthusiasms have proved illogical and their failures are overwhelming.

Not always feeling the confidence manifested, she does though have little fear of people or circumstances, being prepared as she is for all exigencies. This cool poise belies the sensitivity and the strong emotions which flow beneath the surface of her composure. If one looks closely enough, there can sometimes be seen peering around the corner of her reserve, a little starry-eyed, pig-tailed girl who once had illusions of her own—and fanciful convictions—the kind which held no knowledge of the dishonesty and falseness in the world.

When she enters commercial territory (which she usually does at an early age), the Virgo woman soon knows well the sorry face of reality, yet retains an appearance of passivity and impregnability. As a mother, she is tolerant but often strict, expecting the ambition and determination from her children which she herself possesses. Without entering her home one could guess at its arrangements. It is comfortable, colorful and spotless! Not a corner is left undusted or a shelf unlined. Even the cans and jars in the cupboards are placed both for neatness and convenience and the contents of the closets hang in perfect array.

There is likely to be a business-list list upon the door's reverse side which tells one exactly how many peas, or pears or "whatever" repose on each kitchen shelf or the identifying description of each pair of carefully boxed shoes, plastic-covered garments and other accessories that are housed in the closets. Is it any wonder that the Virgo woman is never without work or a gainful occupation even when others are helplessly walking the streets in search of it? Employers instinctively recognize her value and sense that she will never fail them or betray their trust.

Incidentally, although of such practical fiber, she often is very artistic and her paintings may be greatly treasured by those who are moved by the delicacy and intricate detail of her portraitures. (It takes more than a knowledge of color and technique to become a fine artist! One must have heroic patience and a self-discipline which is unyielding. The Virgoan frequently has these requisites.)

Her quick nervous energy, that bloom of health and proud carriage are qualities to be envied. Any lover of finely bred horses, familiar with "The sport of Kings" will recall that same defiant toss of the head and the alerted, mercurial stance of the body—that anxious eagerness for action that is seen at the starting gate of a race track! In the world of the future, women will need that remarkable drive and aliveness which are the mark of the September woman. Conservative men are drawn to her introvertive qualities, to her modesty and to the twinkling eye which is glimpsed only now and again but which always adds that element of surprise which causes a "double take" and arouses curiosity.

Here is a woman of extreme loyalties and worthy motives. Her mate will never find her kissing his best friends behind the door, nor had he better be found kissing hers!

Saturn's obtrusion in the second decan often invokes brooding and anxieties over trivialities or catastrophies which fail to materialize. Her concern here is usually for others close to her but over whose activities she has no control.

Venus of her third decan or her Virgo-Libra cusp brings relief from this and advises less conformity and rigidity before marriage. As a wife, she is faithful in thought and deed.

What kind of person would suit this woman?

The *Aries* man? She would appreciate many of his fine traits. His prudence and his ambition equal hers. Both are conscious of the need to save.

However, while he enjoys displaying the solid evidence of his abilities in his possessions and surroundings, she much prefers the quiet satisfaction attained from her state of solvency and the amount of her bank account. Not that she is penurious—her attractive and flawless appearance refutes that! Would the two agree as to the reasons for dipping into their savings? Or could one of them be adamantly against doing so at all?

Both are sometimes critical yet neither is ready to accept reproach from the other although there can be a certain humility in her attitude when she is in love which would intrigue this man.

The good humor of the second decan native could perhaps overcome some of their major differences of opinion.

He of Jupiter derivation in the third presents hazards in that he would possible prefer an affair to marriage and never, never would be content with a captious manner from a woman!

The *Taurus* man, an Earth affinity, should provoke her attention! He is of that responsible group of humans who seize opportunity and makes the most of it. This, she fully understands, since it is an appropriate description of herself.

His Venus offers promising warmth to combat the coolness of her Mercury. Yet, there is his consuming dislike of anything which he could define as fault finding. Of all the signs, the Taurean is probably the most infuriated by it! Can the Virgoan come to know the vast differences in people and realize that some men rebel at suggestions made even with the best of intentions? Compatibility depends upon this answer which of course is an individual one.

The second decanative division of Taurus produces a man not unlike herself in nature and he, even more than she, while apt to note the weaknesses of others, is quick to condone them as normal—to calmly accept as inevitable the difficulties which arise because of them. For devotion, she could not find a better man to marry!

Capricorn similarity of his third decan could add to the worries which are hers, particularly if she too has Saturn's influence. Still, in commiserating with each other, they might find a bond.

What of the *Gemini* native for a partner? They sometimes make a happy couple but not often, especially if the man is the Gemini resident. Though finding a community of tastes in fastidiousness and a liking for good fellowship and even sharing intellectual and artistic interests, the Geminian needs almost constant evidence of approval which the Virgoan has a proneness to overlook. The possibilities of these two consorting on any enjoyable basis is enhanced somewhat if Venus influence enters the picture (either through his Taurus-Gemini cusp, his second decan, her third decan or the instance of her being on a Virgo-Libra cusp.)

A Gemini native of the third decan, having many qualities comparable to Virgo's, is sometimes not as diplomatic as the others and the Virgo woman might see his possible disregard of her ideas as humiliating.

Mating with the *Cancer* man bodes small satisfaction for either. Their extremely diverse attitudes could injure both psyches. This compulsively driven woman could fail to understand a nature that requires periods of restfulness and freedom from all nagging worries. The home of the Cancerian must provide this else all the neatness and order to which she is addicted, (and to which he too prescribes) is not enough.

If he has Mars as his personal mentor and is akin to Scorpio, Mercury's daughter is sometimes moved to create this atmosphere, being captivated both by his ardor and his aggressiveness.

If of Piscean flavor, he is often too sensitive in his romanticism for her lesser awareness.

Despite her conservative "down to earth" inclinations, she and the often indiscreet and urbane *Leo* man sometimes surprisingly achieve a genuine amity together. Although true that aside from their mutual sexual attraction, they share but a composite of neutral viewpoints on a limited number of subjects—and certainly they are in direct contrast in regard to the method of attaining success—their variances seem but to compliment each other.

In his Jupiter decan, however, while both her comely appearance and unsophisticated manner would appeal to him, the sweep of his unconventionality (especially regarding other women) could be to her a debasement of her own value.

He of Mars influence might remain in her good graces if he were disposed to contend with her somewhat rigid ways.

The native of her own sign, *Virgo* could be favorable only if one of them submerged his own tendencies. Each needs a spark from some other source to kindle the fires that lie buried in that insulated capsule of reserve.

Only with Venus in the third decan or Virgo-Libra cusp in either of their signs is there much happy promise and even that is uncertain.

Two Saturn imbued natives would generate enough depressive skepticism to capsize most matrimonial boats.

With the *Libran,* the Virgo woman has many conflicting traits, unless she is on his cusp or has Venus aid also in her third decan. This man is usually much too "easy going" and lackadaisical for one of her discretion and steady application to duty. He would make no attempt to adjust to her orderly ways, thinking them only an intrusion upon his preferred life style.

There is scant basis for understanding between her and any member of the Libra decans. The third might comprehend her worth but would feel that she failed to appreciate his.

Considering *Scorpio* for the Mercury women, it is found that here (even more than in Cancer's second decan, since Scorpio is the actual native) his mysterious magic works upon her mind and heart. For some reason, this man of Mars, with his regal dignity, perceives in her an essence of truth and virtue not evident to those of less discernment, and seeing this, is able to transcend the pettiness of disagreements upon insignificant varients so that both may enjoy the pleasures which accrue from their relationship.

All three decans are favorable with some slight doubt about one of Piscean genus in the second.

With a *Sagittarian,* much depends upon the woman herself. No matter what fate their birth charts indicate, he would always be attracted to the Virgonian. She would, of course, like his inventiveness but her choice of partner here would be a native of the Scorpio-Sagittarius cusp.

Being impressed by the other two Fire Sign men, Aries and Leo, the two decan natives which represent them here, would perhaps also hold her interest. With him of Mars influence there could be marriage since both have the same objectives, and if she could withstand the hurt caused by the wandering eye which the Sun inspires in the third, combined with the inveterate fleet-footedness which Jupiter itself suggests, her many pleasing attributes might slow his pace sufficiently for mutual investigation.

Although the Virgo worries are often accentuated when added to those of *Capricornial* origin, the two natives of the signs indicated do sometimes find consolation in this. She could see to it that he had the pleasant home life which is so essential to him (if she were wise in keeping household tasks at a minimum when he was there. Capricorn dislikes seeing the domestic wheels go round.) Sometimes though, he surprises this companion by offering real cooperation—not only taking on the burden of shopping but trying his hand effectively at gourmet cooking—this only if she has an outside occupation with which her restless, active needs are satisfied and her bank account increased. He admires such sagacity and industry.

All three decans are often auspicious, although his third, copying her Mercurial temperament, is least likely to provide lasting substance.

As with all Air Sign natives, there could be many problems with the *Aquarian.* The Virgoan's sense of duty prevailing under all circumstances, presents such a contrast to his more relaxed method of accomplishment that there is little chance of their concurring in their ideas. She may think him lethargic when he is only refueling his remarkable energies—often a necessity, particularly if he is of Gemini texture in his second decan.

Venus penetration in his third could cause temporary entanglements with others, deflating her spirits. In case of the

Virgoan herself being overwhelmed with Venus influence (also possible in her third decan or her Virgo-Libra cusp) there probably would be extremes of reaction present—either they would reconcile their differences through delight with each other (an unusual occurrence) or they would pursue tangential courses of secret intrigue.

Lastly, there is the *Pisces* man to consider. Here are seen two opposites whose moods could well be in discord much of the time. The Piscean has more romantic sentiment than is usually seen in men. The Virgoan, having to be awakened from her own virgin-like attitude, may not sense his need of warm communion. It is sad when this is so, since each has commendable traits highly valued by both. It is their misfortune that they seldom recognize this.

He of Moon inheritance looks for more comforting overtures than this Earth woman casually displays, but the nature of the third decan, his Mars dignity notwithstanding, may bewilder and confuse her with his unexpected amorous moments. If she succumbs, all will be well.

Of the men discussed, whom then would the Virgoan choose?

Those of the Fire Signs were found to be suitable in many ways. She could no doubt adjust to Aries if she controlled her own impatience when his was uppermost. With Leo, there could be exciting possibilities but with both the Leo personality and that of Sagittarius, she would need considerable tolerance regarding other women. Would an alliance then be worth the uncertainties?

Of the Earth Signs, Taurus and Capricorn appear to be more likely participants in a successful union than her "twin," Virgo. The latter mating could be worked out satisfactorily only with real incentive prompting the effort.

She apparently would have little in common of consistent value with any of the three Air Signs.

Of the Water Signs, the Scorpio native offers greater probable happiness. All three have the objectives, vitality and perseverance which she finds so important but while Cancer and Pisces both require the attention which she may not strive to give, Scorpio himself, taking the lead in all matters, can fulfill her expectations and his own as well.

It is plain that the Virgo woman needs an outlet for her multiple energies and her compulsive drives. She should never be denied this. Easily capable of keeping a home functioning in high gear, she is just as efficient in handling an outside job or profession. She is physically and mentally able to do both. Wherever she is employed, both sexes like and respect her. Of this she can be especially proud, since it cannot be truthfully said of all women. Also, this increases the number and variety of opportunities open to her, just as her confident fearlessness—her integrity and strict adherence to duty and principle makes for sure success in whatever she undertakes.

LIBRA—September 22 through October 22

THE LIBRA WOMAN

How can one best describe this unique woman with her beauty, her sparkle, her savoir faire? To see her is to imagine that she has been fathered by the Gods of Olympus! Her ability to attract men seems to surpass that of all other women. Her charismic aura begets in them a total, blind bewitchment. As if these were not sufficient gifts from Venus, the Libran has been showered with so many natural talents that her only difficulty lies in deciding which ones to develop and utilize. Anything of beauty, whether it be of sight, sound or touch, awakens in her a deep response. Music is the magic which transforms for her a world of depressing drabness into one of gay fantasy. The theatre awaits her with open arms. It is in this realm that she is most often seen.

Various kinds of reproduction seem to pervade this native's activities. If not enacting with her distinctive flair a character on stage or screen, she is generally arranging musical scores, doing replicas of nature or people on canvas or some more exotic material. If thwarted in these glamorous outlets for her originality and imagination, she may type manuscripts, forms and letters in a business office (although a position in which she greets clients or prospects is more appropriate).

Not overly prolific, to those children which are hers she passes on her creative genius and independence.

The Libran's home mirrors her own personality. It is kept in constant "on stage" appearance. If there is no household help and the Venus ruled woman must do the domestic tasks, they are done unwillingly but as quickly as possible to allow for more interesting and stimulating pursuits. This may include upholstering the furniture or painting the walls (like the Geminian, she would rather paint than scrub them.) Skillful in the creation of delectible entrees or pastries—taking advantage of packaged or already partly prepared foods but adding practiced touches to make them pleasing to the palate and noticeably ornamental, she receives warm praise for her culinary art.

The specialities that are the more time consuming are saved for parties or rare occasions. The day by day routines of cooking and serving are kept at a minimum, with all vestiges immediately removed as if to deny the importance of such mundane activities. Outdoor chores she likes best—especially the care of flowers and pets. Knitting, crocheting—sometimes sewing are within her province although they only fill the gaps between more gregarious occupations. Having a remarkable facility for card playing and other mental games, the October native nevertheless finds them too confining to long hold her interest. If she has no avocation or outside profession, she is apt to volunteer for work with her favorite charities—to serve in hospitals, community enterprises or political causes.

To be accurate in completing a description of this unusual woman will appear contradictory. Despite her multiple talents, the many admirers—both men and women—who vie for her attention, the October woman is normally restless—often melancholic and discontented. She hides well an unbelievable sensitivity. No one would suspect the insecurities nor the fears which color her relationship with others.

Discriminatingly ambitious, she expects her mate to have the necessary qualities for social progress. Her insistence upon proper surroundings sharpens her innately perceptive judgment when selecting a connubial companion. If she is of the second decan with Uranus infiltration, the man she chooses need not be one of monetary preeminence if he is intellectually admirable and culturally aware.

This is true also of Mercury's decan, and here she is more concerned with the problems of others. She often joins organizations having to do with their welfare, thus frequently meeting men who are similarly engaged.

The native of all decans is apt to associate with men of prominence or at least with those of marked ability. Whom then will she select?

The *Aries* man? In all probability she would never be sorry. He has all the qualifications about which she dreams—ambition, aptitude in handling situations and directing people, and a feeling of responsibility in attaining worldly benefits for his family. He is passionate and sentimental. She could hardly ask for more but there is one thing to be remembered: Mars contributed pride is urgent within him, and he needs the approbation that is so precious to her own self-esteem. (He would resent her showing too much interest in other men.) Could the physical magnetism between them and the other complementing characteristics inspire them to mutual understanding?

All parts of the sign offer fortunate omens only if she can bring herself to be somewhat deferential to the Sun endowed man and give him of Jupiter inclination the freedom she likes for herself. Her creative longings would need to be fulfilled within the home unless she were united with one of the last decan.

What of the *Taurus* man? He also would provide the substantial elements which she thinks befitting. His Venus and hers would make for an active love life. Yet this man too has defensive moods; gusty angers waiting for another's thrust. Will she allow him the ego satisfaction that is necessary for his well being? (He will expect strict faithfulness on her part, just as does the Aries man.)

If Virgo-like, in his second decan, he could expect a more conservative attitude than she is likely to possess.

The Saturn influenced native might be deeply interested in her physically but could be a bit condescending toward her. Too, she might think his quiet ways very dull even while grudgingly admiring his intellectuality.

What then of the *Gemini* man of her own element? Idealistic and always in search of romance, his personal appeal for her is stupendous. She would appreciate his sensitive refinements and their mutual enjoyment in artistic and musical areas would be a strong bond. If, in her restless need of change and excitement (which could further blend their union since he likes this also) she still remains constant, this alliance could be a lasting one!

The native with Venus combining his Mercury, with tendencies similar to hers (Taurus cuspal or second decan) could charm her most, even though he is more careless in dispensing his amorous "favors." (She could vehemently denounce this action while inconsistently indulging in the same procedures; yet, if she herself is also sponsored by Mercury, this could be a strong attachment.)

He of Uranus influence would be a little too changeable in his emotions, having "cooling off periods" which are little understood by the Libran although her penchant for similar moods is well known. Neither would be overly trustful, nor in some cases would they be trust-worthy!

As for the *Cancer* man, he is often too addicted to conformity to please the Libra woman, but she would enjoy those very things which she condemns. Wandering around his house and garden, admiring and fondling the lovely objects usually found there, she would admire his taste and perhaps delight in the fragrance of some special blossoms grown only by him, yet at the same time be trying to overcome a feeling of imprisonment.

However, sensuous as she is, she could not resist his winning ways if he is of the second decan with that subtle touch of legendary mesmerism which Scorpio-like individuals have.

If of the third decan, Neptune's surprising moments of adventurousness could add just enough persuasion to attract her seriously. (There are those who believe that the water element natives act as depressants upon those of the air signs. This is not necessarily true. Sometimes they learn to compromise!)

The *Leo* man enters her web very cautiously. He is piqued but amused at her clever maneuvering of those who come within range of her plotting, but he has no desire to be one whom she manipulates. His fire attracts her and she accepts even his flirtatiousness without question since it reflects her own leanings. Both want the "good life" and are ever alert to possibilities of attainment. The Leonian would be agreeable to her having outside remunerative interests even though financially it placed her in a dominant role. He would be always expecting a sudden "windfall" from one of his plans or ideas to more than compensate for this.

If Jupiter is present (second decan), the Libran could have more excitement than she anticipates! If her glove retains its velvet texture so that he never suspects the strength of the hand within, there could be a pleasant partnership.

With Mars in his sign (third decan) he might already have the accouterments she seeks when first she meets him. While his warmth is variable (as is hers) in the process of enjoying their home and busy life, they might adjust to each other.

With the *Virgo* man, many difficulties seem inevitable. He might be captivated by her brilliance and her gay manner especially if he is of the Virgo-Libra cusp. Yet he often lacks interest—even patience—with the social amenities; though his thrifty, settled ways would provide the means for the life style that appeals to her, that very grim, determined application to work which is a necessary adjunct to most success, could leave her without escort to enjoy its dividends and thus lessen the pleasureable aspects of such a combination. It is doubtful if she would risk it.

The Virgoan of the Saturn ruled decan could hardly offer the lively atmosphere upon which this woman thrives although in his enthrallment, he might make an effort to do so.

He with Venus influence—cuspally or from his third decan ruler, would be a good "love" companion and still have the major requirements of prestigious background. Any alliance here though would be fraught with a struggle for the commanding position—a continuing battle which their union might not survive.

The *Libra* man, her own "twin"—directed and activated principally by Venus, could be her ultimate choice. Theirs is a uninimity of tastes, high spirits (alternating with moodiness)—a liking for convivial friends and frequent entertainment.

Certainly they should comprehend each other's foibles, their occasional lapses of attentiveness or even outright unfaithfulness—but one cannot be certain. Few men, even today, actually accept the theory of a single standard of conduct for men and women, particularly if it affects their own lives. The Libra woman, accustomed to much regard, is usually unprepared for the loss of a man's allegiance, even though his interest in herself be of limited tenure. Undoubtedly she would not subscribe to a lifetime of humiliation. They could reach a peaceable agreement only if both made a conscientious effort.

If either or both have Mercury bringing logic (Virgo-Libra cusp or third decan) it could be considered a favorable factor but if the addative were Uranus, the problems of adjustments would increase, mostly through an unwillingness of perception.

The *Scorpio* man presents quite a contrast to the Libran tradition of compulsive erotic wandering. Said to be the most sensual native of all twelve signs, in reality he confines his amours conspicuously to the woman "at hand" and often she is so thoroughly bemused by his knowledgeable methods of subtle inducement that she capitulates completely. Thus he is kept permanently beguiled. The Libra woman is no exception in this, but felicity is more probable with the "true" Scorpio than with one of Neptune or Moon influence since both of them are usually too jealous to contend happily or graciously with the Venus infused nature.

The *Sagittarian,* wayward and teasingly flippant, awakens within her a tittilated eroticism. Her search for stimulation could end with him if he could believe in her sincerity, but he has no eagerness for marriage and his own brand of sincerity is sometimes questionable. Yet, if their many common interests brought strong enough cooperation, and if she allowed him to feel unrestrained while subduing her positiveness in respect for his, they could possibly remain together.

All decans promise like objectives and tremendous incentives but he with the Sun prominant in the third decan would perhaps be in the lead in first attracting her.

The *Capricornian,* like Virgo, would be forced to admire the free spirit who dwells within the enticing Libran body. (Oh to be that liberated himself!) Yet, he is as moral as his carefully constructed role demands. Would she, through concern for his dignity and a fine regard for his accomplishments, submit to such conventionality for herself? If his Saturnian permeations allow him a needed sense of humor and rich wisdom, he might retain her affections and even make sure of her discretion.

In his second decan with that knowing brush of Venus painting pictures of libidinous pleasure, how can his overtures be refused?

In his third, he could also overcome Mercury's solemnity in order to please her. (She could feel free to pursue her own career without serious objections from any Capricornian if they were able to make proper domestic arrangements to leave him undisturbed and comfortable.)

The Libra woman very often marries an *Aquarian,* another Air Sign native. Gratification can be theirs, however, only if each respects the other's independence. This includes allowing for his own individual code of sexual ethics. They are a good team when working together in altruistic matters; both like some spice added to their daily lives and either can provide it.

All three decans offer excellent possibilities for contentment although he of the first may be a bit "headstrong" for her approval and he of the third could have bouts of moodiness surpassing her own. (He of Mercury blend is not so susceptible to melancholy or can better control it.)

Unfortunately, this woman frequently rules out the *Pisces* man without much thought. He disturbs her by arousing feelings of guilt because of his unfailing dependability and his seclusive attitudes.

However, when he is of the third decan, Mars is a powerful persuader. The Libran cannot refuse a man who is discreetly disciplined one minute and amorously purposeful the next. If their association becomes serious, being acutely jealous, he may wish that he could keep a padlock on the door when he is away. Whether his own faithfulness would be an advantage in keeping her loyal is a moot question.

If of the first decan and also when influenced by the Moon, he would feel that the home was of paramount importance and should have first consideration, although the latter native might sometimes sanction her having a career, (especially a glamorous one) but he of the third would accomplish more through his own efforts if she devoted herself exclusively to him and to their home. He would not resent her creative hobbies if they were secondary to this.

Reprising these observations concerning the men of the various signs—as has been said, this Venus favored woman can have as a mate almost anyone she desires.

Those of the Fire Signs could appeal to her for practical reasons as would those of the Earth, although here there is some question as to her making the necessary adjustments.

Air Sign men almost invariably play some part in her "love life" although not necessarily in marriage.

Of the Water Signs, she would be most apt to choose Scorpio or one in a decan of the other two which bears resemblance to him. (For both their sakes, she should never ignore his pride.)

Many opportunities may be hers through affairs, marriages, careers and creative enterprises. She will indubitably encounter jealousy and envy in other women yet almost too easily can command their fidelity and aid. In the very men who most admire her as a woman, she can experience frustrating patronization when she seeks to make use of her mental capacities in areas until recently only occupied by them, yet here too, her charm usually will prevail over their smugness.

In the theatre and in business wherein she conforms with the traditional idea of women's activities, she will have less trouble. Indeed, she may have difficulty in separating herself from the throng of willing helpers. She can attain ego satisfaction so easily through the adulation of others that she may be tempted into a lazy, self-deluding way of life which seems to her expedient, never achieving that which her potential indicates. Yet she is a clever woman, far more capable than is required to secure whatever she wants through her own efforts; rarely will a door be closed to her.

The Libran who is true to her "guiding star" and therefore true to the self that was fashioned so lovingly and optimistically by the Zodiacal Planner when the heavens were wrought, will find the real satisfaction that can be realized through accomplishment from these strivings, and will also know the devotion which comes to those who are themselves, generous and compassionate.

SCORPIO—October 23 through November 22

THE SCORPIO WOMAN

This woman of Mar's multiple attributes is deceivingly cool, inscrutable and reticent—not given to hasty friendships or unconsidered commitments. She is one of strong emotions, passionate jealousies and deeper loves. Grave and reserved, she has yet a look of surprised expectancy which is most appealing. There is about her an air of youthful wonderment; it is as though she has inadvertently tumbled into some enchanted garden from an alien land in outer space, being alternately delighted with the mysteries of this universe and puzzled by the antics of the cavorting humans whose actions she cannot fathom.

She is intelligent, thoughtful, intuitive, perceptive, and despite her casual manner, eagerly interested in everything about her, especially in other people's ideas and ideologies. Seemingly fragile, she is often extremely active in sports such as tennis and golf and at home is always restlessly engaged in keeping things in their place and noticeably free of all disorder. There are no doors or drawers in her home which merely hide the clutter of work undone as is common in many households! Her conscientiousness and innate honesty function here as well as in all facets of her existence.

Although a gracious hostess (the Scorpio woman is capable of entertaining her husband's business associates and pleasing their wives too—an important item often overlooked by some women) she prefers dining out, attending the theatre, going to museums, art galleries and concert halls. Her children—usually few in number as with the Libra woman—are given restrained affection and understanding. Although like the Gemini woman, she makes her own rules, she requires from her children conformity to society, which invites respect.

One cannot even imagine this woman in surroundings of squalor or poverty. She would not long permit herself or loved ones to remain in such humiliating straits. Ingenious and determined as she is, a way would soon be found to exchange these circumstances for those in keeping with her gentility. Although her natural understanding of men would never allow her to appear domineering, she is an excellent organizer and can use this ability equally well at home or in business. She may be quietly obdurate but never openly argumentative, having definite opinions and preferences of her own (reached with due deliberation) but with which she never annoys another. Nor does she undertake to expound upon the logic of her views or wishes, in outright confrontation, but seeks to attain the desired result through tactful, adroit maneuvering.

Men are curiously, irresistibly drawn to her. She appears amazingly helpless and unworldly and they long to protect her from all the evils which beset our kind, yet they sense too, a valiance—a buttressing strength beneath that deceptive gentleness and are thus further intrigued.

There is, of course, that secret place known only to Scorpio natives (and perhaps the elves)—a place of unrevealed mysteries of which they do not speak. Is it the knowledge of this soul-refreshing haven which she frequents unattended that often brings briefly to her eyes that faraway look—that

Mona Lisa smile which lightly touches her lips and is as quickly lost in polite attentiveness? Despite these spiritually attractive qualities, she is though warmly, endearingly human.

Those of the second and third decans are strongly motivated toward careers in which the humanities are involved. It seems unbelievable to the casual observer, but this enigmatic, Mars-directed woman is extremely competent in almost all fields of endeavor. (She is anything but helpless!) It is pure wisdom that prompts her not to usurp a man's duties when it would cause him to be defensive—that leads her to defer cheerfully to his decisions, even when her own might be more practical.

A good politician? Without doubt! And with her comprehensive intelligence, her aptitude for cohesive planning, an asset to any business. She has the same sense of delicate balance in color and form that is so evident in the Taurus and Libra woman. When she is an artist, which is frequently, her paintings reflect this delicacy and an incomparable essence of spiritual beauty.

In the past, however, the Scorpio-born has often contented herself in the home, seeking to enrich her own life through her husband's successes. (The future may bring great changes!) She of Moon vibration may continue for a while in this capacity (her home is the canvas upon which she paints her wordless longings) but she of Piscean leanings more and more will turn for the expression of her deep compassions to fields of medicine and other humanitarian benefits.

Who then—what man—is the logical companion for this incredible woman?

The *Aries* man? It could be, although this union calls for either strict self-discipline from both or an almost complete submerging of the dominant instincts of one. Both have Mars ruling which means that both like to lead. In the household of an Aries man, it must be he who heads it. Can the average Scorpio woman be as tactful and self-effacing as is here required? The Aries man provides the way of life that is almost a necessity to her; they agree on the importance of appearances and both are initially prudent in being willing to

mark time as they safely accumulate monetarily for possessions suitable to their life plan.

There is this to consider: as a new order comes about in
our land, and the Scorpio woman takes her rightful place in
making pertinent decisions concerning human values and
welfare, will the Aries man accept this with aplomb? (Some
of them may, since they are always generous and proud of
their loved ones.) At present, this woman might gladly offer
the ingratiating respect which the Aries native needs. The
problem here would be whether he were willing to adhere
strictly to monogamy. (She is not one to take infidelity lightly, if at all!)

The Aries native of all three decans is romantic and
idealistic and he of the first and second, if happy in his marriage, usually is willingly faithful. (He of the second may be
aware of feminine allure elsewhere but still adhere to his
code. He of the third is never as interested in his home as
the others, yet is often beguiled by this woman's elfin qualities. Even he might be held spellbound.

What about the *Taurus* man? Here is seen the same picture. The cultural advantages or at least the financial means
would be available. The Venus native has a special rapport
with Scorpio women. (They can be quite enraptured with one
another.)

She is more sensitive than is evidenced in her behavior.
While she could please him immeasurably with her hidden
warmth and her discretion, would his own often unwar-
ranted irritations lead to the anger and recriminations which
neither can afford? (Some Taurus men are extremely kind,
considerate and just—extremely empathetic.)

Those of the first and second decans are the most likely
candidates for a union here, although obstinancy or jealousy
could be harmful hindrances.

Saturn in the third is an intruder that brings no joy to this
particular combination.

What of the *Gemini* man? He could be a fortunate choice if
his Mercury allows him a steadiness of purpose and great
perseverance. (The Taurus cusp area provides this.) The
Scorpio woman often has a streak of the wanderlust despite

her liking for formal backgrounds and the Gemini man could support this leaning with his own. They often establish bonds of great spiritual strength which is an advantage in effecting a permanent relationship. Both would require faithfulness and for either to abide by these rules, there must be meaningful attachment.

The Mercury native with gifts from Venus in the second decan is a fine physical affinity, but he with Uranus influence could never settle down to the usual conservative life of Scorpio, who may like travel but only with the sure knowledge that her home awaits her return.

The *Cancer* man? He could be the ideal mate for Scorpio since they have the same motivations, although Cancer has even more conformity in his make-up than she has. Both are Water Signs and are so much in tune that there should be few difficulties between them unless they forget that either can be depressed by the moods of the other. With Mars in the Cancerian's second decan, he could be very like her in nature. (He could be discreetly tactful and would also then resent any capriciousness on her part.) In his third decan, he can be easily offended if she is one who is quickly angered. Scorpio's wary woman however, has usually learned to quell the sign's tendency in this direction.

The *Leo* man? He is not often compatible with the November woman. Both are prideful and he is too unaware of her encouragement needs in the dilemma of his own. Without that constant strumming on the strings of his ego (the tunes he most likes to hear) he could never perform in a way to make possible the environment they both want. She may fail to perceive this and could also find him pugnacious when he was striving to be dynamic, vain when he was being regal and predatory with other women when he was only accepting the praise she had failed to supply. This is usually a deleterious situation for both.

This applies to all three decans, Jupiter even adding other problems, although as has been indicated, the native with the Mars of Aries' genre as his personal ruler might qualify if its rays were more potent than those of the Sun.

The Scorpio seems to have some special communication

with the *Virgo* man. They are always attracted as lovers. Also, she finds his shrewd business ability admirable and his thrift commendable. (They match her own.) He would fulfill her expectations as to fidelity and no doubt she would respond in kind though both must watch the inclination to be censorious else there will be bitterness which neither would know how to overcome. The first decan and also the third (with Venus blessing here) are most favorable, since Saturn in the second might cause the native to seem (to her) overbearing.

How would she feel toward a *Libra* man? The magnetism shared by this twosome could hardly fail to work its magic, yet he would need to be especially ambitious and energetic to win the Scorpio woman as a wife. While an alliance of some duration could develop into marriage if he can prove himself worthy, she is not apt to be rushed into a permanent commitment unless she sees that he can produce, financially. This is not to say that she would fail to be cooperative if after making a marriage together, financial difficulties were then to occur. In this instance, she would be both patient and helpful. If she were successfully emersed in a career of her own, she might not be so adamant as to his money-making proclivities. However, under these circumstances, she would naturally assume a more important role in their relationship, in which case, it is possible that more tact than even she can provide would be necessary to keep him feeling contentedly secure.

Uranus would only add greater obstacles here, unless this native in applying himself with his extra vigor in the process of obtaining worldly goods, could forget his longing for convivial friends and the delectation of other women's company.

Mercury in his third decan would give a mutuality of intellectual interests but he too likes more personal freedom than the Scorpio woman might offer. (She of the third decan would be more forebearing.) Also, there are many instances in which the sensuous Mars woman keeps a man so intrigued and so busy keeping up with her, that he willingly foregoes outside pleasures. (This could be one of them.)

Of her own sign, the *Scorpio* man should be significant in

her considerations. Since the ideals, concepts and desires of these two are identical, a union could prove fruitful. The outcome would hinge entirely upon a perfect understanding and a magnanimous spirit. This would not be a union in which it is enough for one of them to make the concessions; each would need to keep ever in mind the pride and sensitivity of the other.

Although all decans threaten more possessiveness than either subject enjoys, sometimes it is helpful if one or the other is in the third decan with the Moon as a conspirator.

Women often get a sparkle in their eyes at just the mention of a *Sagittarius* man! This one would be pleased with his inventiveness and prodigious accomplishments—his flights of investigation into philosophy and science, yet would resent his penchant for adventurous erotic variety. As do so many men, he finds the Scorpio woman utterly enchanting, but while she admires him for the very qualities she fears in him (since she too has his need of freedom) she usually finds it difficult to accept him on a serious basis.

If of the second decan, he might curb his wanderings for her but probably not, if of the third.

The *Capricorn* man might be bewitched, seeing in her the femme fatale he conquers in his dreams and molds into his more sedate desires, yet he deceives himself—he would actually prefer her with the siren qualities he imagines her to possess. In reality, she would adore him for his extensive knowledge and that keen facility for expressing his ideas. However, both can be sarcastic under duress, yet neither can tolerate its barb without feeling a growing malice.

If he has Venus in his sign, their mutual attraction would warrant a trial together, and, as with Virgo, Mercury influence lends promise. Whatever decan is his, she must remember that this man's home is truly his castle!

The *Aquarius* man? It has been found that the Scorpio woman fears or scorns a man who wanders far from her side, so obviously, she should not attempt to unite with this man. If he could slow his pace long enough, he might perceive in her the soul-mate of his fancies. Both cover well their "thin skins" but Scorpio can be easily bruised. Seeming unassailable, she could yet be badly scarred by the Aquarian without his comprehending the cause. One has to dig deeply through his impregnable shield to find his vulnerability. It is there, and he can be a loving person under the proper set of circumstances, but Scorpio would back away too quickly for adjustments.

If of the second or third decans, the Aquarius man would be more perceptive, yet a combination of Scorpio and Aquarius bodes too much emotional friction.

Finally, there is the *Pisces* man, of her own element—one who is in accord with her in many ways. It seems that they should be able to find a common meeting ground. Their longings and their passions are much alike at times, but their habit of retreating into themselves when offended or in order to refresh their vitality, while useful to them individually, often precludes an attempt at reconciliation after a misunderstanding. As with her own sign, these two must recognize and respect each other's moods. Mars in both signs augers reprehensible struggles for power but if either is of the Moon's viable directives, there could be smooth sailing.

Of all the signs, with whom will this woman fare best?

Of the Fire Signs, Aries seems most probable although Sagittarius is in the running.

With those of the Earth, Taurus or Virgo seem more favorable, although Capricorn should not be over-ruled.

Gemini and Libra of the Air Signs should be considered as well as Cancer and Scorpio (and sometimes Pisces) of her own element, Water.

There will be many hours worth treasuring by whomever she chooses. Not always the easiest person to be understood—sometimes bitter or harboring unreasonable resentments, she nevertheless has great awareness, deep sympathies and the rare capacity to fully forgive.

Her intelligence is such, however, that if she confines herself to wifely and household duties alone, annoying frustrations are certain to be hers. Either she should have meaningful hobbies, devote herself to worthwhile "causes" or else prepare for a career early in life. Furthermore, it should be one in which she uses her own ingenious ideas, in which she is unafraid to express the novel and the untried.

She can adapt well when the necessity demands but within her is a wild bird of unrest, beating its wings against its cage of enforced conformity. (It would be better for her to find an outlet through achievement than to lose forever her true identity.)

SAGITTARIUS—November 23 through December 22

THE SAGITTARIUS WOMAN

When thinking of descriptive words for this woman, those of honest, diligent, reliable, foresighted and poised come immediately to mind, yet in actual fact, she is also impulsive and quite emotional. No woman is better equipped, however, to attempt and execute tasks which are baffling. Even in areas usually reserved to men, she seems to have a certain prescience as to how things are done.

Certainly not male in appearance or action, her forthrightness, her self-sufficiency and leaning toward the enjoyment of "single blessedness" are traits often attributed to men. (Whereas it is the Virgo man who can more easily forego the companionship of the opposite sex than can those of most signs, it is the Sagittarius woman who can do so.) Her determined energies are limitless and she constantly refuses to accept defeat in anything she undertakes. It hardly needs to be mentioned that household tasks do not disturb her, since she does them with the same dispatch and automatic planning that would normally be applied only to a business or vocation. Good, substantial cooking is her forte although this may include traditional pastries which put to shame those of more modern vintage. As to food preparation, she accomplishes her purpose here with effortless ease, while having a repertoire of which many women are envious.

If needful, she becomes a capable seamstress although preferring garments already made so that she can better judge their suitability to herself or the occasion. Gardening and growing flowers are a part of her regime when location permits.

Disliking commands—indeed, even suggestions from others—wanting complete freedom of thought as well as action, she still maintains a detached, reluctant acquiescience to the morals and conventions of the community in which she resides. The principles and precepts of her Church remain as important to her as are the affiliations and social activities that are a part of religious customs.

Generous and extremely helpful to those in need of her attentions, possessing a fine sense of subtle humor, she can though, be quick of temper and resentful of those who would take advantage of her good graces or who attempt to impose their will upon those less fortunate.

Her friends are unlikely to leave her to feminine pasttimes such as cards, sewing or frivolous parties when they go fishing or traveling across country to enjoy nature's offerings. She likes being out of doors, finding it more relaxing and pleasurable than domestic pursuits. Foreign lands hold for her a marked fascination.

The Sagittarius passions are unpredictable, which may explain that self-sufficiency and easier adjustment to living alone than is common to most women, yet it accounts too for the possibility of varied partners in her "love affairs." While there is nothing lacking in her sensual response when her mood so indicates, she has little taste for dissembling about anything and certainly will not pretend to amorous emotion when the circumstances or the person do not please her! Sometimes, when traveling, she is inadvertently caught up in a pattern of romantic design, when she would much rather be "on the wing," exploring strange places or customs than libidinous pleasures.

Perhaps it is the injustice that she feels she suffers in being a woman that so infuriates her at such a time (thus alienating her deeper emotions) as she realizes that were a man in the same predicament, he would probably not hesitate to indulge in the moment of passion—using it to his advantage—while planning a quick escape into the exciting uncertainties awaiting him elsewhere. The warmth is there, beneath her angry discontent but it may be that her keen perception and intuition are a hindrance also to what she sees as subjugation.

She plans to be faithful when she marries and is often true to this intention. A proud mother, she expects her children to be obedient and well-mannered through suggestion rather than discipline (although she can be very firm if the occasion warrants it.)

She needs marriage neither for protection nor security since she can make her own provisions for both and often prefers to do so. Sometimes she lives happily without companionship—at other times is involved in rather serious affairs of long standing, as is her male counterpart. (In this, she is most discreet, in consideration for regional conventionality.) Thus, without commitment, she is free to follow her own inclination, whether it be to travel or to live in seclusion, whether in applying herself to successful enterprises or in enjoying an easy studious existence.

If of the Scorpio-Sagittarius cusp, conformity is a burden to her restless nature, but if of the second decan with Arien leanings added to Jupiter's strong emphasis, her home and prevailing customs will be of greater importance.

If Sun infiltrated, her interest in men's attentions and admiration is more noticeable.

With what man could she then best be happy?

The *Aries* man? A Fire Sign also, he should understand her well, but since women are not yet allowed the latitude of men where freedom is concerned, it is doubtful whether the Aries man would consent to her obvious independence. Many of her qualities would be to his liking, but he looks for an agreeably pleasant companion who defers to his judgment in most matters. However, their similar tastes and habits of thrift present amicable possibilities.

If the Arien is of the second decan, though, with more awareness of the allure of the opposite sex, what then? (She is capable of leaving him instantly if he even casts an eye in the direction of someone other than herself!)

Supposing she has Sun influence also? (Each would be furious with the other if their reactions were similarly cavalier.)

If he is of the third decan, and as freedom loving as she, the partnership would have to be one as modern as today's predictions to survive. If each went his own way and then returned home to a hearth of warmth and bliss and refreshing camaraderie, perhaps they could find surprising satisfaction in a union, but how often could this happen?

What of the *Taurus* man? Since the Sagittarius woman is not much interested in the financial benefits to be derived from marriage, knowing that she can handle her own acquisitions, she would hesitate to long restrict herself in such a manner as would here be required. (The self-complacency of both is too great for either to be comfortable when together.)

An affair might be in order but would have no bonding qualities. All three decans indicate the same negative situation. (Actually, only the native with Venus two-fold in the first decan would even try to inveigle her into an affair!)

He of Virgo or Capricorn likeness would be too restrictive for this woman.

The *Gemini* man then—what of him? Need one even ask? He possesses her same liberty-seeking qualities—is often even less amenable to rules than she. Human nature is not such that one excuses in others the deplored faults in himself. A temporary alliance, yes—he refuses none that provides a semblance of romance, but that perfect idyllic love for which he searches is not evident here. To begin with, she would find the Geminian too optimistic and too unworriedly sure that everything is going to be fine no matter what he does.

Also, if he were of the second decan with Venus persuasiveness, he would give her keen competition if she should stray from the fold and if of the third, he himself would be too independent to countenance so much of the same trait in her.

Could the *Cancer* man qualify? Obviously if the Geminian distrusts the need of the Sagittarian for time to herself and unexplained "wanderings," Cancer would do so with still greater suspicion! He could not live in the state of uncertain emotional weather this union could produce. If he were of the second or third decan, transitory appeal might be theirs.

What of the *Leo* man? This combination suggests good results since he is of another Fire Sign with similar aims and plans; yet both like most the ego encouragement which their associates of the opposite sex induce. Leo men need a constant catering to their vanity; would she be there to "cater" when he returned home from an evening out with a gaggle of adoring women? (Or even seriously trysting with some new admirer?) She might be off on some lonely jaunt! (A practice to which she is addicted.) Or, like him, basking in the warmth of erotic adventure. If he is of the second decan and hence more like her, this could be favorable to some extent.

If he be of the third decan, there is a chance of their staying at home long enough to become really acquainted. They might then find both their home life and the recreational excitement which they could generate together, very entertaining.

Would the *Virgo* man be a marital prospect? Only if he has learned to disparage less and praise more and she plans to be less liberal in her conduct and more willing to follow the lead of another (difficult for most Sagittarians).

While commending his sagacity and his bank account and perhaps sensing a physical affinity, especially if he were of the third decan with Venus lending impetus, her spirit could still feel earthbound by his (to her) severe attitudes. If Saturn intruded in the second, that would further add to her miseries.

The *Libran?* This man of vibrant personality could subdue the dominance of the Sagittarius woman, if anyone could! Strong ties are often formed between these two. Libra always admires those persons who, while working hard, seem to do so many things easily—his own bent often being limited to the theatre or to sedentary positions in which the mind and emotions chiefly function. All women want either to be a lover or a mother to him and the Sagittarian with her own unique self-confidence for ballast, could well be both and enjoy every minute of the association unless her mothering instincts were too discomfitting to his flirtatious ones. Since she has similar patterns, though—both seeking self-aggrandizement rather than deep affection, there is hope here for mutual acceptance.

This holds true for his second decan though some doubts

arise concerning the third, Mercury invasion always prompting that dissatisfied search for perfection. (The two do have
corresponding interests in philosophy and literature,
however—a fact that might cast the deciding vote.)

The *Scorpio* man? He, of course, would never concur to the
managerial efforts of any woman, thus would not have the
patience or the will to attempt a lasting union. An affair
could be indicated except that a Scorpio man is known to refrain from surreptitious dalliance. To him, such a relationship is serious and carries responsibilities including constancy, while to her, this might not seem so obligatory. Also, her
undependable erotic moods would seem offensive to one of
his dignity and pride.

Those of the second and third decan are not likely to
please her because of the tight reins held upon their loved
ones. Uniting Mars and Jupiter invariably presages many
clashes.

The *Sagittarius* man? At initial glance, the marriage of
these two appears to be a wise arrangement. One thinks of
the many interests they could share and of the natural understanding each would have of their common eccentricities
and inclinations. However, there is a question as to who
would be the leader and whether the Sagittarius man would
sanction in his wife, the same flighty indecision in romantic
areas that he reserves for himself.

If two Sagittarians "fall in love," it would not necessarily
lead to marriage, especially if either or both were on the
Scorpio cusp with Mars interference although Mars in their
second decans could lead to agreement through greater sincerity and respect for a conservative and conventional home
and social life.

In the third decan, his Sun bequeaths more congeniality
but brings a possibility of harmony only if she can accept a
place of lesser importance than she usually needs in any association and if both can refrain from jealousies.

The *Capricorn* man? His unpretentious living habits and
knowledgeable discussions often attracts the Sagittarius
woman. She is also amused and unbelieving at his lack of
sexual peccadillos, sometimes even using seductive methods

and persuasive blandishments to test his apparent indifference. Piqued by her failure to succeed in this, she may try for marriage itself (sometimes—not always—to her later sorrow.) His somber, pragmatic outlook often weighs too heavily upon her more carefree tendencies.

Mercury influence in his third decan does not alter this fact but a union with one of Capricorn-Aquarius cuspal region is sometimes satisfactory; Venus in the other part of his sign relieves the tension and often makes for felicity.

What of the *Aquarian* himself? As just noted, the native on the Capricorn-Aquarius cusp is sometimes compatible and the "true" Aquarian sometimes is a good mate for her also. (This is surprising in that both are independent, headstrong, audacious and changeable.) Yet the variety of activities, the disregard of rules, the expansive ideas that are expressed in their respective ways of life, all are an inducement that neither can ignore. If he is of the second decan, his defenses may not be strong enough to withstand her more authoritative ways although he of the third may be undaunted. Obviously, cuspal and decan origin are extremely important here.

The *Piscean,* with his conservative business-man image— his intrinsic affability and unaffected 'elan combined with such marked self-restraint and incredible naivete makes him a sure target for this capricious woman's wiles. Yet her repugnance to any sort of confinement or limitations gives cause for reflection. He is a jealous, possessive lover! Too, his creative impulses could be vitiated by such self-assurance as is hers.

With the Moon's interposition in the second decan, his protective care could seem suffocating to her while impatient expectations borrowed from Mars in his third would negate his making necessary concessions for long-term companionship.

Rechecking, it seems indeed fortunate that the Sagittarius woman is so complete within herself. For all her fine qualities, sometimes men fail to claim her in marriage because they fear and resent such strength in women. One questions auspicious reactions of Fire Sign men, mainly because they recognize within her the ingredients with which they are familiar and which they constantly utilize in accomplishing their own ends. (Dubious but open to deliberation.)

In the Earth Sign men, she would find a stubborn rigidity even greater than hers (and thus confining.)

Of the Air Sign men, Libra and Aquarius should rightfully be given thought. A union with either, perhaps presages the greatest chance of all for permanence.

The Water Sign men, Cancer and Pisces could suppress her natural instincts with their deeper affection or freeze into immobilized coldness of manner because of feeling dominated. (Scorpio's indignation is a certainty.)

Obviously, with the widespread scope of commercial, and professional opportunities afforded because of her efficiency and dependable skills, the Sagittarian has no need to worry. One of industrious nature, her variety of knowledge and her inclination to investigate and implement innumerable business processes, could hardly fail to succeed and she is usually discontented unless utilizing these abilities.

She is not, however, a cold woman and often she definitely prefers a sound marriage to the affairs that some of them enjoy. While it is more difficult for her to restrain her aggressiveness than for many women, like others of her tendencies, she can do so when it is necessary. The choice is always hers. She is attractive—sometimes very beautiful in an aloof, sophisticated way.

Many men will fight for her favors. One thing she must remember: her contempt for a man whom she thinks may be a weakling, is often unfounded. (There are many varieties of ability and success and many types of bravery.) It is true though that there are men who unconsciously sensing in her the fortitude they so sorely need, turn to her with real loyalty and affection. Sometimes both are woefully disappointed from such a union yet among such men there are those who, having love as an incentive, rise to greater heights of performance than they themselves believed possible.

If a woman in love does marry a man weaker than herself, in will and self-discipline, often the faith and expectancy indicated begets determination which leads to accomplishment pleasing to both.

There is within the Sagittarius woman, that spirit of adventure that knows no surcease. Which road will she take? Many a one is apparently happy in making a man so by hiding her true nature under a facade of quiet gentleness and satisfaction in homemaking, though today, the majority of them seek other rewards through a career. When women "come into their own," the Sagittarian could be off on a safari in the East Indies (with a camera—not a gun), overseeing the building of a bridge in Jamaica, (unlikely as it seems at this time) or merely working on a coffee plantation in South America, but meantime, she plods along, doing that which is expected of her and to which she applies herself with an enthusiasm difficult to comprehend since one suspects that she is filled with frustration and longing to be seeking those new, far, horizons and fresh experiences.

CAPRICORN—December 23 through January 21

THE CAPRICORN WOMAN

It is particularly important here to first mention the cuspal area of Sagittarius-Capricorn since the women of this combination are remarkedly outstanding. They are worldly oriented, progressive in their ideas and competent in areas usually thought to be restricted to men.

They are coldly logical and have a detachment and insight that serves them well in business and political as well as social life. They head political committees and organizations—are interested in community undertakings, improvement of school and teaching facilities—often are striving to overcome discrimination of races or women. Even in smaller matters such as seeing the need for special street lights or new traffic signals, it is very often the Capricornian who initiates the plans or suggests the circulation of petitions to effect these accomplishments. She is indefatigable in her zeal and personal efforts, her dedication and concern being genuinely in the public interest and not in selfish ego fulfillment.

In the "true" Capricorn, one finds many of the qualities and inclinations that are inherent in the Sagittarian nature and in those of this cuspal region, but she is a woman of noticeable extremes—almost certain to be either prettily, feminine in appearance and manner or robustly vigorous, cool, self-reliant and regally proud. Seldom is she a mixture of both.

Her interests range from historical studies, and perhaps the musical realm of the theatre, to the most modern, advanced plans afoot by statesmen and politicians. She may be equally able as a participant in any of them, like her "cuspal sister" just described.

Seeming without trepidation concerning her acceptance by others, she is though, like the Capricorn male, actually assuming an identity which is not quite authentic. She cares a great deal about the opinion of others, sorely needing their approval—not so much to maintain a feeling of confidence but as proof that she is successful in hiding her vulnerability. Often she denies this even to herself, since her courage is great and her ambitions mighty. It is as though she has been forewarned of Saturn's testing, punishing habits, and is prepared to fight tenaciously to overcome the obstacles it places in her path.

Only one thing ruffles the placid waters of her self-esteem—Saturn's morbid melancholia which senselessly sweeps over her at times, provoking a feeling of dark portent, unworthiness, and deep pessimism which curtains the reality of good friendships and ethical ideals. Yet these moods may be only transient. (Fortunate is she who learns early to conquer them or pay them little heed.)

Usually, as her personal achievements multiply, she finds it far easier to quell the forebodings and turn such moments to good account by losing herself in the books she loves or by joining congenial friends in an atmosphere of jollity and good fellowship. She "has a way with words," a wry wit and a vast fund of information on many subjects on which she can discourse at great length when she has an appreciative audience—and no other activity can better scatter the gloom for her. Furthermore, if she is active (as is probable) in civic affairs or in the performance of tasks which tax her intelligent attention sufficiently, she may avoid altogether the unpleasantness of unwanted hours of brooding.

Home is that place in which the mask can be removed to reveal her true self without loss of prestige. Actually, she wants a home for a refuge more than for the domestic life involved, disliking physical tasks as she often does. If ever a woman should have household help to free her from monotonous drudgery, it is the Capricornian!! Her better talents lie elsewhere. However, if "house-bound" her expertise in cooking and serving as well as her facility as a hostess is usually pronounced. (Often, this surprising knack is utilized commercially in one way or another.)

The January woman is normally quite strict with her children, not so much in making rules for them to follow as in expecting them to be sensible enough to make their own and to abide by them, and in providing their own interests without infringing upon hers. As self-sufficient as the Sagittarian, she nevertheless prefers marriage to the uncertainties of bachelor-like existence. Passionate, though often appearing indifferent or unaware of the romantic nuances which are an essential part of complete fulfillment in the marital bed, she requires a mate of infinite tact and wisdom to awaken her to genuine responsiveness.

If she is of the second decan, her Venus may bring more need of affectionate gestures from her spouse. (It scoffs at perfunctory "love-making!")

If of the third decan, Mercury may lead her into unexpected adventures, soothing her flagging spirits and vexation (when necessary) and much of the disappointment that seems so inevitable to the Capricorn woman.

If she happens to be of the Capricorn-Aquarius cusp, Uranus, while not disclaiming seclusiveness, rejects its perpetuity and also adds that superior strength which the Capricornian needs for her proud image.

What man will best understand her?

The *Aries* man? This is quite doubtful. When Aries is impulsive, Capricorn is cautious. Although this man could be captivated by her intellectuality, the fixity and somewhat critical attitude germane to those of her sign would arouse his displeasure, and he in turn would antagonize her with this reaction.

If of the second decan, there would be no further advantage, since, although allowing greater good humor, its native still cannot be placating.

If of the third decan, the Jupiter influence could cause him to be less predictable than she expects.

The *Taurus* man? Alike in many ways, it is still questionable whether two persons of such sternly, inalterable precepts could make pertinent adjustments to one another. Being Earth Signs, both are imperious and taciturn of manner yet his Venus could grant him an intensity of feeling which she secretly might welcome. (Perhaps, if she were of the second decan, with her own Venus interceding?)

If he were Mercury favored (second decan), there is reason to believe that they would benefit, and if of the third, a blending of two Saturn natures (if his austerity were not too disconcerting to hers) could make a stimulating partnership.

There is no need to ponder long about a Capricorn association with the *Gemini* man. These two persons, so dissident of viewpoint and traits could rarely be reconciled. The Geminian's restlessness and seeming lack of serious application is little understood by one of Capricornian purpose. This man, too, would be fretted by the dictatorial ways which disguise her incertaintude.

Neither the second nor third decan offers alternatives. (While Venus in his second could augment the Taurus Venus in her second, in providing enticements, the Libra-like subject is much too outgoing and would require too much leeway in social activity to settle down with one of Saturnian nature and the native of the third, enriched by Uranus, needs an even longer leash.

What of the *Cancer* man? The Earth woman might do well to choose for a companion the Moon sponsored native! One can visualize their comforting home life, providing as it would, the safety and protection both so persistently seek. Yet, there is a question as to the emotional aspects of such a union. Moon people are sometimes as easily depressed as are those with Saturn's proprietary hold. Would they be concerned enough with each other's vagaries in this regard? Could she overcome her diffidence in "love-making" if he be of the second decan with Mars' importunate expectations?

If he be of the third and inclined to long silences when aggrieved, would she of somewhat corrollary bent, accept this with nonchalance and offer cajoling banter which might be beneficial to both? (Each individual must decide this.)

The *Leo* man? Rarely, if ever, with this woman, could he retain that necessary *self image* of proud sovereignty and magnanimous condescension to mere mortals—that carefully nurtured interpretation that is a great part of his attraction for women. How can he feel important without those about him furnishing the food for ego inflation? The Capricorn woman could neither delude herself nor him to this extent. And she would not enjoy remaining at home alone nor care to join him for his social forays which would almost certainly prove embarrassing to her.

No improving differences are presented in the second and third decans. (While in the delineation of the Leo man's personality earlier, a native of lesser pomposity was described, in this instance a mutually happy relationship probably could not be maintained because of the dominating qualities of the Capricornian herself. However, this native of such disarming quietness is like her in disdaining false amenities and too much social activity. He is a voracious reader and "the good life" to him means a comfortable chair and a bright light in a quiet spot. Can one not see possibilities here?)

As to the *Virgo* man, many astrologers suggest that he may make an agreeable partner for the Capricornian, but there is much to be taken into consideration. While both are Earth Signs and thus alike, is it not perhaps this very likeness which might inhibit their congeniality? Both have fixed opinions and little patience where there are arguments. The Saturn controlled subject is usually more sedentary and studious while the Virgoan is more constantly active. (One's imagination here raises doubts of needful cooperation.)

If either is of the decan where Venus disposes, this might

be helpful, yet he could seek or display more affection than the other. If both were in that decan, this could solve that problem to their delighted satisfaction.

If both suffers Saturn's character strengthening manipulations, they could accomplish together all that they desire unless Mercury's restlessness keeps them at crosspurposes.

What of the *Libra* man? This son of Venus could, without question, mesmerize the Capricorn woman. She could be aroused to a degree almost foreign to her nature, but she might look for steadier effort in financial areas than he deems necessary. Also, as with Leo, she would either find herself alone much of the time or must learn new habits of sociability with convivial associates—otherwise the Libran himself would rebel. She could establish cogent ties with him before marriage but whether the tensions would prove too great for them to prolong the association indefinitely would probably depend upon her willingness to make the adjustments.

With the "true" Libran, there is more possibility of a continuing union than with the natives of either the second or third decan who are never content where the atmosphere lacks flexibility.

She might capitulate to the *Scorpio* man's special brand of seduction if he were free at the moment to become involved, but this happens infrequently. Also, as a rule, her cool indifference does not pique the interest of the Scorpio. He looks for more fire and reciprocative rapport.

Venus in her second decan offers some hope but his Mars temperament and her normal Saturnian coldness are seldom adaptable to one another unless the Neptunian influence in his second decan quiets her disapproval of his audacious ways or the Moon's additive in his third gentles his impulsiveness.

The *Sagittarius* man would not stand still long enough for her to catch up with him. He would always have "too many irons in the fire" away from the marital hearth. She might tend to be a bit jealous of him since he appears to have few restraints—to have everything he wants and still remain free. Secretly, she would like this very thing for herself but that something within that represses her tendency toward a lack of conformity is ever on guard.

The *Capricorn* man? Ah! Who could gainsay this for a good combination? They would have the same aims—the same ideas as to propriety and be comfortable as new-born puppies in surroundings appreciated by both. The decanative differences can offer only increased satisfaction if one or both are of the second decan to afford greater erotic pleasure but the most difficult "set-up" would perhaps be one in which both had Mercury's positiveness (third decan) although even in this case Saturn's traits could provide a necessary balance.

The *Pisces* man? An alliance here also often portends real compatibility since he is generally as methodical and decorous as she could ask. If she has genuine, protecting love to give this man, he will never fail her and will provide the home and financial security she thinks appropriate while still respecting her as an individual and admiring her talents. What else could she want? It should be remembered that the Piscean needs assurance and romantic participation as a steady diet. If the Capricornian expects faithfulness, she should supply a rich mixture of these ingredients.

Moon inclusion presages the same favorable outlook but Mars of the third decan brings a risk of clashing wills.

Thinking back, it can be assumed that although the Capricorn woman is aggressively active and very independent, she probably will marry. However, none of the Fire Sign men seem quite suitable for her, since, though being extremely aggressive themselves, they perversely dislike this trait in women. Regarding the Earth Signs, she should consider well the facts before mating with either Taurus or Virgo though her own sign, Capricorn, offers fine potentialities. Those of the Air Signs are definitely not reliable prospects with the exception of Libra and in his case, it is she who must make most of the concessions. Of the Water Sign natives, Pisces shows greater indication of accord although Cancer could be a good choice. (In both instances, she must not forget the need of tact and diplomacy.) With Scorpio she has little chance of effecting a tolerable alliance.

It may be that she will seek marriage only for reasons of

feasibility, advantage, prestige, social position or opulence. Undoubtedly, these factors will weigh heavily in her decision as to a marital partner.

Rarely is the Capricornian content, however, without furthering her own career, nor should she be! As women try more and more to establish themselves in high political and executive positions, she can lead the way. Her aptitudes are instinctual, and furthermore, she has the insight to realize that education and preparation are essential for opportunity and continuous advancement along these lines.

Not every woman is adept at coping with such responsibilities and "keeping the home fires burning" simultaneously—this woman is! The necessary facility to thus compartmentalize her time and her life (as does the successful man) comes natural to her. The penchant for placing "first things first" and concentrating fully upon that which is important at the moment, while firmly closing her mind to all else, is hers! Why should she "hide her light under a bushel" when women of her stamina and mental caliber are so greatly needed throughout the world?

AQUARIUS—January 22 through February 20

THE AQUARIUS WOMAN

As was noted concerning women of the Sagittarius-Capricorn cusp, natives also of the Capricorn-Aquarius cuspal area have distinctive aggressive traits and are frequently capable of extraordinary accomplishments. (Others may be as forceful, yet not turn their tendencies to productive use as these do—particularly if they have had encouragement in their formative years.)

Those of the three different decans of this sign have vastly dissimilar characteristics but motivated by Uranus, all have a compelling verve which is manifested in every facet of their existence. Of the three Air Signs, the Aquarian is by far the most determined and self-actuated, having the persistence which promotes success when utilized in practical matters. The decans of Gemini and Libra which borrow this strength of purpose, are often greatly benefited, while on the other hand, any overly resolute attitudes of the Aquarius subject may be modified when she herself has Mercury or Venus as leavening agents in her second or third decan. Mercury gives her imagination and a greater sympathy for others while Venus offers affable warmth and provides more reciprocal pleasure in her "love life."

She is intuitive and perceptive under some circumstances but strangely unrealistic in others. When she reads of violence, rape, robbery or murder, she remains unconvinced that these misfortunes could befall *her!* She is unappalled at darkened streets or lonely isolated places of residence. Distrustful of men as to love and romance, she still cannot believe that they would harm her otherwise. (Perhaps this imperturbability is her only defense against panic?)

Considered by many to be unpredictable and unconventional, where her conscience demands, she is untiringly dedicated to the comfort and care of those she loves, often not so noticeably to her children (of which she has few) as to her parents or other elderly dependents—giving of her attention more unselfishly—at least at times—than do her Air Sign "sisters," Gemini and Libra. Librans are often blinded to another's needs; when the Geminian sees, she is almost too empathetic, yet she too may be absorbed in personal difficulties of the moment and not properly attentive.

Although Uranus does charge one with the urge to try new experiences and go into strange places, the Aquarian still relinquishes the past very reluctantly. Her unusual attachments to family members never wavers, her loyalties are steadfast and constant. She has great pride in family background, often extolling the virtues of her ancestors and glorifying their exploits beyond strict accuracy. (Could it be possible that some of the renowned self-confidence of this native, derives from the fantasies that were deliberately woven into her "subconscious" as actual memories, to replace the unacceptable or unglamorous when reality failed her youthfully illogical standards? (She is so vulnerably expectant!) Could it be that without this shield, she would be as assailable as her Air Sign "triplet" Gemini? (Libra, one remembers, has escape in one form or another, as protection against hurtful events or fears.) Certainly the Aquarian has seized upon every incident in her childhood that could justify her cherished memory pictures of the past, or could lend their support.

If she is tactless, it is through a lack of comprehension; she does not always realize that her ways may be overpowering to those of weaker fiber. She is shrewd and money wise but undeniably generous.

The February subject is an outdoors person, appreciative of all gifts of nature; the plants and flowers she tends respond to her ministrations as naturally as do those persons for whom no sacrifice—no service—is too great. Fundamental in her need and ability to create with her own hands articles in original form—a ribbon and a flower becomes a hat, a scrap of silk a sarong or some "odds and ends" of almost anything, a decorative montage.

She is never a strict copyist, though like the Libran, is often engaged in activities of reproduction or those requiring manual or artistic skill. Those of Gemini vintage are often teachers or secretaries. Only Mars influenced natives equal her in the drive and the energies required for participation in fields of entertainment. Whatever her business or profession, there must be allowance for a certain freedom of action which is essential to all Aquarians.

Unless compulsive in her urge for perfection, as a homemaker, she chooses the decorative tasks—the flower arrangements, and the special touches that make for an attractive setting, in lieu of systematic housekeeping. The laborious, the tiring, the repetitious should be done by outside help if she is to follow her bent for walking away from such dreary but necessary chores.

One of the Pisces cusp may develop a real talent for this dull drudgery. It is usually she who appears to have a fanatical urge for cleanliness and neatness—a seeming overcompensation in exorcising some fancied flaw of dilatoriness within herself which she suspects and rejects. These are the women whose houses are kept in rigid order and whose tables are graced with delicious, appetizing and healthful foods. It is surprising to see the ease with which they perform their feats of cuisine. The natural result is that they are called upon again and again for such services at their clubs, churches, and other functions. The Aquarian loves excitement, variety and the social whirl and should be free to mingle with people and savor the pleasure that this gives her, without being so unfairly deprived of it.

It was once accepted that Saturn was the Aquarius ruler; seeing her unaccountably in a miasma of depression occasionally, one could believe that there are untoward influences here. Understandably, those on the Capricorn cusp are in line for some of Saturn's disciplinary measures, and even those subject to Venus influence in the third decan may be temporarily morbid, but fortunately, the Aquarian bounces back with rapid consistancy and thus is gregarious, friendly and extroverted most of the time. (She of the second may be as genial but often is also more reclusive, her sacrificial gestures mostly to her own family.)

Where men are concerned, this woman "of many faces," is blithe, detached and complacent, an attitude which often deters their advances, yet she can evince such wistful interest in romantic situations that sometimes they are taken aback. Just as a man decides that she is too overweaning for his tastes, she may surprise him with a quick reversal, offering a yielding, apparently unlimited, even though casual, affection.

Here, through the contradiction of her nature, she finds her greatest punishment. Desperately wanting sincerity in love relationships, the secret knowledge of her own uncertainties and pretenses and her fear of disappointment or rejection, causes a regime of trial and error with men which rarely brings her satisfaction. She may refuse marriage altogether or marry late in life for the sake of convenience although those of Mercury blend seldom avoid alliances of some kind and those of the third decan may marry early and sometimes exert real initiative and zeal in making the union a mutually pleasant one.

With whom will she attempt a serious commitment?

The *Aries* man? While she would be attracted by the solvency of his financial affairs, the possibility of amicable
years together is very doubtful. Both are born to be leaders
and with the male-female situation still as it is today, her
abilities and aspirations would certainly be eclipsed by his;
moreover, though she would be resentful of this, she would
unreasonably lose her respect for him and be unhappy with
any other arrangement.

His Leo likeness in the second decan could lessen her resistance to his ways but he himself could not be comfortable
in an environment in which he would be less and less
deferred to in decisions affecting them both.

He of the third decan, with Jupiter reigning, might understand her desire for sudden change and recreational pleasure
but not care to confine himself to her elected itinerary.

It should not be forgotten here, since there is such divergence of decanative traits, that she of the second and
third decan might be more adaptive and be willing to accept
a role of lesser importance in this relationship. It is remembered that Gemini and Libra with Mercury and Venus respectively as rulers, have a good chance of happy adjustment
with Aries. Though the Aquarian would still have Uranus
interfering, an alliance might work out favorably.

Almost the same presumption would be forthcoming with
the *Taurus* man in view of the fact that a similitude of varying traits is operative. If both remain true to the dictates of
their own signs, they would disagree on many subjects.
While sharing a desire for thrifty, progressive patterns, the
Aquarius woman might spend money in ways which would
seem foolish to the Taurus man (although if he loved her, he
would probably not mention it.) Both are often unyieldingly
determined yet in dissimilar situations.

As in Aries though, the decanative structure could alter
these conditions. While none of the three decans of Taurus
seem logical in relation to Aquarius, she herself might provide those qualities which would make feasible such an association. Although, in his second decan, Mercury's additive
has little advantage nor is Saturn favorable in his third, if
she has a Venus wrought warmth in her third to combine

with his Venus, the inflexibility of both might be mitigated through their mutual erotic desires. It would be helpful also were she of the Pisces cusp, since Neptune and Venus controlled individuals get along amazingly well.

First to be noted in regard to the twosome of Aquarius and *Gemini* as marital partners, is the oft repeated fact of his need to feel important in order to accomplish. He will be defeated in effectiveness of his career strivings as well as in his sexual life from attitudes which might deflate his ego. Will she be able to subdue her sometimes unwitting captious manner? Although much has been said by astrologers to lend credence to the supposition that this couple is compatible, much depends upon the decanative bequeathment of both.

Those of the first Gemini decan are often amenable to suggestions made by others. (It would be simpler if the Aquarian were the man and the Geminian the woman.)

He of the third, with Uranus matching hers, will either wage a continuous battle to maintain his prized "masculine status" or will helplessly succumb, leaving all plans and decisions in her hands. In this case, each may go his own way, returning to the conjugal interests only when the mood permits. It does sometimes happen that she cares enough to conquer her own fixed ways or to at least pretend to concurrence with his views. When this comes about, they have wonderful "fun times" together, sharing as they do a liking for pleasure.

If he is of the second decan (and especially if she is of the third) Venus is sometimes so persuasive in physical attraction for one another, that many halcyon hours result. This may mean marriage.

The *Cancer* man? He with his devotion to duty—to convention, the home and planned certainties of life? She with her wayward inclinations and her liking for many outside activities? This combination would usually produce too much stress for both. Neptunian intervention in his third decan offers the only possible compromise, with one exception. Both have great regard for elderly persons. If by coincidence, they are interested in the same individual, the respect thus engendered for one another could lead to further understanding and tolerance.

The *Leo* man? A marriage here is seen surprisingly often though the participants do not necessarily live in harmony. Like the Cancerian, the Leo native often commits himself to a number of humanitarian projects and this can lead to a relationship with Aquarians who seek the same outlet for their protective instincts. True, each is bent upon having his own way but sometimes, objectives coinciding, they meet on common ground.

If both are of the first decan there are apt to be frequent clashes, but if she has Mercury or Venus influence and he has Mars, they are often drawn to each other, despite their differences.

If he is of the second, with Jupiter prevailing, only if they each had separate occupations and experiences of consequence and came together briefly at the times when the pleasure in these diminished, could they likely sustain a bearable alliance.

The *Virgo* man? A unity here is ill-starred from the outset. He would not be pleasantly impressed by either her ideas or her loquaciousness concerning them, notwithstanding their meritorious substance. He is looking for quiet efficiency in the home and a depth of seriousness in all things, and she could not abide an atmosphere minus all gayety. Her bright pertness would vanish and her lively banter be stilled.

The second and third decans are as negative as the first unless one considers the possibility of her Venus decan (third) linked with the Venus in his third. Physical allure could then intrigue them for a while.

The *Libra* man? Here in her Air Sign compatriot, the Aquarian finds real contentment and congeniality. They enjoy rare companionship since the tenor of their ways is identical. One difficulty, however, presents itself. Both have phases of moodiness. She perhaps can accept his and even find methods of lessening their intensity, but she must learn to deal with her own without disturbing him. (Will she grow weary of this lack of reciprocal empathy?)

The decanative variations play a part here as they do so strongly all through the Aquarius combinations. Her Mercury and Venus influences are extremely advantageous. His ruling Venus and his borrowed Mercury in the third decan are especially favorable.

If he is of her own Uranus influence, there can be combativeness too great to surmount, although Venus is always alleviating, especially where there is real sincerity of affection.

The *Scorpio* man? A marriage between these two is highly improbable. She often wonders at his singular lack of interest and even flirts a bit out of curiosity. He hesitates because he sees that any commitment with her should be serious and knowing that the pronounced independence in both could then be fatal, he wants to avoid taking such chances.

All three decans present a sameness of problems. Both the natives of his second and third decan might stumble into this situation, but should be on guard and realize in advance what this could mean. The Aquarian must be ever "on the go" a tendency not consonant to Scorpio's need for occasional solitude. She hides away only when melancholic and this itself could frustrate him. Too, her passions are often changeful and unpredictable, thus seeming aberrant to one of his nature.

The *Sagittarius* man? The likelihood of marital bliss between these two depends entirely upon their mutual tolerance for each others foibles. They usually have a fondness for each other, recognizing an existing affinity between them at first sight. However, this is a man who often chooses his companions with no serious purpose in mind; the idea of his "Amour Object" pursuing the same course could be objectionable. It must be remembered that her dalliances are often experimental, not going beyond the platonic stage (a great surprise and shock to some of the victims of her conquests). The Sagittarian, prone to "love and leave them," may not comprehend that there is a variance of motive here.

If she is of the second decan, despite Mercury's "flightiness" she might curb her own wandering in his behalf but would be more susceptible to hurt by his. Would it be worth a trial?

He of the second decan would probably reject her decisive manner. Not always completely tactful himself, he does expect it from others—particularly women.

Sun in his third decan gives him some of the qualities with which the Leonian pleases women. If spell-bound by him (which is possible) the hurts would be greater if he failed to show her the consideration she wanted.

How would the Aquarian regard the *Capricorn* man? Unless at least one of these natives is of the Capricorn-Aquarius cusp, there is little hope for agreement. It has already been seen that the Earth Sign men are usually too serious minded for her and in turn they find her ebullience annoying.

The *Aquarius* man? It would seem that here is this woman's ideal mate—her look alike—think alike (must *be alike?*) partner, but would this conjecture be over-optimistic? One wonders if his knowledge of her leanings, though similar to his, necessarily encompasses their acceptance? Men have always allowed themselves more leeway, especially in their erotic experiences, than they will condone in their women.

In today's world, since many of the old ideas and conformities are outmoded, will the Aquarian willingly allow his wife or sweetheart the same freedom he demands for himself? It is questionable. Then must she still assume a submissiveness she does not feel? Undoubtedly. Whether either would attempt to cope with the assertiveness of the other largely depends upon their respective decans. As could be expected, if either or both are strongly enough influenced by Mercury or Venus, there can be greater expectancy of harmony. This is especially true when one's Venus decan is duplicated by the other.

The *Pisces* man? What of his qualifications? The "true" native falls very deeply in love with the Aquarius woman; thus her distrust of "double harness" could be at an end. Faithful and adoring, he would share her interests with gratifying eagerness and a willing participation beyond her fondest dreams. This is what she has always wanted. It is to be hoped that she would not feel trapped or smothered by his constant presence and attention—that she could give of herself in the unstinting, unreserved way needed by him. Otherwise his diffidence would be increased so that he could no longer express his affections. Some adjustments would be necessary since she likes perpetual movement and he normally prefers a substantive, fixed orderly existence. Despite his fondness and faithfulness, he might tire of continuous turmoil. This applies most to the natives of his second decan, although some of them do enjoy a certain amount of sociality. (They are the ones who could share her outside excitements.) Still, a comfortable home must be waiting in readiness for their return. As with Scorpio, he of Mars moodiness requires refreshing interludes of rest from time to time. If they coincided with her melancholy periods, this could be disenchanting.

To recapitulate: of the Fire Sign men, Leo and Sagittarius should first be considered.

Of the Earth Signs, Taurus is probably the only one with whom she might find real communication.

Among the Air Sign natives, Gemini is a less likely prospect than either Libra or her own sign, Aquarius.

Pisces of the Water Signs is favorable if her own decanative pattern indicates ameliorating adjustment but neither Cancer nor Scorpio can be counted upon for fruitful relationship.

Here, one thinks back to the Leo woman, who, wanting marriage, must submerge her own instincts of leadership in order to attract men. (Those of Aries and Capricorn sometimes find this necessary also.) The Aquarian, too, may see it as expedient. Paradoxically, in addition to her assertiveness, like the Geminian and the Piscean, she is always searching for a romance which is actually somewhat mythical and so she is insecure in any "love alliance."

In this regard, it is essential to mention the Aquarian only infrequently seen, and therefore not considered typical. She is found sometimes working in little out of the way shops, away from the main stream of commerce where articles of beauty are sold or small animals cared for—in mountain resorts or other places offering tourist attractions. She seems to possess a peculiarly fascinating, challenging quality which men cannot resist even though they sense in her seductive fragility and virgin-like innocence an ironical nemesis.

Though the physical characteristics vary, she is often small, slight, as if trimmed down from running—pixieish and ethereal with eyes unhappy, perhaps from useless quest. She is almost always single, although there are a few exceptions. (She may arouse in men their deepest, paternal-like, protective feelings which they recognize as a threat to their more "eathy" natures, and thus to their real freedom.) Being herself a "free spirit," the Aquarius woman shies away like a wounded doe fearing capture, yet that very gesture exudes a sorcery which may seem a trap to those men of conscience who know that they would be expected to give too much—a love of greater depth than they are capable of feeling. It is she whom the Scorpio and the Pisces men of the third decan often find irresistible, yet they usually flee from her vulnerability in self-protection. (The men who do marry this type of woman rarely understand her. Therefore, she has the same puzzled, questioning look as the others.) Any Aquarian can marry if that is her primary desire.

No one is more anxious to serve where she is needed than the Water-bearer, but she should not confine her energies to domesticity where her greatest talents are wasted. No one has more commendable aspirations than she. Just as there are for other women many open fields of highly rewarding occupations, so too will these various opportunities be available to the Aquarian in which her many skills, her unswerving urge to overcome difficulties, and her amazing vitality can be put to worthy use.

PISCES—February 21 through March 20

THE PISCES WOMAN

Describing this woman is like hesitating with brush over palette, wondering whether to dip into the purplish hue of the delicate, gentle violet with all its subtle serenity and inscrutible poise or to dip and lift the brush with lavish, careless hand, splashing the canvas instead, with the bold, vivid, fearless colors of the flaming coral-red hibiscus!

Perhaps only the Piscean herself could suggest the choice, yet indisputably she has within her the essence of both, with all their disparate qualities—thus a true portrait can but disclose this fact.

Visionary and imaginative—imbued with Neptunian mysticism, she is often demure, modest and docile appearing yet in a certain sense is only masquerading, though usually without conscious intent to mislead, since she conceals a nature, not always adequately discussed, that is stridently vigorous and emphatically forceful as well as sturdy and courageous in times of difficulty. She will readily undertake new ventures which lead her into unchartered territory.

Flexibly adaptive, strongly maternal, she is vitally concerned with every aspect of her family's lives and will forego her own pleasures for their benefit without question. It follows that she is a superb homemaker. Almost without exception, such women are excellent cooks and fine seamstresses. If their "life style" makes these tasks superfluous, they see that the work is done by others who are able to do it in an effective and knowledgeable manner. The Piscean's family can be proud to ask their friends to the house at any time although she is not overly fond of extensive entertaining, enjoying as she does, the close intimacy of their personal contacts.

One has the impression of a strongly domesticated woman, dedicated only to her home and family, yet the very qualities which make for efficiency here, are often as aptly applied to business or the arts. In fact, this is frequently her preference and she finds a welcome in many positions where not only her reliability and deep sense of duty serve her purpose, but her pronounced artistry and dexterity are useful as well.

Often said to be without great confidence in herself, she constantly contradicts such an assumption by attempting and executing that in which others have failed. Moreover, the arduous, tedious details which are likely to have been overlooked or slighted by them, are competently, assiduously done by her without fuss or complaint, even though this dedication is not always appreciated.

Having a rare feeling for color and a true perspective of

what she views, it may be through these talents that she ex-
presses her creative ability. Rhythmic music does for her
what alcohol may do for another, lifting her spirits and intensifying her pleasure in all activity. Her vocation often includes some phase of this art—composing, singing and more
often dancing.

She is chary of close friendships but is constant and loyal
to those she trusts. Perhaps she often hides from herself the
desire for friendly companions although there is the Piscean
who displays (and apparently has) no such need. Of queenly
carriage and demeanor, she projects a self-reliance which, if
only an assumed bravado, is nevertheless so real in its pre-
sentation, that it is translated by others into inviolable
aplomb. (Could it be that like some of her gentler "sisters," she
has earlier had a timidity which she despised and sternly
overcame or buried beneath her courage?). Like the Capricornian, through fear of being hurt or to hide the intensity
of her quivering emotions which she never quite understands, she may have erected a facade of steely indifference
which is impenetrable.

In pondering this, one remembers that whereas the Aquarian firmly, optimisticly refuses to see danger to herself, the
Piscean may know fear but either disregards it or seeks to
destroy its source. One is reminded too that it is a brave person who goes into the fray frightened but determined to meet
the enemy with a formidable front and a show of fearlessness. Sometimes though, the Piscean sees enmity where
there is good will; her eyes look inward and seeing the
shadow of her own unadmitted dislikes or fears, mistake it
for an adversary.

Whatever her true identity, she manifests complete independence and often shows little interest in intimate contacts
even when gregarious to an extreme and functioning well socially or in any situation requiring fortitude and daring.

Almost as if to defy this characterization, there is that better known native, unassuming and retiring, who, while
sometimes shyly flirtatious and cognizant of the quick response this evokes, is seemingly unworldly and untouched by
the grosser facts of life. Gracious of manner, there is a de-

tachment about her—a self-containment not natural to many women (unless it is the Scorpio individual)—her personal identity never quite coalescing with any other.

Since her ideas of "love" (like the Geminian's and Aquarian's) are too spiritual to be realistic, one wonders if she can ever actually accept life's realities or if in accepting, she is deeply disappointed. Can it be so strange that there is seen in this woman of contradictory traits a multiple of persons?

Moon in her second decan adds secret longings to her Neptunian impregnability, giving her a greater need of care and affection than is required for those of the first and third, who are more self-sustaining.

The latter decan is augmented by tempestuous Mars which dispenses more energy and immeasurable support. These natives have a remarkable resistance to adversity. They are discerning in their knowledge of human nature and possess a depth of feeling not always recognized by those not analytically inclined. Even the most quiet Pisces woman has incredible staunchness and strength. She desperately disciplines her emotions, valiantly striving to solve her own difficulties, meeting her own obligations, asking no quarter and expecting none.

She is intelligent but wary, intuitively knowing much but revealing little—capable of predicting many incidents yet certain, like Cassandra, she would never be believed. Thus, she is either silently insular, living the outward untruth of serene passivity or (less often) that of blustery self-assurance.

Could she be happy in traditional marriage?

What of the *Aries* man as her mate? Both he of the Pisces cusp and the Sun decan, might employ the adroit finesse essential in dealing with her special "love needs." If the Arien could read aright her sensuousness and respond with thoughtful comprehension while controlling inadvertent cold rebuffs in day by day proximity, there could be a comfortable "togetherness." If she were of the patient, unassertive type, he would be filled with admiration for this lack of brashness (a trait which he intensely dislikes in a woman). If by chance she were one of the "blusterers," he would never even approach her!

The Jupiter controlled native offers slight promise since he must have a scope of action which would leave her feeling rejected.

The *Taurus* man? If the Piscean is wise, she might look no further. She would see in him a man who would love and protect her for the rest of her days. His strength of character—his inclination toward monogymous marriage—his sense of responsibility would provide the balancing reassurance that is right for her. Even if she herself exhibits rugged aggressive proclivities there could be real communication between these two.

The second decan echoes the first but if he is of the third, both should strive to combat the Saturn depressant. Hopefully, the joint influences of their Venus and Neptune would allow them to overcome this disadvantage.

Another thought also concerns her third decan: the Taurus man might find her independence a threat to his masculine ego. With so much in their favor, however, surely they could work out judicious compromises.

The *Gemini* man? This might offer a situation of tension too great to be of viable consideration. Her joyless solemnity when disturbed could be vastly unsettling to him, just as his Mercurial, changeable ways would be disquieting to her. (If of the Taurus-Gemini cusp, his own seriousness under such circumstances might equal hers, resulting in unusual rapport.)

There are some instances too in which he of tne second decan would grant her the appreciation so often denied her but the more dominant tendencies of the third could be disruptive even though thus equipped, he might personally accomplish more.

The *Cancer* man? These two should be ideally mated—two Water Signs, both of whom value home and family above all else. Real compatibility is certainly possible but in honesty, one must call attention to the amount of moodiness, jealousy and possessiveness present in this combination.

Decanative influence could alter the edict but the Moon's presence itself does not. The fact that the Piscean of the second decan has the Moon as her ruler also adds to further speculation.

Unpredictable Mars could affect either or both signs, whether favorably, depending upon the predilection of each individual to follow his own natural bent. One thinks of the word "indomitable" in relation to Mar's subjects yet there are emotionally vulnerable Scorpio natives who make most of the adjustments in their love relationships. This would suggest that either the Piscean or Cancerian of Scorpio likeness could be similarly generous.

If the Cancerian is of the third decan, Neptune's light touch in uninimity with the Pisces Neptunian ruler, could produce an everlasting romance. As with the Taurus man, concessions might be called for but can one expect to avoid all challenge?

The *Leonian* is a man of vigor and fire but he is sometimes flattered by the quietly interested and adoring Piscean. Flattery is an offering dear to him yet his suave but possibly domineering manner could antagonize her. Also, her relentless needs could be too confining for one of his expansive, enterprising activities. Many heartaches could be hers from such a union.

All three decans must be rated equally doubtful—not only from problems arising in marriages of fire and water, but because Jupiter urgencies in his second would leave her too little security, and Mars in his third, while giving an Arienlike personality which could please her, would also mean either conflicts for supremacy or the hiding of her more audacious instincts. It should be reiterated that the meekest appearing Piscean is only so on the surface. (She must sometimes become very weary of continued pretense.)

In passing, one must not forget that rare Leo man who is almost too intellectually passive and kind for his own good. One questions whether he and the gentle Piscean would be suitably mated or whether he might need one of more aggressive inclination to fight the necessary battles for the family and provide them with psychological security. (This could of course apply to women of other signs as well as Pisces.

The *Virgo* man? Felicity with him could be hers if she would simulate weakness so that he could nurture the association and feel protective; he is at his best when someone depends upon him. (Normally, though, she would disdain such pretense.) If he could sympathize with the recreational interests which even the home-oriented Piscean seeks for stimulation, or if she would remain loyal despite his worried suspicions, and her indignation because of this attitude, they could complement each other's natures well.

He of the second decan should be carefully considered; there is sometimes a surprising attraction here. Also, the warming rays of Venus in his third or in his Libra cuspal area (where they are doubly operative) could encourage lasting bonds.

Virgoans must never forget that the Pisces woman blooms with wooing. Taking her for granted sexually is a mistake which she does not easily forgive.

The *Libra* man could give her rapturous moments but those hours spent in waiting for them could defeat any pleasure in marriage. The second time he returned home from an all-night's outing, he would likely find her gone. While this he would no doubt prefer to reproaches or accusations, the forecast here could only be one of bitterness and regret.

Her varying decan influences offer no alternatives nor do his. Uranus in his second and Mercury in his third prompts a greater impatience of restraint and since the Piscean's well-being is contingent upon her mate's willing attention, no peaceful arrangement seems indicated.

On the surface, *Scorpio* and Pisces with their many corresponding traits—especially their romanticism and passion, seem well mated. They could be pleasurably companionable, possibly spending many lazy hours at the beach, not only swimming and "making love" but lying together on the sand, listening (perhaps) to soft music on a transistor as they made bright plans for travel to unknown lands or dreamed their dreams of other worlds on the distant stars.

How could one ask for more contentment? Ah! but could she be happy on those times when he seemed uncommunicatively insulated with his books or sat raptly engrossed at the piano improvising his own music and creating new, sad cadences or plaintive melodies?

Natives of all three decans merit true appraisal despite

this preoccupation but he of the second, with her Pisces own Neptune prompting gentleness, would probably magnetize her most because of his awareness of the more delicate nuances of courting overtures—although he of the third, as strongly sensual but with Moon supplement, has also this idealistic concept of love. (Ties that bind too tightly would be frustrating to any of Scorpio nature.)

She would do better to accept some restiveness from Scorpio than to attempt a union with the *Sagittarius* man of many dissimilarities. While her hesitancy would be tantalizingly effective in drawing his erotic interest, marriage is rarely in his planned agenda and this she would resent.

Mars in his Scorpio cuspal area could be somewhat helpful but the Mars of his second decan as well as the Sun in his third, are not propituous. They might only provide the additional problems found in Aries and Leo.

As with Scorpio, Pisces and *Capricorn* have an intellectual and musical basis for their mutual interest and to both, this and their homes are of primary concern. They also share other likenesses. Both are parsimonious at times and extravagant at others. They are generous though different in their attitudes. Pisces cannot bear to see a loved one in need of anything without offering aid and Capricorn, though appearing reluctant, will do so if he is convinced of the actual need. Like the Virgoan, he is apt to think that the recipient should have used better judgment, thus not incurring the necessity of help. Of lesser import is their noticeable agreement regarding simple likes and preferences such as gourmet food and pastel shades of wearing apparel. In their case, it is often these simple things of their daily existence which constitute communion.

It is questionable whether he could be relied upon to sprinkle their days with enough romantic spice to satisfy the subtlety of her erotic tastes—to be openly affectionate so that she could justify her tender but disquieting passions.

A native of the second decan could be so inclined and he of the third, being a romantic at heart, especially he of the Capricorn-Aquarius cusp—might qualify. If Saturn's captious tendencies are not too persistent, the Pisces woman could favor such an alliance but must herself respond with commensurate effort if it is to be one of permanence.

What then of the *Aquarius* man? As already indicated, the cuspal area is auspicious but the Pisces woman asks for an assurance of real sincerity in her relationships and the Aquarian might be only "questing" and still uncertain where or with whom to settle down. He likes excitement and feels that a woman should accept this and approve his frequent unexpected changes of plan. Often, home for him is the place to go when all else fails to pique his curiosity or pleasure. If these two were equally in love, they could resolve their differences; without this incentive, neither would have the will to try.

She could form close ties with the natives of the first and third decans but not necessarily of enduring quality and the unrest of the second decan native could keep her tensely apprehensive and unsure of her status in his eyes.

Lastly, the *Pisces* man, her own sign affinity, is an apparent fortunate choice for her. They could travel around the world on a freighter, operate a nursing home, have a dance studio, a dress or hobby shop; they could own a travel agency or promote tours in which they were guides; there are a hundred projects in which their joint ideas could be implemented enjoyably and profitably—the possibilities are endless. Furthermore, this procedure would be wise since both are serious, possessive and inclined to brood discontentedly when not actively engaged in pursuits of their choosing. Moon influence could but add a further measure of closeness. If either mate had Mars inclusion, their business efforts could prove more lucrative but if both were subjects of Mars, they would need to stabilize their emotions—to deal with the occasional dark shadows of self-doubt that haunt these natives—a double amount of which could be disasterous to both marriage and business.

To summarize: it is questionable whether the Fire Sign men would offer the tranquility which should prevail in the life of the Piscean, although Aries and Leo are capable of doing so when the decan influence permits.

Of the Earth Signs, any of the three could be favorable—

again, with decanative discrimination.

The Air Signs are all problematical for cohesive understanding, but the Water Sign men of her own element all present virtues compatible with her own.

Thus it is seen that the Pisces woman will never lack for admirers—that she may even find in marriage the "knight" of her improbable fantasies. While she has the attributes which are essential in many types of endeavor, and is extremely versatile, endowed with intellectual and artistic gifts which are consonant with rewarding self-expression, she possesses an inherent longing for a loving companionship in which she would offer a willingness of cooperation. (Almost invariable she utilizes her earning power whether married or single.)

Today, these multiple goals are not inappropriate and there is an unprecedented opportunity for their attainment. If she is (as has been intimated so often through the years) too modest, too distrustful of her own talents (and of other people), if Neptune has bestowed upon her a sensitivity which sometimes inhibits her drives, she has only to remember that the very awareness which is responsible for these feelings is an advantage for accomplishment and a weapon against all antagonists. None there are who should deny her the right to her true heritage!

Chapter 8

Supplementary Information Pertaining to Women's Signs

Their Amours

Any of the Fire Sign women might find affairs diverting or amusing (except the Sagittarians who are more disinclined to do so. They are of strong fiber and can take in stride the inevitable results or terminations without the wounds sustained by less vigorous women.) The Arien might yield in an impulsive moment to a liaison with one who piqued her curiosity, although more probably as a gesture of independence. She cannot bear the thought of any man not wanting her and so could deliberately investigate the reason if she found one reluctant.

The Leo woman though, would rarely jeopardize her position as the wife of a man whose talents or abilities impress her (which they normally do or she would not have married him). She is not apt to accept another sexual partner except for the purpose of increasing her own prestige through an eventual permanent arrangement.

The Earth Sign women, disliking infidelity in "their" men as they do, are slow to allow themselves any lapses of integrity. Moreover, they are not really interested. The Taurus woman is thought of as being erotically "earthy" and so she is, but all other aspects of a relationship must be resolved before she can find satisfaction in such moments. She seeks commitment—not dallying episodes!

The Virgoan has much the same attitude. Not so cold and apathetic as she may appear, her needs are well supplied by "her" current man—otherwise, she chooses another or lives alone—a state which she sometimes enjoys anyway.

Either she or the Capricorn woman can be quite contented with a partner who treats her as an equal. (The September woman might even conceal her impatience at having to show considerable deference to him.) The Capricornian thinks also of her image in the community and would hesitate to take chances of losing the respect of her associates.

Of the Air Signs, while it is the Geminian who is the most defenseless in these matters, the Aquarian is a close second in her reactions. Both are fundamentally romantic, with a combination of emotional and physical needs which men seldom fathom. While seeming easy prey to advances by men other than their mates, it is their search for the *right* man, his gentleness, his awareness, the close rapport which so often urges them into situations of false promise. However, the Geminian sees and responds to what she believes to be true communion while the Aquarian may fear and distrust it. In both instances, they may mistake their own feelings for those of the suitors, being misled by their hopes. Both seek permanent, fulfilling relationships and both are constrained by duty and loyalties, but it is the Aquarian who most often does not recognize the quality of that which she may already have. (Love has many faces but commitment least often brings disillusion.)

Like the Leonian, the Libra woman has few of these problems. Generally her husband offers substantial benefits (often the reason for her initial interest), one who can provide her with the life style to which she feels entitled. If cheated of this, her affairs may be numerous although usually clandestine. They are often as much for the need of fostering her self-esteem and to vent her disappointments as for physical enjoyment. (An exception is when she herself is especially capable or talented and this source of satisfaction replaces that of lovers. Another is that of the native of the last decan who, like the Geminian of the first, might be consistently loyal under all circumstances through a fanatical sense of duty).

Concerning the Water Signs, since the husbands of these women are so often faithful, their perspectives differ from those of other signs. Cancer women always seek the lasting alliance. Even when they have affairs before marriage, it is only in the belief that they have found "the" men! They would prefer postponing all sexual indications of affection until after the ceremony.

Scorpio, deceptively detached, wants no trivial matings. In marriage or out, her "loves" are not only passionate and enduring, they are conspicuous for their loyal and steadfast qualities. (She demands acknowledgement of her worth but this is usually freely given.)

The Pisces native though, like the Geminian and the Aquarian, never ceases to look for that mythical mate who will support her ego and warm her heart!

Women's Differing Attitudes Regarding Unfaithful Partners

Women of varying signs react diversely to the infidelity of "their" men. The Fire Sign natives are hotly indignant and usually vocally vituperative.

The Aries woman is quick to notice a lack of personal attention and attributes it at once to an interest in someone else. Whether it be husband or lover, she is apt to leave a man whom she cannot trust. If she remains with him there are usually many recriminations. Nor would she hesitate to retaliate with affairs of her own, although in a mutually satisfying union, she would rarely do so.

The Leo woman, equally prideful, is just as bitter, but she may rail with less vigor since she finds it almost impossible to believe that "her" man would turn from her to another, with any serious intent. Often she has chosen him for position or wealth and is therefore capable of accepting at least those less flagrant cases of unfaithfulness in order to maintain the status quo and its advantages. She may have a carefully constructed self image also and be aware that there are always other men if the current one fails her too conspicuously. (She might console herself with others meantime— sometimes quite openly.)

The Sagittarius woman, contrary to her male counterpart, is often circumspectly faithful even in the event of overt disloyalty or humiliating lack of attention, countenancing her mate's outside liaisons with grim tolerance. She employs many extra-curricular activities to fill her time and thoughts, often traveling when feasible since these separations are more bearable than the silent aquiescence she must affect in his presence. All three natives of the Fire Sign tripplicity cling to their pride but react differently because of it.

The Earth Sign women are adamant in their denunciation of infidelity in marriage and those of Taurus and Capricorn would rather be single than be condemned to a life of pretense or uncertainty with a man who has no principle. After they are mature, neither of them (as a rule) seek other men for sexual companionship. Being as interested (and adept) in money-making activities as their trigon "brothers," they normally become absorbed in lucrative projects and often are thus very contented!

The Virgo woman also proclaims a preference for loneliness to being with a man who is not trustworthy but often she will wait patiently (though sullenly) for him to change. She could live in solitary manner without too much difficulty unless she has had a husband or lover who gave her the affectionate arousal she craves. Her sexual emotion she keeps subdued unless the circumstances for its continuance are favorable. (Once truly loved, she relinquishes her partner with stubborn unwillingness.)

Perhaps many Earth Sign women do not find it worth special effort to keep "their" men intrigued. They, themselves, have a code of honor which prohibits their disloyalty and they expect as much in return.

Women of the Air Sign trigon differ considerably from each other in their reaction to perfidiousness. The differences may seem minimal, but they are distinctive. Like the Aries, Taurus and Capricorn natives, they may all look for a quick exit but some do not even mention or appear cognizant of "their" men's infidelity if this suits the purpose.

The Gemini woman, being generous and maternal, wants to forgive and often believes she does, even though never completely trusting him again, once she finds a man untruthful. His wandering robs her of a feeling of worth as a person. It is a real blow to her self-esteem, which she may immediately seek to restore with other alliances.

The Libra woman is not so easily appeased by cajolery and promises as the Geminian and is more outspoken. The Venus-ruled woman may already be engaged in an affair of her own or have a man not too far away with whom she *could* have one if she desired. (This fact often serves to "hold" the one she has. Nothing dulls a man's romantic interest so much as being too sure of his partner.)

The Aquarius woman, because of family ties, often weds late or not at all. Once a widow, she rarely changes this status. (It could be that the responsibilities she assumes are but sublimating subterfuges, preferable to making the compromises required in marriage.) She is extremely independent—unique in having a consuming need for affection while reluctant to give of herself in a way to attract or at least retain it. As vulnerable as the Geminian, like the Capricornian, she learns early to surround herself with a simulated imperturbability which is a protection if her lover or husband wounds her by going adventuring elsewhere.

The Air Sign women differ from each other according to their personal signs more than Fire and Earth but not more than the Water element natives.

The Cancer woman tends to be a warm, "mothering" wife and is slow to believe ill of her husband. Indeed, she has a way of holding his love so effectively that he seldom *does* stray! If he should do so, she would find it very difficult to adjust to the idea or to cause a permanent separation, and although heartbroken would probably not retaliate with like dalliances. (She is not apt to have serious "love affairs" at any time without the sanction of marriage vows or similar assurances of continuity.)

She differs appreciably from those of the Scorpio native, who, (like the Geminian and the Arien) is suspicious and instantly alerted when "her" man's attention wanders. Conceivably she could run straight into the arms of another although she is far more likely to cause such a lively, berating commotion that he may henceforth settle for monogomy. Obviously, this solution could not be expected were he not deeply involved in his affections for her, but this is usually the case. Like her Cancerian "sister" she is adept in providing her partner with the incentive to remain faithful. Scorpio women usually know "their" men!

The Pisces woman also has these attributes of her trigon "sisters." She is as domestic as is the Cancerian and indulges her loved one in every way possible as long as she is certain of his love. However, she is mystical and unrealistic in her attitudes toward sex and a man may go elsewhere for entertainment while retaining his Piscean "love nest." If she learns of this, "hell hath no fury" like hers. She usually leaves him at once, although, instead—in what would seem uncharacteristic of one of her nature—she may initiate many casual affairs of little meaning, not bothering to keep them clandestine. Certainly, the three Water Sign natives, while noticeably alike otherwise, have very different defenses against infidelity.

As one thinks about these variances and similarities in the respective signs, he should bear in mind the many influences which are brought to bear upon the particular decan and cusp of each, remembering the fine nuances of changing pattern that could result.

Chapter 9

Protest

The wild desires are not enough for youth
The ecstasies that break the heart are not
Then there are dull, hard, unrelenting years
When constancy and patience mark each thought
And sacrifice and loyalty prevail—
A pattern, which engendered by young fears
Is wrought in sure belief it cannot fail
For woven in the tapestry of time
'Twas ever taught as quintessential truth
That service brings its own reward sublime
And this is all one dares to think about
For so the ego has recourse from tears!

But Oh! When leaves are turning red and gold
And all the world is bathed in Autumn's glow
There stirs within, rebellion and regret
Cognition mocks the virtues so extolled
(Despairing of the hopes held long ago
Beleaguered and unable now to doubt
That there are sweeter goals than duty's debt—
Tradition, nature's trap—outworn and old—
Submissive yet, not looking for redress)
Then—vagrant winds betray the truant heart
Beseeching still with songs of loneliness,
Beguiling though with hints of mystery,
Seducing through their tales of heresy—
In one exultant moment set apart
Defying even love, *the Self runs free!*

While the list of women's grievances begin in the home,
those outside are more discernable. Some women have fine,
keen minds and remarkable business acumen; others have
untapped sources of creativity. There is rarely one without
skills which could serve others. Often, they are as driven as
men toward goals of achievement, yet because of outmoded

ideas are prevented from demonstrating their talents.

Among the ones who for various reasons prefer only domesticity (caring for the home and playing supportive roles to husbands) some find contentment thus, but in this group also there is restlessness and resentment. Many women in all areas of life are frustrated and dissatisfied. Now, that of necessity, there must be fewer children (or none at all) these feelings will be even more prevalent. Is there any quick, equitable solution to their problems—a catalyst which can bring immediate relief? Perhaps not, but real efforts are now being made in this direction. In the realm of commerce, politics and the arts, it will come first. This is because of the numbers and groups to uphold each other as they demand action in their favor. In recent years as a few were given elective positions with the government and others permitted to enter such alien fields as Research, Medicine, Publishing, Advertising, Brokerage, Banking and Broadcasting, they were lulled into a belief that their number was rapidly growing and that they were commanding equal respect as independent, freethinking individuals. However, it soon became evident that men still received preferential treatment in the filling of most important posts.

This has been embittering to those who have earned promotions through great effort—women who have proven themselves as competent as the men who are favored. They have been thwarted so long in their competitive strivings, suffering disdain, insults or at best an amused tolerance that it is little wonder if their voices now raised in complaint sometimes seem shrilly vindictive.

In any restaurant near an office building, one can always see dozens of men during the day, sipping their coffee, relaxing, telling jokes, sometimes boasting of deals they have been negotiating, often not even discussing business issues. Back in the office, secretaries are typing, filing, researching, writing notes of reminders, monitoring the phone calls—all to spare the "boss" from being bothered with "insignificant" details! This is fine, except for the fact that if some of those "Girl Fridays" had had the same opportunity for promotion, based upon their knowledge and ability, they could just as well be the ones on the extended coffee breaks! (They might be less relaxed as they worry about their children, the evening's meal preparation and other innumerable duties which await them at home.)

The present denouement has not come about suddenly. Many women have always felt belittled—not only in the intimate contacts with men whose brash smugness too often left them with little dignity or pride, but in Society's unfair appraisal of their abilities and intelligence. Long ago in the cities (as now), the young married girls who had other jobs kept up their home as well. They worked long hours in the factories, stores, laundries and offices, always at a lesser wage than that paid to men for identical work. They did heavy labor, lifting and carrying heavy merchandise while men stood aside to allow them room for their strenuous efforts. Yet when the whistle blew or the gong of release sounded, these same gallant fellows, bowing and smirking, vied for the privilege of opening the outside door for them! (Many girls held their jobs only through the sufferance of sexually attracted men and lived with the constant knowledge that those smarter or more obliging might take their places at any time.) They were besieged for their favors and feared the reprisals of any who might be angered by refusal.

Through the years, denied of all other means of ego sustenance, women cultivated culinary skills, became proficient with the needle and strove to keep each family member in clothing and surroundings which were comfortable and clean, while gradually realizing that regardless of this, they could never attain stature not considered secondary to males.

Men frequently left fastidious, meticulous, hard-working wives for those who were "slap-dash' housekeepers as well as blithely indifferent to their own appearance, and if they did remain at home were often unfaithful. So what was the answer?

Some women attempted to find it in applying themselves to other jobs but as has been stressed before, with about the same results. They nibbled around the edges of Jack Horner's luscious pie of opportunity and self-aggrandizement, but were never allowed a full portion and barely a whiff of the plums!

They have not found it easy to be ascribed with less emotional stability, intellect and business judgment than men, when having to give them vital assistance without due credit. They have always been the "chinkers" of the world, filling in wherever needed—("fetching the nails") whatever the occupations or the projects, while doing their own tasks without aid. Furthermore, they have been found to be able in much that in normally done by men, while still retaining greater dexterity and facility for that allotted to themselves. (This may be because men lack patience. Women's work is too much like that of Sisyphus, the legendary King of Corinth who was condemned to rolling a stone up a steep hill in Hades only to have it roll back each time as he neared the top!)

Men speak proudly of male success in fields of art and music as well as those of business, yet only a very small percentage utilize their own full potentials. When their personal accomplishments in such areas are not spectacular why do they call attention so gleefully to those of others? Few women can devote full time to such activities. One who is capable, and has the stamina, to establish a business or do any kind of marketable productive work in the midst of her domestic responsibilities deserves a medal both for bravery and accomplishment. She who can produce creative juices for writing, painting or composing under these conditions which are certain at times to be defeating and stressful, must have inner resources seldom found in men since the latter rarely attempt such ventures where there is not available privacy.

Members of minority races have asserted that they are required to be far better prepared than others for similar jobs. This, women can well understand—it is their own dilemma. Their paintings or compositions rarely have comparable exposure or recognition. In a position formerly held by a man, a woman must not only be as knowledgeable as her predecessor, her performance must excel his!

There is constant mention of the pressure under which men work, yet a women has the aggravation of crowds, noise and traffic and even keener competition. In addition, she frequently has as many household chores as the woman who is a full-time homemaker! If a family member is ill, she has the care of him during the night and the worry during the day. Is this not pressure?

A man, in being both self and job oriented, can usually concentrate upon his work, forgetting all else until it is completed. Strangely, while a woman cannot forget the anxieties pertaining to family life (in spite of this handicap) her execution of similar tasks is as commendable as his. When adequate child care is available or better domestic arrangements possible, men may find the competitive results somewhat disconcerting!

Nothwithstanding the fears or lethargy of some women, many have grown so bitter at being taken for granted at home or in places of employment that they are diligently pursuing ways of amendation, surprising to those who know them best. Theirs is not a fight over who changes the baby's diaper or who dictates the letter and who writes it. It goes much more deeply than that, although it is this very dull, prosaic aspect of activity which, without gratitude finally wears down a woman's spirit! They refuse to continue bolstering male egos to the detriment of their own. Those with outside jobs expect more helpfulness at home. Many demand the sexual freedom long enjoyed by men.

They can no longer afford to be passively silent, but they are hampered by a lack of genuine communication. Both sexes are victims of former premises. Many men, well meaning and astute in other ways, ask anxiously and a little contemptuously, the cause of all the shouting. They use crude invectives to describe leaders of Liberation Groups, either calling them frigid and undesirable or accusing them of lesbianism. They seem to fear emasculation or reduction of their pride, not realizing that women admire strong, aggressive men even while shielding, protecting and often loving with greater intensity those who apparently need it. Some males confuse muscular prowess with courage, and robust appearance with masculinity. They even show a reprehensible scorn for others of their own sex who are gentle toward wives or sweethearts, interpreting this as milquetoastian. (These same men are apt to imagine that women are weak, but they are in error. Some women have been overly permissive and lax—too generous and self-deceptive through their need of love, but those who are now alerted will never again close their eyes to evident truths.)

When one considers old standards and Society's illogical belief in women's inferiority, the tasks toward change seem Herculean, but today's women are beginning to make vital progress.

The Liberation Groups have been accused of "playing games" but their true motives are too serious, their interests too broad and the increasing need of their enterprise in projects affecting all humanity so great that they have no time for games. In a "civilization" which is predicated upon competition in which one person loses that another might gain, there is much to be challenged. Men who are too old to fight, establish the rules of war which force younger men to kill and be killed or suffer permanent disabilities, against their convictions and even without a voice in such decisions; then they smugly discuss the ethics of women's abortions! Such inconsistency is appalling!

With the existing blatant conniving, dishonesty and lack of ethics so rampant where it is most deplorable, women must take action. Their immediate concern includes many areas. Conditions in Nursing Homes need further investigation. There are elderly persons with irreversible ailments who have no funds for nursing care. Many should be removed from inadequate living quarters and supplied with decent incomes and medical services. More individuals on welfare could be trained and prepared to support themselves, so that these funds could be used more appropriately elsewhere. Selected families could be quite comfortable and healthy in semi-rural districts where a garden, several fruit trees and a few chickens would furnish a large part of their support. At least a few children from the slum districts would have a place to play other than the streets. Experimentation could reveal unsuspected advantages. How much longer must people live in rat-infested and over-crowded houses?

Are there not more humane, effective ways of dealing with

the criminals than those based upon revengeful premises? (Laws which fail to accomplish their original purpose surely should be revised or canceled.) While those dealing with speeding and drunk driving need to be more rigidly enforced, further facilities for the treatment of alcoholics and drug addicts must be provided. Child neglect and abuse must be ferreted out and dealt with wisely. Women dare not rest as long as there is one hungry child in the world—one child forgotten behind bars or incarcerated with older hardened criminals.

Feasible methods for their supplemental care is a subject that deserves much thought and ingenuity. For some, "Centers" financed by the Government are the only solution. (There is never enough volunteer help in day-care homes.) Circumstances vary. Many arrangements could be made between the women themselves. In some neighborhoods there are already "block mothers" and phone advisors for children's greater security and comfort. (These should be increased.) There could be exchanges of all kinds to lighten the burdens of many. (There are unexplored possibilities here, involving cooking and house cleaning as well as child supervision.) There could be residential cooked food suppliers as well as "crews" of home cleaners. Innovative ideas along these lines are certainly as essential as those for pollution and ecology control! As more women get together on these plans, their objectives will be better understood. A million women with zeal, courage and perseverance can change tradition beyond belief.

The justice of measures to insure equal pay and equal opportunity for all, regardless of sex or race is generally conceded. As to birth control and abortions, there can be no question as to who has the *right* of decision here!

These are only a very few of the most significant undertakings to which women will address themselves. Why do they hope to succeed where there has been little done in the past? Because the projects deal directly with human beings. Men are more interested in abstractions; women in individuals. This essential difference in male and female has been discovered in tests with even very young children. People are women's special charge!

The list of crucial situations is endless, but in many cases, they will be forced to fight first for the "right" to help, so progressive action may seem slow. Unbelievably, there are only a few more women in the House and none in the Senate in Washington than there were some years ago. In the State and City Governments, while there is improvement, the more important offices *usually* are not theirs. (An exception is a female governor of Connecticut.) Nevertheless, women now constitute over 38 percent of the working force of this country and over 20 million individuals are living in households solely supported by them.

Too, as more women accept their accountability, not being afraid to voice the protests which they have kept in abeyance through fear of ridicule or anger, the scoffers will have to acknowledge the sincerity and legitimacy of their requests. Much can be accomplished if women will work together. Perhaps the first requisite is for them to better understand themselves and thus each other. (Mort Sahl once suggested that if women were not competing for the men, they could see them more clearly. Certainly, they could have a more empathetic feeling toward their own sex.)

There are some very fine leaders in their organizations— intelligent and personable. They apparently are not only well informed and articulate, but have a vast compassion for humankind. Most effective in presenting their precepts are those who realize that it is futile to attempt to sell a product unless the package is presentable. It is not necessary to adopt the appearance or the manner of the male in order to have his advantages. The bright plummage of the Cardinal does not negate his masculinity nor does it make him any less aggressive. In the same context, women whose appearance betrays their gender do not suffer the loss of efficiency or the interest of their listeners. As their unlimited abilities become common knowledge, they can be proud of looking like themselves! Sufficiently sure of the principles for which they fight, they can continue to dress according to their own tastes.

Radical changes do not come about easily. Just as the Blacks knew that moving into a white neighborhood would not insure them of immediate invitation to dinner by their neighbors, these women realize that discriminative practices in business will not be replaced overnight. (Each will be required to offer proof of her worth.)

As new laws and amendments are enacted, they will begin to enjoy the advantages they seek—a choice of life style— options which have not been theirs before—a right of self-determination in all things. This is certain to come first. In the public domain, the process of change is already evident.

Privately, in interpersonal matters, those involved must find their own way through a maze of bigotry, outmoded concepts, deceit and wounded vanity—not to speak of disloyalty and philandering!

Many a woman devotes herself to her family, encouraging, praising, lending moral support to each member and serving them day after day, living only vicariously through their activities, gearing her life to theirs without thought of personal preferences or interests and repressing any resentment which may struggle for utterance as they accept her ministrations and labor as a matter of course. Is this not her sole purpose? Every one of them, including the woman herself, has been led to believe so! (Indeed, she might be the first to deny her exploitation, actually deriving pleasure from the many monotonous tasks which are performed in a spirit of love and offered as a token of its constancy.)

Does this willingness of subjugation make it any less unjust, or excuse the others for their lack of reciprocal concern? Does it inspire their appreciation or greater affection for her? Not necessarily. They may, though subconsciously, resent her creating a dependency in which they feel helpless or uncomfortable. Too, male ideas of superiority begin in such a home. Her husband may even speak of her facetiously but with betraying arrogance, as "the old ball and chain," which is no more humorous but just as commonplace as are the mother-in-law jokes. His words are not only tasteless and cruel, reflecting his masculine restiveness and a desire to have no commitments, but they encourage the disparagement of all women. Furthermore, their innuendo is without foundation, since it is the woman who has hitherto worn the shackles of restraint—dominated throughout her life by the men with whom she is associated, denied the independence afforded her brothers when young, later on controlled or coerced by a husband who was often unfaithful, and always bound by a multiplicity of never-ending tasks—having a lifetime assignment to serfdom! (The double-entendre of the word "house-wife" is very appropriate!)

Even back in the days when farms were the backbone of America and were family enterprises, the work load was frequently unequal. On a farm of any size, although the man had "hired help," the woman, with an incredible amount of chores to be done, both in the house and outside, often had none until there were children old enough to help when not in school. (As the boys grew, they worked outside with their fathers.) They often worked far beyond their strength and with the poorest equipment on the place. (The big barn, the fine machinery, were badges of the men's success. It was not until recent years when the exodus from the farms had already begun, that more pretentious houses and inside conveniences became prevalent.) Death sometimes came at an early age, giving the men two or three young wives each during their life spans. Peritonitis may have been the diagnosis of the cause, due to improper attention at child birth, but being over-tired and returning to work too soon were contributing factors.

If they had less worry about their husbands' infidelities than those in the city had, it was only because of limited opportunity in the rural districts for clandestine meetings. When a wife made her trek to the fields in mid-afternoon with coffee or iced tea and sandwiches a bit earlier than expected, there was always the chance of her finding the horses (in later years the cultivating equipment) standing idle while her mate reclined in the shade of a tree in tete-a-tete with a maiden from a neighboring farm—sometimes the one who replaced her when she was freed forever from her monumental tasks.

The young mother of today, besides doing the customary housework, laundry, shopping and cooking, is often the chauffer for the family, belongs to the P.T.A., attends school and Church functions, assists in Scout activities and manages somehow to read enough to converse intelligently with any of her peers. She tries to keep herself youthfully attractive in an effort to compete in appearance and sex appeal with any woman whom her husband knows.

Can she hope though to successfully compete, romantically or sexually with the younger, sleek, predatory girls he sees in his daily rounds of business and recreational diversions? The labor that a household and family entails, keeps her busy and harried—often tiredly worn from child bearing and rearing (the constant loss of sleep when they are fretful), the confusion and the rigor of her duties. Can she be the carefree erotic partner which she could be under other conditions? When night comes, can she suddenly turn into a seductive courtesan? How many husbands understand or expect to help? Their number is few. Often, a man is concerned only with his feelings of being pushed aside—ignored. He may become extremely jealous of the children. This provides a good excuse for him to seek consolation from one of the "chicks" of his acquaintance. He probably knows many of them who, confident and naive in their inexperience and sudden power to attract and having no thought of loyalty to their own sex, eagerly join him in his sexual errances. (They themselves are pathetic, when in their innocence they become entranced by the married men who are only flitting from flower to flower in the garden of their shallow emotions. It never occurs to these girls that they are faceless puppets, providing transitory moments of pleasure, only to assuage men's wounded vanity. Even the pampered Sweetheart of a married man may lose him at any moment. She has no assurance of his constancy; the "partying" girl of today may be the neglected and overburdened wife of tomorrow!)

Despite these factors, a woman is very lucky whose circumstances make possible her remaining at home while her children are small, although she needs some time of her own away from them in order to retain her equilibrium and a spontaneity in her relationships. No one can be continuously confined with very young children without losing something of herself, nor can she provide the constant atmosphere of

security and affection in which a child thrives, unless she
has periods in which to revive her energies and recapture
her resources. When the children are old enough to help, her
burdens may be reduced, although with each additional family member, the work is also substantially increased.

For the woman who is a home-maker and has another job
as well, it is particularly difficult. Her husband may be opposed to her employment even though, while there are undoubtedly some women in business or professions for self-
satisfaction alone, most of them are there for pressing financial reasons. (Frequently it is to supplement the husbands'
inadequate incomes, to educate various family members or
contribute to the livelihood of parents.) Such husbands usually do little around the house. It is not uncommon for a
woman, hurrying in late with groceries purchased on the
way home from work, to find her spouse already waiting—
beer can in hand—feet on chair—avidly watching the news
or a sports event on T.V. This he continues to do while she
prepares the evening's meal, after which he returns to his
favorite program, naps or reads the paper while she cleans
the kitchen and does any number of other nightly chores.
Still, he often is the man who complains to his male companions or "girl friends" that his wife is cold and unloving.

A perennial drudge is deglamorized. Her real worth is be-
clouded by her image of servitude. Thus, even as a sex object
her attraction is diminished. She loses her own self-respect
and in doing so begins to distrust her husband and all
females. A woman who does sedentary work during the day
might actually enjoy some culinary activity in the evenings
and upon week ends if there were someone else to clean and
keep the house in order, but she must have an inordinate
amount of energy to function well in all capacities.

Certainly, her family or even she herself does not like to
admit that a woman is virtually a servant in the home, but
much of the work done there requires far more strength than
that which is needed for many financially remunerative positions outside. (It is no wonder that so many whom Society
call "domestics" have left jobs in which they were ill paid,
unappreciated and humiliated, finding others less tiresome

and more rewarding. Yet, who advanced the idea that women alone were then responsible for the arduous tasks they left behind?)

Clearly, affluence changes the picture completely (as it does in all areas). Herein, the concern is not for those who have sufficient means to provide for even part-time help (when they need it)—they are of a minority, but there is a preponderance of families with incomes far too small to allow for this relief; it is for the millions of this classification that women protest!

Sometimes one's husband does not readily see the difference in her gladly doing something for his own comfort but feeling resentment at being entirely responsible for the care of the children or the cleaning of the house. (Nor does he realize that while she actually enjoys a service for him, the improbability of his ever reciprocating bothers her.)

Every household has its special needs and each individual his own energy quotient. While some men have recognized imbalance and assumed responsibility for its correction, those who are vain or doubt their real masculinity are not quick to offer. (The man who needs constant sexual variety or ego stimulating erotic contacts can rarely be found in the kitchen. He it is who suffers the "castration pains" if faced with any household task!) Obviously, not all men fit this description. Many simply do not comprehend the extent of work to be done although there are those who would notice quickly enough if it were left undone!

Even when retirement age is reached, men leave their jobs but the women in the homes of average incomes must continue with their housekeeping as long as they live. In Condominiums, Town Houses, and other housing facilities for older couples, outside maintenance is often included but this does not relieve the women from the many duties which are still theirs! Many of the men find new, interesting occupations, usually not menial or energy absorbing. Women too, might enjoy such self-fulfilling projects if they were freed from their normal enervating tasks. (What of the ones who have held both jobs through the years? This applies to approximately half of those of our culture between the ages of

18 and 76.) Should there not be some feasible plan of complete retirement for them if they want it?

Although each existing marriage is unique, if the disadvantages are too numerous, they must be dealt with accordingly. No matter what bequest a woman has from her Zodiacal sign, if sufficiently optimistic she can keep on investing "her" man with the qualities she wants in him; if her love is great enough, she will see only this image and ignore all else.

Sometimes a confrontation with truth is inevitable and this is particularly painful if the years have been allowed to pass as she resolutely sought to hold together a marriage which was completely one-sided. It is demoralizing when attempting to draw the marital surrey in double harness if one member of the team keeps dallying along at a different pace or goes off on tangents of self-indulgence, regardless of the effect upon the other. It is heartbreaking to a woman to finally have to acknowledge to herself that she is only the much discussed "sex object" or a mother substitute. Usually, if of the latter group, she will continue in her efforts to retain her husband's approval or preserve his good humor, perhaps realizing that it had been his immature need of her which initially brought them together.

If she feels that he wants her only for sex, she has no such duty. He can obtain this for the price of a drink or a phone call at any time. (Every woman is beginning to realize that she is a fool to spend 10 minutes on a bed with a man who has no further interest in her after attaining his personal, selfish objective. A man in this age who does not understand that a woman's responses depends upon pre-tenderness or at least some show of affection, does not deserve her cooperation.) It is doubtless only habit that has kept him around at all. Actually, her chief attraction may be that of a servant since it is more difficult to obtain this kind of help than it is to find a participant for erotic pleasure. In any case, why should she allow such an association to continue? While it may be a fear of loneliness, she endures that now and probably is ashamed of her need of his presence. (She could fill many hours in cheering the aged or ill, and if she wants male companionship, that poses no problem. There is little excuse for any woman of today not making an appearance which would merit the attention of some equally personable man of like status and then finding mutual interests to be shared.)

Unless there are small children to be considered, in a union *without love*, wherein a woman lives with a man only for financial support, is she not actually only a licensed prostitute? If she is the housekeeper, she further belittles herself by being his servant as well as his sex object.

Needless to say, in this "new world," there should be no children begotten without thoughtful consideration and unless both parents plan to share in their personal care and in their financial support (if necessary). Each will want to be sure that he is good parent material. (This precaution alone would solve a great number of family problems!) There are many children already without homes who could be cared for by those who would love and cherish them. More adoptions are needful.

In an unhappy household, even if there are children, a woman still has alternatives. Albeit the ideal may be for them to have a father, they can survive divorce with less traumatic result than may be theirs in a home where there is no affection. A young girl needs to revere her father and a boy also fares better when he has genuine respect for him. (Loving his mother, he may despise her meek subservience even though contrarily he would resent a matriarchal attitude in which she sought to dominate the family.)

Incidentally, new attitudes will begin to be cultivated in young children. School subjects will be based more upon individual leanings and interest. (Hopefully) home activities will include each family member. It will no longer seem strange when sister prefers digging in the garden or feeding the rabbits while brother makes the supper's souffle! Fathers may even prepare dinners while tired mothers rest. And when the more unpleasant chores are allotted, it will be done without reference to gender. How can there be more willing, helpful husbands unless different ideas are implanted at an early age?

One aspect in today's talk of abortion and birth control (the advisability of having fewer children—or none at all) should be the care given in assuring those one has of their welcome and right to be here. Arguments can have serious effects upon both sexes.

A young girl sensing for the first time her mother's frequent displeasure, often fears and distrusts any heterosexual alliance for herself. She may be disdainful of boys, shun their company altogether, or seek short-lived relationships only for the purpose of dominating or embarrassing them. Obviously, much will depend upon the manner of the father toward his family. A boy could be strongly influenced by this also, and apt to pattern his own upon it, first toward his mother (and sisters), later toward his wife.

As career women without children find their proper niches in the world, some may prefer to occupy separate quarters from their spouses or lovers—a plan which could be more suitable for both. Sex may begin to assume a more rational proportion of interest and come at long last to be a pleasure available and acceptable to a couple only when the desire and need is mutually manifested. Then each will be responsible for the other's enjoyment. It is possible that romance itself will flourish once again if thus encouraged.

There will be more "trial" or "open" marriages—"serial alliances" and "serial monogamy." How can two people know whether or not they will be compatible until they have lived for some time in the same household? (Those who seek astrological information have a better chance of initially choosing wisely.) Without pre-knowledge, it is sheer luck if they do get along together well enough to sincerely want an association to continue. While cohabitation without marriage seems to suggest a lack of commitment, it could be just the opposite, since under these circumstances each partner would feel the necessity of making an effort toward pleasing the other. Since neither of them would be expected to contend with grouchiness, ill humor or habits lacking in fastidiousness, the association might take on the flavor of "courtship." However, one cannot refrain from wondering how much women themselves will benefit by these experiments. Will men only have still more leeway in their erotic adventuring, while women, as always, will be left "holding the bag?" One recalls that divorce and alimony laws, though later becoming unwieldy and often unrealisticly burdensome, were originally adopted because many men could not be trusted to support their families once they tired of their wives or found them sexually less appealing. Surely though, it has been well demonstrated that to try to hold an unwilling partner by law or through a feeling of obligation is usually not only futile but results in self-contempt.

There are many women who are kind, generous and loyal for years as they silently contend with temper outbursts, moroseness or infidelity, knowing that if they dare to criticize "their" men, such reproaches will be used to excuse all future indiscretions and even possible separation. Whatever the circumstances of an intolerable and irremediable situation, once a woman faces reality, she can usually find feasible ways of handling it. The domestic incongruities encountered daily, vary according to the persons involved.

Although in the future, mama may use her special skills to bring home the "bread," while daddy does the home chores and cares for the small children during periods when this proves logical, (already there are couples sharing equally the work at home and that outside) a large percentage of this present generation of males will never be able to feel other than downgraded when doing housework. Too firmly imbedded in their minds is the conviction that it is "unmanly," and at best he can only submit reluctantly through the wish to avoid his spouse's displeasure. This outmoded belief is defended by recalling that their mothers did it all with fewer conveniences. They overlook the increasing number of duties besides housework which women of today perform.

Some now grudgingly admit that if a woman also holds an outside remunerative job, she should be able to count upon help at home. Yet it requires only small insight and a knowledge of people in general to perceive that in many cases she will have to accept the old pattern as irradicable. One reason for the increasing number of divorces is that with the stigma now removed from this way "out," many who have long borne unfairness, quietly but resentfully, are now seeking escape and freedom. It is not the males alone who are looking for new mates!

It must not be forgotten that women themselves are as imbued as men with misconceptions as to "men's work" or "women's work." This *attitude* must undergo adjustment. The difficulties of all will be greater if through selfishness or blindness a few continue to live in Ivory Towers of smug satisfaction and ignore significant facts. Until women get together on changing ideas, there will be those without proper respect for men who attempt to reverse such roles to overcome the inequities in their own family circles. Many a man will wonder whether or not to hold open the door of the Laundromat when a woman arrives there as he does with an overloaded basket of clothing! (Is she a feminist or a "happy housewife?") It is ironic, now when many have decided to seek a greater freedom—to insist upon their rights in a world which has so long withheld them—that some of the women themselves are to be the most feared. (This could have been condoned when they had no avenues of support except through men.)

Although the status of the housewife is not the same as it was in the days when all Mom had to do to feel "superior" was to be a better cook than her neighbor, still, the women who prefer only domestic roles are free to continue thus. Should they not be sympathetic toward those of different viewpoints and objectives? The time will come when a young woman in good health and without small children will be looked at askance if she has no interests or involvements other than keeping house.

Many, safe in the knowledge of their own talents and efficiency and secure in their careers, are quick to recognize that only because of this they are spared the problems faced by others, but there are those who are not so generous. Having excellent positions, they fear to jeopardize them by expressing opinions which might displease their employers. It has been suggested that many well educated young women with "fine writing jobs" have kept silent on women's issues. The implication is that this means disapproval. Since they are often in far greater danger of losing those jobs if they express agreement, such reasoning is absurd.

Of course, there are a few females who renounce women's vocal dissentions, knowing that in so doing, they improve their image with men whom they hope to impress. Also, by criticizing a Movement with motivations beyond their ken, for the first time they may find a way in which to feel important! (As for those coy, preening ladies who giggle "I *like* being a woman!", can they for one minute suppose that there are many of their gender who do not?)

Some dread disfavor of male family members or lovers— the anger, derision and reprisals of men who, having been Kings so long now have no intention of sharing their thrones with parvenues. Such women do not like being obliged to do domestic chores while the rest of the family indulge in recreational activities or pursue other interests, but they know that any mention of exploitation would bring only perplexed defensiveness. It is conceivable that they might gain more respect if articulate about their resentments.

The female who would bear anything rather than lose "her" man is very insecure. She may have come from a home where it had been expedient in her formative years to be always agreeable—obedient—a "good little girl" in order to be in the best graces of either Mommy or Daddy—sometimes both. If this masochistic pattern has been continued in her marriage, it can rarely be broken. Talented and capable of having a rewarding career elsewhere, in the process of becoming personally indispensable she has lost her identity.

Women who resist "facing the world," needing male support and protection, are frightened by any thought of change. Some are inept or untrained at anything but keeping a home. They may even enjoy the mechanics involved, although much rationalizing can be done in this regard when other factors are predominant.

There are wives who though not necessarily pleased with their situation, nevertheless when possible avoid the mention of alternate ventures. They deny any agreement with those who seek equal status with men since they are usually maintained by those who would disapprove. Those with growing children justifiably minimize discussions of women's unrest because of the deleterious effects upon the children themselves.

Older ones who have had marriages based upon the theme of men's supremacy remain silent. They will not admit that their relationship has taken on an aura of servitude.

Some who have not had outside jobs for a while feel ill-equipped to return to former activities even though they might like it better than their present arrangement.

Many employed in plants, offices or stores, upon being offered better jobs which entail increased responsibility refuse them, preferring routine tasks with lesser pay so that their primary interests can still be focused upon their families. Highly skilled or educated women, capable of holding excellent remunerative positions, often feel that the care of their children through the formative years is of first importance.

In the transitional period ahead, many women will be faced with new, perplexing decisions. There are men who will be offended and embarrassed by suggestions offered, or at fear of losing status. Those who have not previously known of their wives' discontent may now welcome it as excuse for more flagrant infidelity. A number may want divorces.

Whatever the circumstances, women will need courage. For some, the time is late for self-deprecation and knuckling down just for the sake of peace. (Two angry cats in a sack can rarely be reconciled!) Yet, in the search for truth, each kernal must be garnered carefully without rationalization or misinterpretation. Some changes will bring rewards—others, disappointments. Disagreements can only be resolved if there is a true comprehension of all facets of their origin.

In the outside world, there will be defenders by both sexes. In the home, a woman's personal happiness and that of her family, will usually depend upon her own wisdom.

What does astrology have to do with the foregoing? Those versed in its lore believe it has *everything* to do with it! Certainly, the influence of the planets through Zodiacal heritage (as well as a person's own genes and environment) determine reactions to traditional beliefs and encourage—or limit—

acceptance of new and unexplored ideas.

Women seeking to retain or to find their preferred life pattern, and simultaneously their deserved societal status should allow no instrument for this achievement to go unstudied. The better one knows and understands his associates in any enterprise the better chance he has of promoting concerted effort and willing cooperation. A real awareness of tendencies and differences of all the persons involved can help in meeting almost any difficulty.

Groups of women working for various causes could well profit by knowing the signs of their leaders and co-workers. For instance, it has been verified that Mars-blessed women have remarkable drives. This applies not only to those of the Aries and Scorpio signs but also to their respective cusps and to the appropriate decans of Leo, Sagittarius, Pisces and Cancer in which other attributes abide. (Those of Aries genre are particularly successful in managerial positions where they direct and initiate new procedures. Subjects of Scorpio vintage have a remarkable understanding of others; they are innovative and persistent.) Sun imbued individuals are extremely convincing in presenting plans. Jupiter gives expansiveness, sound "know-how" and an eagerness toward action. Neptune provides vision and inspiration, the Moon courage; Venus harmonious sociality. It is often those with the greatest influence from Mars, Jupiter and the Sun who lead the way—but this is no positive criterion.

Taurus women tend to be steadfast and persevering— unequaled as financial advisors. Virgo natives can be counted on for detail and meticulousness. Where children and the elderly are concered, Gemini, Cancer and Aquarius women will work indefatigably, just as will those of Libra's last decan. (All Librans attract willing helpers.)

Aquarians have extraordinary energy and enthusiasm. Saturn influence adds to their dependability. With Neptune aid they can anticipate future needs as can the Piscians who work without fanfare and are dependable in emergencies.

Capricornians make fine public speakers and many are capable of seeing a situation dispassionately. Sagittarians have widely diversified abilities and will serve well wherever their interests are aroused.

While the special characteristics should be noted, anyone dealing with the public should study the more detailed resume. Those of all signs have important talents with which they can contribute creditably in any cause or upon any project, and each decan offers its own advantages.

Without doubt, astrology will be used more and more in places of employment or wherever it is helpful to have pertinent knowledge of character and personality traits of various individuals.

As has been explained, women vary in their reaction to infidelity according to their Zodiacal signs. This is true also of those who contend with divorce forced upon them by unhappy spouses. Most of the Fire Sign women adjust rather quickly, although those of Aries' second decan, Leo's first and the third of Sagittarius do so less easily.

Of the Earth Signs, only those of Taurus' first decan and those of the Virgo-Libra cusp have any real worry. Most Capricornians are stoics.

Air Sign women require men for emotional support. This is best descriptive of those on the Gemini-Taurus cusp, Libra's last decan and some of those on the Aquarius-Capricorn cusp.

Water Sign women fare better with masculine companionship, but those of Piscean genre staunchly abide the other condition if necessary (especially those of the third decan.)

In reference to those who themselves want change, it is hoped that this time around women will be wiser in their choice, deciding first what characteristics they want in a man—then assessing each prospect according to his Zodiacal qualities.

Why does a woman often select her mate so carelessly? If she wants him for support and tangible assets, why not look for one with dynamic and aggressive qualities? This does not necessarily mean that she must forego the sentimentality of a gentler man although the possibility bears consideration. He who is devoted to business and the attainment of material success could be too occupied with this to give a woman all the attention she craves. Some men of more artistic bent may do as well financially through this source and be very interesting companions. On the other hand, neither altruistic nor ethereal traits guarantee perception. Congeniality and a man's choice of vocation gives little notice as to his innate leanings. An artist or a musician can be as selfishly obtuse and as blindly bigoted as the man concerned only with accumulation of wealth.

One should first analyze herself and recognize her own requirements; then search for a companion who will be most apt to be cooperative. (Her Zodiacal sign in relation to various men will indicate the kind of future likely to be hers.) Would she be compatible with those she admires? Or live up to their expectations?

Men want wives for disparate reasons. One may be thinking of the social advantages to be gained, another will plan to fit her into a certain life style which he has in mind, still another may think only of her physical appeal, disregarding all other important attributes. Then there is the man who desires a combination of nurse, housekeeper, business manager and sweetheart, but if he finds such a one, feels so threatened by her efficiency, that he is restlessly discontented.

All of these facts should be taken into account. However, many women will not risk a second or third marriage. Instead, they will seek further education and training for future contingencies, preferring careers and the headiness of being single again.

As women ponder whether it is wise to change the pattern of their lives or to continue with situations not to their liking the decisions eventually reached will be due, at least in part, to the discernment provided by their respective Zodiacal signs.

Chapter 10

The Alchemy of Love

So hopelessly you gaze across the miles
With saddened eyes that glow sometimes with dreams
Of days when miles were steps and you a King
(Do you recall that then it was enough
To know that every breath I breathed was yours
That every plan I had was filled with you?)
I hear your sighs that have replaced the smiles
And feel with sharpening pain your discontent
And pray that once again the things you do
Will give you naught but hours of rich portent.
Although your sighs denote regret, they bring
You closer to the memories which we share
For even as you long for other days
Your thoughts retrace rare moments treasured there
(Perhaps a recompense your need ignores)
Oh! listen to my heart, for now it seems
A record of our love it plays and plays!

Is this a soliloquy of anguish? Hardly; on the contrary, it
reflects the triumph of a woman who has been able to conquer loneliness and resentment and retain her tender regard
for a man despite his lack of full reciprocation. She may
have spent years in spinning sturdy webs of trust with which
she hoped to hold him while unconsciously knowing that he
would destroy them again and again as his fancy wandered.
At the termination of each episode, she may even have held
him in her arms in utter forgiveness, cherishing the rare
moments that were hers as he refreshed himself from the
fountain of her generosity, thus preparing for future exploits.
   She who so unselfishly devotes herself to an unapprecia-
tive (sometimes unfaithful) husband might be expected to be
extremely unhappy, but often she is too well adjusted to allow herself the "luxury of discontent." Even though he may

only know her through her services, seldom seeing her as a person, (being distracted by the enticements of the other females in his vicinity) her loyalty remains intact. She would have learned early the symtoms of his various phases of interest in other women—some harmlessly innocuous—others more serious. He may continuously have had some special person in the offing who helped to satisfy his unquenchable thirst for feminine flattery, changing to some one new as each conquest paled in significance. While always reacting with the familiar pain to his feeble efforts at lying or deceit, since both are products of a passing era, she has accepted her role, if not gladly, at least without rancor. Any assurance of his affectionate need of her would be ample reward for her devotion, but often she suffers only his dissatisfactions—particularly, as time passes, his regret at his lessening virility. (She is not unaware of his covetous glances at the bodies of young girls nor of the fleeting memories which momentarily brighten his mood.)

Only a woman of infinite compassion could thus refrain from an accusatory attitude, donning an armor of serenity which protects her pride and allows her husband to keep his. In recalling her own nostalgic pictures, she may for a brief moment entertain the hope that at long last he will turn to her with undiluted fondness—that he will read in her eyes the indelible words written on her heart, but most of the time, she is reconciled.

There are many such women. It is too late for them to change the habits intensified by time. It would be futile to expect any change of attitude in their spouses.

Many of them have had deeply buried longings and unfilled dreams of personal accomplishment and self-aggrandizement which they have renounced in favor of their husbands'. Yet they are cheerfully affectionate and uncomplaining. They are strong and self-reliant. Like the woman in Helen Reddy's song—they are *invincible!* While there are a number uninterested in domestic changes or the "liberation" which women's groups espouse, whose reasons are those of expediency, these women are motivated by unselfish concern for their loved ones.

The farm women mentioned earlier, although overworked, often loved their husbands without reservation. Had there been other options than the way of life which was theirs, few would have chosen them.

Married couples who have muddled along for years, taking the "bad with the good" in their marriages, are somewhat aghast at the thought that they could have reneged and tried new experiences long ago. While there are more and more divorces now obtained by this group, in many cases, ties long established are unbreakable. Even where there is little physical attraction there are feelings of sympathetic affection and responsibility.

For a pleasant family life, obviously each member should put forth his best efforts for the good of all, but what of the household in which the man, long used to a hierarchy which he heads, could not endure a partnership of joint tenure or a role for himself which he sees as demotion? Has the wife here any alternative (if she loves him and wants to keep the family together) but to face the truth graciously and without criticism? (While some persons can be guided into paths of cooperative behavior, few respond favorably to demands!)

Will there not always be the woman, seemingly responsive who accepts her loved one's sexual embrace without prelude—a gaucherie on his part that no woman ever really excuses—yet whose affection keeps her silent?

What of those desperate females of all ages who are starving themselves, doing strenuous exercises and even resorting to pep pills as they pretend to a vivaciousness that is often false? It is seldom true as has been intimated that they strive for an appearance admirable to other women; they only compete with them, each to hold the attention of the current particular man! Dare they abolish such measures in their bids for loyalty?

The young newly-married woman in the midst of her rapture wonders at the impatience she hears in the voices of those who are dissatisfied. She is so enamored by her youthful partner that if confronted with his disloyalty, she might not believe it. Even in the face of obvious proof, she often remains constant and begins the customary pattern of adjustment.

Although she may not admit to the fact, many a woman with a promising career or a lucrative position would willingly give it up if by so doing she could exchange it for a loving companion! She would prefer that he be romantic and faithful but would settle for one she could love and serve.

Even with new opportunities in sight, and having always given more than they received in devotion and genuine concern, there are those who still cling with unabated fervor to a relationship which has long been dead. The reason? Women need tender relationships so much that they pretend to mutual feelings which do not exist. They have a right to equal opportunity and far more consideration than has been theirs in all areas of their lives, yet they cannot deny their instincts nor the hungers which beset them.

Even among those feminists professing disdain for men, there is frequently that belligerent voice which is too loud—too vociferous, as if designed to relieve an aching heart and delude the proud declaimer herself!

One of today's writers has suggested that these are women who "do not want to put out anything," yet if one listens closely he will detect another note beneath the stridency of the most bitter. Here lies disappointment and in many cases, loneliness and fear! As the song goes "You're nobody until somebody loves you." (It would be more accurate as "You're nobody until you love somebody.") Who is more aware of this than the disillusioned?

Those who vocalize the loudest, would be just as quick to defend their own as were the Sabine women 2700 years ago. Fond of the men who had once been their abductors and rapers but were now their husbands and the fathers of their children, in their frightened anguish they had the courage to rush upon the battlefield screaming and pleading as the two armies—the husbands on one side and the fathers and brothers on the other—fought in hatred and vengence. (The combatants were so taken by surprise that the war was immediately terminated.)

Most wives of today would be no less defensive! Even those who have had bad encounters with men may have sons for whom they would give their lives! A son can be as chauvinistic as his father but provoke his mother's indignation less. Has she not helped to shape his opinions? When the two heatedly disagree, she can never summon the same antagonism which she would feel at another male's disparagement of her sex.

Despite the protests, many will continue familiar patterns of adaptation. Still, among them are some who, though caring deeply for their husbands, antagonize and alienate them without conscious intent. A woman may bewail "her" man's lack of sentiment while being herself guilty of imperceptiveness, forgetting that he also may be unhappy. As she looks across the table, she no longer sees him with eyes that were once alight with the admiration which he may require. In her tiredness and resignation, she may fail to recognize the symptoms of depression, the feelings of bewilderment and frustration which besiege him. Is it not possible that a kinder assessment would prevent the traitorous thoughts which may be his as he contemplates the empty years ahead and deliberates upon the feasibility of seeking a more meaningful arrangement?

Some husbands are like guests in their own homes. They would willingly help with household tasks but somehow can never do them satisfactorily. (There seems to be certain mysterious rules of procedure which they never quite master.)

The bungling Dagwoodian mystique may prevail. Cartoons and commercials have pictured wives not only attractive but as efficiency experts, correcting their husbands' ineptness and mistakes. Men may laugh as heartily as women at these characterizations but the laughter could be a whistling in the dark.

Recently there has been considerable talk about males not being needed. It is true that their original primary function was to provide the seed of propogation and that this has been grossly overdone, but now when it is suggested that a man is actually expendable, not being required even for sexual pleasure, he may feel somewhat like the male Black Widow spider who is destroyed by his mate when once his purpose has been served.

Since doctors and psychologists report that many a man, far from being the confident, arrogantly self-satisfied person in the bedroom which his bravado indicates, is now instead, timid, insecure and even impotent at times because of having become aware that his wife (or sweetheart) may only have pretended to orgasmic pleasure in the past rather than embarrass him with the knowledge that he was an incompetent lover. Can any woman tell a man she loves that he is not the smart, perceptive fellow she has pretended he was? Will he ever try to "make love" to her again?

Most women dislike being controlled. Indeed, if they are to be successful in their jobs or even contented in their homes, they need to retain their identities. Yet, traditionally, men have always been at the helm. Probably very few will take kindly to female authority which comes about so suddenly. that egos are threatened. It is well known that a man who is dominated loses initiative and vigor. He must be "his own man" or he is nothing. Paradoxically, while a woman resents the air of superiority in males, she grows contemptuous of one who is weak. In joint ventures, as her own power increases, her respect for him diminishes. Whether the role of leader is thrust upon her by his lesser fitness or is due to her own decisiveness, if she "takes over," no matter how stubbornly he tries to overcome his sense of worthlessness, the impatience in her voice or gestures will eventually subvert his spirit.

Possibly from babyhood on, males try to escape from females, although when doing so they frequently only run to others. The old adage implying that a daughter retains this relationship forever while a son is lost in marriage to another woman is also significant. Trouble in families is not necessarily caused by friction between mother and daughter-in-law but is a result of the son's attempt to cut the apron strings when he gets away from home. (Unconsciously he may choose a woman who will help him in this.) Alas, he only substitutes them for those of even more binding fiber! Here he has both maternal and erotic ties.

Eons ago, the men did not stay around the Caves long at a time. (They hated the turmoil and still do. They are glad to leave, no matter what labor is entailed elsewhere. Some even go to war to escape!) They were the Big Hunters in those days. They went off together, combining the search for food with jolly comaraderie. They were the first to be indentured with family obligations, women pacifying them with sexual accommodations and praise. Is it not this use of sex and undue deference which shackled women originally and brought them to their present untenable state?

They justly complain that they have been the victims of incredible prejudice and discrimination through the years, but is it not true that their oppressors have but borrowed from them some of their own weapons to use in appeasement? Their bondage has been camouflaged and even sweetened with honeyed words, patronizing gestures of commendation and bright promises. Somehow, these procedures seem uncomfortably familiar! Incidentally, many a man has had the superiority crutch most of his life. It will take him a while to learn to walk without it; patience is required. Also, since the disparity in sexual attitudes remains the underlying cause of much grief, it is easy to forget that unless he is of that male chauvinist group who actually believes women are intellectually inferior, Dick, Harold or Inglebert is no more responsible for women's *general* woes than are the women themselves! However, if personal grievances could be alleviated, that would be a mighty step in the direction of compromise. Thoughtful women are considering all aspects of their difficulties.

Without the meliorating, healing balm of true compassion and its unbiased insight, there can be no appreciable concessions made by either men or women to bridge the widening chasm between them. Only through a discerning blend of independence and cooperation can a couple or a marriage long withstand the awesome stresses of modern Society. Call it "compassion"—call it "love"—it is the only magic which can be effective in fostering their greater harmony. What else is there? Recriminations and accusations have never helped to bring couples to a reconciliation. After all the shouting is over, if its resulting harm is not irreparable and if each of them is sincere in the desire to establish a workable partnership, sometimes it can be done, but without a loving attitude—never! As always in such matters, it must be the woman who leads the way.

Men whose Zodiacal influences encourage them to have affairs will probably continue to do so (and presently, their wives and sweethearts may be more likely to indulge in their own.) Where a tranquil home life is appreciated above all else, there at least will be caution to insure this comfort. Those who have genuine affection for their companions will not be loth to show it; others will be amenable temporarily while their ardor lasts and then move on to fresher attractions.

As women request change, they will see that in the process of achieving their own emancipation, men will also be manumitted. There will be unprecedented freedom of action— more flexibility in intimate relationships. Men may feel less obligation toward their families. Still, some marriages might then lose the dullness of prosaic custom which now robs them of the sponteneity and joyousness which should be the foundation for such unions.

Can women ever come to condone men's erotic conduct without so much bitterness, viewing it not as a phenomenon or a breach of faith but as the natural expression of normal male instincts? Can they acquire an equinimity that no longer depends upon absolute constancy? (Just as taking from sex the alluring qualities of sinfulness diminishes some of its overt appeal, perhaps loosening the bonds of previous expectations will reduce men's desire to prove them foolish. If so, is it worthwhile?) As Edgar Guest said, "It will take a heap o' lovin'," but women have the capacity for it. One is reminded of the prayer requesting the serenity to accept the things which cannot be changed—the courage to change that which is possible—and the wisdom to know the difference.

An early philosopher (probably Plato) likened Humanity's sorry interpretation of the truth to that of a man sitting in the rear of a cave, with his back to the entrance where a blazing fire made shadows upon the wall which he faced and from which he drew his conclusions. (It takes genuine insight and *caring* to get along well with others!)

Vexing ways are common to all, yet when he is irritated does one ask himself which of his has sparked that of the other? It is so easy to see clearly another's faults while not perceiving one's own. If in constant proximity with spouses or various family members, it is certain each has played some part in the development of the other's attitudes.

In the midst of malcontent and displeasure, the need for appreciation is universal. When the boosts to self-esteem do not come from expected sources, a person may seek to replenish his confidence in sexual adventures unless he can find some spectacular way through outstanding accomplishment to revive the waning respect of those he hopes most to impress. (Where the needs are greatest, they may be hidden under cover of facile arrogance.)

Some turn to alcohol or drugs to allay their feelings of ineffectiveness while there are those who retreat within themselves, closing the door upon reality. Hypochondria serves a purpose here also. Too many trudge passively along a lonely road of life, defeated by abrasive, crippling reproaches cast upon them by disappointed partners. (The silent, sullen treatment is more cruel than words.)

Injured pride can camouflage facts. Present over-reaction is not always caused by new dissatisfactions but from the memory of past wounds never relinquished or forgiven. (Are they ever really forgiven or only stored away as a basis for later quarrels or silent brooding resentment?) It should be remembered also that many wrongs suffered in the past were magnified then because of one's own immaturity or were inflicted by one who himself was immature but who has since grown in reason and intent!

Although our species has been given what is called "free will," an individual functions in a prescribed orbit of performance imposed upon him by the combinative factors of genes, early environment and Zodiacal nudging, the latter including not only his birth inheritance but the subsequent coincidental meetings with other humans which lead to serious implications. Who, then, has the right or the temerity to sit in judgment upon another?

Every day will not offer parades and stimulating speeches

to bolster determination and morale, but then these are only
the signals of women's distress—not the remedy. Their
homes will always be of paramount interest and should be
pleasant havens for all who live there. Constant strife is un-
thinkable; it is incurably destructive, only intensifying problems and availing nothing. Often, if those who are at odds
would only slow their frantic pace long enough to really see
one another, they would be surprised at how quickly their
angers evaporated.

Sometimes, after a thoughtful walk in the garden or the
woods—"taking time to smell the flowers" as Walter Hagen
said, the layers of antipathy and self-righteousness will drop
away, leaving only consternation at the impasse which honesty and awareness could have prevented. There should be
hours of this quiet contemplation—a taking stock of innumerable situations with a view toward better relationships.
Without this, as the days fade into years, can the attainment
of personal goals compensate for the losses incurred?

Women ask only to share men's place in the sun—not
usurp it. They would like to have freedom, but they also
need love, for a woman without love in her life is like a leaf
blown fretfully by the wind from one insecure niche to
another; she is like a boat which has loosed its mooring and
drifts aimlessly upon indifferent waters.

Both sexes have been programmed to seek sexual partners.
If women find more pleasure than men where affection lends
enchantment and additional impetus, this too is a part of
their heritage.

Now that the old bug-a-boos of sex are discredited and new
notions of commitment being tried, must a woman forever
bury the dreams that once she treasured? This would be regrettable for underneath the facade of modern, sophistic attitude there still lives that woman of yesteryear—a strange
creature, always secretly, poignantly longing for tenderness
and romanticism.

However, romance in itself is a game which the senses and
the imagination play. Love is that which whets her sexual
appetite! It is the seasoning which makes palatable the un-
leavened sexual bread offered by the obtuse or unconcerned

man whom she otherwise adores. Sex may be the magnet that entices, but love is the bonding agent!

After the trials and experimentations, the pendulum of change may swing in an arc which becomes almost full circle as new ways are modified and older ones regain favor. It may be found that unions of lasting quality (even though not necessarily in conventional marriages) can be comfortable and even exciting.

Few women will ever be contented with those of only casual nature. Although the female's chief occupations may no longer be linked with reproduction, her nesting proclivity is so strongly entrenched that it cannot be repudiated altogether without pain. Her protectiveness and her need to give are her strongest instincts. Thus it has always been and thus it will ever be. Yet, where there is honesty there must be a willingness to see what lies ahead. Both sexual and romantic love can die. If this happens, she must be quickly generous. Locks and doors cannot restrain the spirit or the mind. Indeed, it is the thought of fetters which often induces the restiveness leading to the separation she would hope to circumvent.

There are those who find none of this important. They believe that soon we will go the lonely way of the hapless dinosaurs, following them into some unknown limbo—that here there will be only the whispering of the wind over the desert wastes and the splashing of the surf in the waters of the seas.

If this be true, "within the twinkling of an eye" it could all be over—the dichotomy between the sexes—the ridiculous posturing, the pitiful pretenses, the self-deceiving prejudices, the ego trips, and the eternal fight for supremacy.

However, this would also mean that the strivings, the hopes and dreams of the human entity have been for naught. Such a purposeless theory of creation could never be approved by women. It would deny the very essentiality of themselves and make illogical the fundamental function of all living things.

More probably, after each individual has served his Karmic purpose through numerous lives of Zodiacal design, he will become a part of some vast, intricate *splendid plan* which is far beyond the comprehension of his recently evolved minute mind. Meanwhile, in this present phase of existence, the rewards are many. Personal relationships offer the greatest challenges; they also promise the richest benefits.

CRCS Books

THE ANCIENT SCIENCE OF GEOMANCY:Living in Harmony with the Earth by Nigel Pennick
$12.95. The best and most accessible survey of this ancient wholistic art/science,
superbly illustrated with 120 photos.

AN ASTROLOGICAL GUIDE TO SELF-AWARENESS by Donna Cunningham, M.S.W. $6.95. Written in a
lively style, this book includes chapters on transits, houses, interpreting aspects, etc.
A popular book translated into 5 languages.

THE ART OF CHART INTERPRETATION: A Step-by-Step Method of Analyzing,Synthesizing &
Understanding the Birth Chart by Tracy Marks $7.95. A guide to determining the most
important features of a birth chart. A must for students!

THE ASTROLOGER'S GUIDE TO COUNSELING: Astrology's Role in the Helping Professions
by Bernard Rosenblum, M.D. $7.95. Establishes astrological counseling as a valid and
legitimate helping profession. A break-through book!

THE ASTROLOGER'S MANUAL: Modern Insights into an Ancient Art by Landis Knight Green
$10.95, 240 pages. A strikingly original work that includes extensive sections on
relationships, aspects, and all the fundamentals in a lively new way.

THE ASTROLOGICAL HOUSES: The Spectrum of Individual Experience by Dane Rudhyar $8.95.
A recognized classic of modern astrology that has sold over 100,000 copies, this book
is required reading for every student of astrology seeking to understand the deeper
meanings of the houses.

ASTROLOGY: The Classic Guide to Understanding Your Horoscope by Ronald C. Davison $7.95.
The most popular book on astrology during the 1960's & 1970's is now back in print in a
new edition, with an instructive new foreword that explains how the author's remarkable
keyword system can be used by even the novice student of astrology.

ASTROLOGY FOR THE NEW AGE: An Intuitive Approach by Marcus Allen $7.95. Emphasizes self-
acceptance and tuning in to your chart with a positive openness. Helps one create his
or her own interpretation.

ASTROLOGY IN MODERN LANGUAGE by Richard Vaughan $12.95, 336 pages. An in-depth inter-
pretation of the birth chart focusing on the houses and their ruling planets-- including
the Ascendant and its ruler. A unique, strikingly original work.

ASTROLOGY, KARMA & TRANSFORMATION: The Inner Dimensions of the Birth Chart by Stephen
Arroyo $10.95. An insightful book on the use of astrology for persoal growth, seen in
the light of the theory of karma and the urge toward self-transformation. International
best-seller!

THE ASTROLOGY OF SELF-DISCOVERY: An In-Depth Exploration of the Potentials Revealed in Your
Birth Chart by Tracy Marks $8.95, 288 pages. Emphasizes the Moon and its nodes, Neptune,
Pluto, & the outer planet transits. An important and brilliantly original work!

ASTROLOGY, PSYCHOLOGY AND THE FOUR ELEMENTS: An Energy Approach to Astrology & Its Use in
the Counseling Arts by Stephen Arroyo $7.95. An international best-seller, this book
deals with the use of astrology as a practical method of understanding one's attunement
to universal forces. Clearly shows how to approach astrology with a real understanding
of the energies involved. Awarded the British Astrological Assn's Astrology Prize. A
classic translated into 8 languages!

CYCLES OF BECOMING: The Planetary Pattern of Growth by Alexander Ruperti $12.95,
274 pages. The first complete treatment of transits from a humanistic and holistic
perspective. All important planetary cycles are correlated with the essential
phases of personal development. A pioneering work!

DYNAMICS OF ASPECT ANALYSIS: New Perceptions in Astrology by Bil Tierney $8.95,
288 pages. Ground-breaking work! The most in-depth treatment of aspects and aspect
patterns available, including both major and minor configurations. Also includes
retrogrades, unaspected planets & more!

A JOURNEY THROUGH THE BIRTH CHART: Using Astrology on Your Life Path by Joanne
Wickenburg $7.95. Gives the reader the tools to put the pieces of the birth chart
together for self-understanding and encourages creative interpretation by helping
the reader to think through the endless combinations of astrological symbols.

THE JUPITER/SATURN CONFERENCE LECTURES: New Insights in Modern Astrology by Stephen Arroyo & Liz Greene $8.95. Talks included deal with myth, chart synthesis, relationships, & Jungian psychology related to astrology. A wealth of original & important ideas!

THE LITERARY ZODIAC by Paul Wright $12.95, 240 pages. A pioneering work, based on extensive research, exploring the connection between astrology and literary creativity.

LOOKING AT ASTROLOGY by Liz Greene $7.50. A beautiful, full-color children's book for ages 6-13. Illustrated by the author, this is the best explanation of astrology for children and was highly recommended by SCHOOL LIBRARY JOURNAL. Emphasizes self-acceptance and a realistic understanding of others.

NUMBERS AS SYMBOLS FOR SELF-DISCOVERY: Exploring Character & Destiny with Numerology by Richard Vaughan $8.95, 336 pages. A how-to book on personal analysis and forecasting your future through Numerology. Examples include the number patterns of a thousand famous personalities.

THE OUTER PLANETS & THEIR CYCLES: The Astrology of the Collective by Liz Greene $7.95. Deals with the individual's attunement to the outer planets as well as with significant historical and generational trends that correlate to these planetary cycles.

PLANETARY ASPECTS: FROM CONFLICT TO COOPERATION: How to Make Your Stressful Aspects Work for You by Tracy Marks $8.95, 225 pages. This revised edition of HOW TO HANDLE YOUR T-SQUARE focuses on the creative understanding of the stressful aspects and focuses on the T-Square configuration both in natal charts and as formed by transits & progressions. The most thorough treatment of these subjects in print!

THE PLANETS AND HUMAN BEHAVIOR by Jeff Mayo $7.95. A pioneering exploration of the symbolism of the planets, blending their modern psychological significance with their ancient mythological meanings. Includes many tips on interpretation.

PRACTICAL PALMISTRY: A Positive Approach from a Modern Perspective by David Brandon-Jones $8.95, 268 pages. This easy-to-use book describes and illustrates all the basics of traditional palmistry and then builds upon that with more recent discoveries based upon the author's extensive experience and case studies! A discriminating approach to an ancient science that includes many original ideas!

THE PRACTICE AND PROFESSION OF ASTROLOGY: Rebuilding Our Lost Connections with the Cosmos by Stephen Arroyo $7.95. A challenging, often controversial treatment of astrology's place in modern society and of astrological counseling as both a legitimate profession and a healing process.

REINCARNATION THROUGH THE ZODIAC by Joan Hodgson $6.50. A study of the signs of the zodiac from a spiritual perspective, based upon the development of different phases of conciousness through reincarnation.

RELATIONSHIPS & LIFE CYCLES: Modern Dimensions of Astrology by Stephen Arroyo $8.95. Thorough discussion of natal chart indicators of one's capacity and need for relationship; techniques of chart comparison; using transits practically; and the use of the houses in chart comparison.

SEX & THE ZODIAC: An Astrological Guide to Intimate Relationships by Helen Terrell $7.95, 256 pages. Goes into great detail in describing and analyzing the dominant traits of women and men as indicated by their Zodiacal signs.

THE SPIRAL OF LIFE: Unlocking Your Potential with Astrology by Joanne Wickenburg & Virginia Meyer $7.95. Covering all astrological factors, this book shows how understanding the birth pattern is an exciting path toward increased self-awareness.

A SPIRITUAL APPROACH TO ASTROLOGY: A Complete Textbook of Astrology by Myrna Lofthus $12.95, 444 pages. A complete astrology textbook from a karmic viewpoint, with an especially valuable 130-page section on karmic interpretation of all aspects, including the Ascendant & MC.

For more complete information on our books, a complete booklist, or to order any of the above publications, WRITE TO:

CRCS Publications
Post Office Box 1460
Sebastopol, California 95473
U.S.A.

**A JOURNEY THROUGH THE BIRTH CHART: Using
Astrology on Your Life Path $7.95**
by Joanne Wickenburg, 168 pages. An
excellent introduction to astrological
basics with a modern slant, in which the
author gives the reader the tools to put
the pieces of a birth chart together for
self-understanding, rather than relying
on traditional "cookbook" interpretations.
This book is a journey that carries the
reader through continual discoveries of
what the planets, signs, and houses mean
in his or her particular birth chart.

**THE ASTROLOGY OF SELF-DISCOVERY: An In-Depth
Exploration of the Potentials Revealed in Your
Birth Chart** by Tracy Marks, $8.95...240 pages.
A guide for utilizing astrology to aid self-
development, resolve inner conflicts, discover
and fulfill one's life purpose, and realize
one's potential. In modern language, the author
explains how the Moon and the outer planets
reveal potentials for self-discovery and
personal growth at an especially deep level.

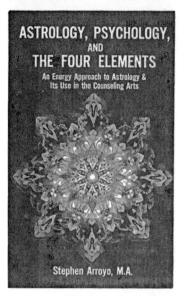

ASTROLOGY, PSYCHOLOGY,

AND

THE FOUR ELEMENTS

*An Energy Approach to Astrology &
Its Use in the Counseling Arts*

Stephen Arroyo

$9.95

This book deals with the relation of astrology to modern psychology and with the use of astrology as a practical method of understanding one's attunement to universal forces. It clearly shows how to approach astrology with a real understanding of the energies involved, and it includes practical instruction in the interpretation of astrological factors with more depth than is commonly found in astrological textbooks. Part I was awarded the 1973 Astrology Prize by the British Astrological Association as the most valuable contribution to astrology during that year.

PART I: ASTROLOGY & PSYCHOLOGY

Part I thoroughly explains how astrology can be the most valuable psychological tool for understanding oneself and others. Analyzing the scientific, philosophical, and intuitive dimensions of astrology, it is oriented toward the layman with no astrological knowledge, astrology students and professionals, and those engaged in any form of the counseling arts.

PART II: THE FOUR ELEMENTS
AN ENERGY APPROACH TO INTERPRETING
BIRTH-CHARTS

Part II deals specifically with the interpretation and practical application of astrological factors based on the actual energies involved (air, fire, water, & earth). It presents a dynamic application of astrological knowledge that clarifies and illuminates traditional techniques and meanings by placing them in the perspective of understanding the vital energies inherent in all life processes.